D1201098

"Todd Wilson's exposition of Galatians admirably meets the goals of the Preaching the Word series. Wilson knows all the issues in this letter and treats them with remarkable fairness, always making clear just what the text is communicating to God's people today."

Douglas J. Moo, Wessner Chair of Biblical Studies, Wheaton College

"Todd Wilson has written a deeply pastoral and theologically competent commentary on Galatians that is an exemplary effort at Biblical exposition. There are some doozy passages in Galatians, especially on the Law, and Wilson provides a plain explanation and then shows readers how these texts relate to modern Christian living. A wonderful synergy of homiletical energy and honest exegesis."

Michael F. Bird, lecturer in theology, Ridley Melbourne College of Mission and Ministry

"Todd Wilson's exposition of Galatians is both Biblically grounded and theologically rich. But it doesn't stop there. Wilson powerfully and astutely applies the message of Galatians to contemporary life. Galatians isn't left on the shelf; the Word addresses us as those who are tempted to walk according to the flesh, and we are reminded of what it means to be led by the Holy Spirit."

Thomas R. Schreiner, James Buchanan Harrison Professor of New Testament Interpretation, The Southern Baptist Theological Seminary

"A wonderful combination of clarity, insight, and passion. This commentary captures the great big-picture message of Galatians without avoiding any of the difficult details, whether the curse of the Law or remembering the poor. Anyone reading or preaching on Galatians will benefit from this book."

Simon Gathercole, reader in New Testament studies, University of Cambridge

"Every pastor knows the need for really great resources that unlock the text in meaningful ways. Todd Wilson's exposition of Galatians does just that. His perspective on this important letter is grounded in outstanding exegesis and seminal preaching ideas. Don't preach Galatians without this commentary!"

Joseph M. Stowell, president, Cornerstone University, Grand Rapids, Michigan

"Surprisingly little has changed in our thought processes since Paul wrote to the Galatians two millennia ago. We humans love to add one thing or another to the simple gospel message just in case Jesus isn't enough. Todd's commentary is full of fresh insights for our generation and a timely reminder that God really does want us to embrace the freedom that was won for us by the finished work of his Son, Jesus."

Phil Tuttle, president, Walk Thru the Bible

"Todd Wilson has written an excellent commentary for those preaching and teaching the book of Galatians. He combines sound, insightful Biblical exposition of Galatians with warm, relevant personal application. As a deeply committed Christian who is both a gifted pastor and scholar, Todd provides a perspective on the book of Galatians that the church desperately needs: we must continue to go back to the gospel and to God's grace if we are going to move forward in the Christian life. I highly recommend this commentary!"

Jim Samra, senior pastor, Calvary Church, Grand Rapids, Michigan; author,
The Gift of Church and *God Told Me*

"*Galatians: Gospel-Rooted Living* is a powerful reminder of how important it is for Christians to cling to the most fundamental aspect of the Christian endeavor: the relationship with our Lord and Savior that can only come by grace, through faith. This book is a scholarly work written in a conversational style that makes it easy for readers to identify with and to value the book of Galatians."

Gene Getz, president, Center for Church Renewal

"Galatians lives! Reading this commentary seems like sharing in deep conversation with Todd Wilson. His acute questions and insights give many 'aha' moments. Wearing scholarship lightly, yet always intensely informed, he opens up this essential epistle to make a vital impact on us today."

Michael Quicke, CW Koller Professor of Preaching, Northern Seminary

GALATIANS

PREACHING THE WORD
Edited by R. Kent Hughes

(((PREACHING *the* WORD)))

GALATIANS

GOSPEL-ROOTED LIVING

TODD WILSON

R. Kent Hughes
Series Editor

CROSSWAY®

WHEATON, ILLINOIS

Galatians

Copyright © 2013 by Todd A. Wilson

Published by Crossway
      1300 Crescent Street
      Wheaton, Illinois 60187

All rights reserved. No part of this publication may be reproduced, stored in a retrieval system or transmitted in any form by any means, electronic, mechanical, photocopy, recording or otherwise, without the prior permission of the publisher, except as provided for by USA copyright law. Crossway® is a registered trademark in the United States of America.

Cover design: Jon McGrath, Simplicated Studio

Cover image: Adam Greene, illustrator

First printing 2013

Printed in the United States of America

Scripture quotations are from the ESV® Bible (The Holy Bible, English Standard Version®), copyright © 2001 by Crossway, a publishing ministry of Good News Publishers. 2011 Text Edition. Used by permission. All rights reserved.

All emphases in Scripture quotations have been added by the author.

ISBN-13: 978-1-4335-0575-1
ISBN-10: 1-4335-0575-4
PDF ISBN: 978-1-4335-0576-8
Mobipocket ISBN: 978-1-4335-0577-5
ePub ISBN: 978-1-4335-2284-0

Library of Congress Cataloging-in-Publication Data

Galatians : Gospel-rooted living / Todd A. Wilson.
    p.   cm. — (Preaching the Word)
    Includes bibliographical references and index.
    ISBN 978-1-4335-0575-1 (hd)
BS2685.53.W55   2013
227'.4077—dc23   2012023659

Crossway is a publishing ministry of Good News Publishgers.

VP		31	30	29	28	27	26	25	24	23	22	21
16	15	14	13	12	11	10	9	8	7	6	5	4

To Kent Hughes and John Piper
who've shown me how to live the gospel
and preach the Word

For am I now seeking the approval of man, or of God?
Or am I trying to please man? If I were still trying to
please man, I would not be a servant of Christ.

GALATIANS 1:10

I have been crucified with Christ. It is no longer I
who live, but Christ who lives in me. And the life
I now live in the flesh I live by faith in the Son of
God, who loved me and gave himself for me.

GALATIANS 2:20

Christ redeemed us from the curse of the law
by becoming a curse for us—for it is written,
"Cursed is everyone who is hanged on a tree"—
so that in Christ Jesus the blessing of Abraham
might come to the Gentiles, so that we might
receive the promised Spirit through faith.

GALATIANS 3:13, 14

Brothers, I entreat you, become as I am,
for I also have become as you are.

GALATIANS 4:12

For through the Spirit, by faith, we ourselves
eagerly wait for the hope of righteousness.
For in Christ Jesus neither circumcision
nor uncircumcision counts for anything,
but only faith working through love.

GALATIANS 5:5, 6

Contents

List of Abbreviations of Journals and Book Series

AB	Anchor Bible Commentary
AGJU	Arbeiten zur Geschichte des antiken Judentums und des Urchristentums
BBR	Bulletin of Biblical Research
BNTC	Blackwell New Testament Commentary
CBQ	Catholic Biblical Quarterly
CRINT	Compendia rerum Iudaicarum ad Novum Testamentum
CurBR	Currents in Biblical Research
ExAud	Ex Auditu
JBL	Journal of Biblical Research
JSNT	Journal for the Study of the New Testament
JSNTSup	Journal for the Study of the New Testament Supplements
NICNT	New International Commentary on the New Testament
NIGTC	New International Greek Testament Commentary
NovT	Novum Testamentum
NTS	New Testament Studies
ProEccl	Pro Ecclesia
SBJT	Southern Baptist Journal of Theology
SBLDS	Society of Biblical Literature Dissertation Series
SEÅ	Svensk Exegetisk Årsbok
SP	Sacra Pagina
THKNT	Theologischer Handkommentar zum Neuen Testament
WBC	Word Biblical Commentary
WUNT	Wissenschaftliche Untersuchungen zum Neuen Testament
ZNW	Zeitschrift für die Neutestamentliche Wissenschaft

A Word to Those Who Preach the Word

There are times when I am preaching that I have especially sensed the pleasure of God. I usually become aware of it through the unnatural silence. The ever-present coughing ceases, and the pews stop creaking, bringing an almost physical quiet to the sanctuary—through which my words sail like arrows. I experience a heightened eloquence, so that the cadence and volume of my voice intensify the truth I am preaching.

There is nothing quite like it—the Holy Spirit filling one's sails, the sense of his pleasure, and the awareness that something is happening among one's hearers. This experience is, of course, not unique, for thousands of preachers have similar experiences, even greater ones.

What has happened when this takes place? How do we account for this sense of his smile? The answer for me has come from the ancient rhetorical categories of *logos*, *ethos*, and *pathos*.

The first reason for his smile is the *logos*—in terms of preaching, God's Word. This means that as we stand before God's people to proclaim his Word, we have done our homework. We have exegeted the passage, mined the significance of its words in their context, and applied sound hermeneutical principles in interpreting the text so that we understand what its words meant to its hearers. And it means that we have labored long until we can express in a sentence what the theme of the text is—so that our outline springs from the text. Then our preparation will be such that as we preach, we will not be preaching our own thoughts about God's Word, but God's actual Word, his *logos*. This is fundamental to pleasing him in preaching.

The second element in knowing God's smile in preaching is *ethos*—what you are as a person. There is a danger endemic to preaching, which is having your hands and heart cauterized by holy things. Phillips Brooks illustrated it by the analogy of a train conductor who comes to believe that he has been to the places he announces because of his long and loud heralding of them. And that is why Brooks insisted that preaching must be "the bringing of truth through personality." Though we can never perfectly embody the truth we preach, we must be subject to it, long for it, and make it as much a part of our ethos as possible. As the Puritan William Ames said, "Next to the Scriptures, nothing makes a sermon more to pierce, than when it comes out of the inward affection of the heart without any affectation." When a preacher's *ethos* backs up his *logos*, there will be the pleasure of God.

Last, there is *pathos*—personal passion and conviction. David Hume, the Scottish philosopher and skeptic, was once challenged as he was seen going to hear George Whitefield preach: "I thought you do not believe in the gospel." Hume replied, "I don't, but he does." Just so! When a preacher believes what he preaches, there will be passion. And this belief and requisite passion will know the smile of God.

The pleasure of God is a matter of *logos* (the Word), *ethos* (what you are), and *pathos* (your passion). As you preach the Word may you experience his smile—the Holy Spirit in your sails!

R. Kent Hughes

Preface

I've spent a number of years studying Paul's letter to the Galatians, and have created a modest paper trail reporting what I've learned.[1] As a student and scholar, I've always been intrigued by the argument of this fiery epistle. But as a pastor and preacher, I've come to appreciate more fully the stunning realities to which this letter points—the promise of costly grace and the power of gospel-rooted living.

Galatians exists for grace. We find grace at the beginning (1:3) and end (6:18) and in the middle (2:21). But the grace in Galatians is not cheap grace—it's *costly*. "It is costly, because it calls to discipleship; it is grace, because it calls us to follow *Jesus Christ*. It is costly, because it costs people their lives; it is grace, because it thereby makes them live. It is costly, because it condemns sin; it is grace because it justifies the sinner."[2]

Sadly, the Christian Church, going back at least to Marcion (d. c. 160), has had constantly to fight the temptation to turn this *Magna Carta* of Christian liberty into a charter for cheap grace. As pastor-theologian Dietrich Bonhoeffer famously asserted in the face of a spiritually insipid Protestantism dithering in a sea of cheap grace: "Cheap grace is the mortal enemy of our church. Our struggle today is for costly grace."[3]

Today, some seventy-five years later, our situation is still the same. Much of the church in North America is awash with cheap grace—and not to good effect.[4] Ours, then, is the same struggle: the fight for costly grace, for gospel-rooted living. And Galatians, I trust you the reader will agree, is perhaps our choicest weapon!

Many have had a hand in helping this project come to fruition, and to them I owe a debt of gratitude. First, I'd like to thank Kent Hughes, who kindly invited me to contribute this volume to the Preaching the Word series. Special thanks also go to Lane Dennis, Al Fisher, Ted Griffin, and the entire Crossway team for their leadership in publishing and support of this project in particular.

The elders, staff, and congregation of Calvary Memorial Church in Oak Park, Illinois, where I'm the pastor, have, with their encouragement and prayers, shaped and sustained my preaching. To them I'm profoundly grateful.

My wife Katie is vital to everything I do. She deserves my warmest thanks in this—as in much else. And to our happy brood of five (with two more on the way!)—thank you for providing me more delightful diversions than I deserve and the necessary grounding I so need.

I dedicate this book to my two pastors, Kent Hughes and John Piper. Kent was my esteemed pastor and mentor in college and graduate school. I then served as his associate at College Church in Wheaton, Illinois for several years prior to his retirement. His life of grace and discipline continues to inspire. For a two-year stint after college, I had the joy of serving on staff with and studying under Pastor John at Bethlehem Baptist Church in Minneapolis, Minnesota. Those were formative days, and John's influence continues to shape my life and ministry in countless ways. I thank God for them both.

Soli Deo gloria!

Todd Wilson

Paul, an apostle—not from men nor through man, but through Jesus Christ and God the Father, who raised him from the dead—and all the brothers who are with me, To the churches of Galatia: Grace to you and peace from God our Father and the Lord Jesus Christ, who gave himself for our sins to deliver us from the present evil age, according to the will of our God and Father, to whom be the glory forever and ever. Amen.

1:1–5

1

Go Back to Grace

GALATIANS 1:1–5

I WOULD LIKE TO TELL you a story. It's about a young man who ruined his life. He left home, traveled abroad, and wasted his fortune on shallow pursuits and empty pleasures. Eventually he came to the end of his rope: he was out of money, out of food, out of help, and out of hope. This profligate is better known as the prodigal son in Jesus' famous parable.

> There was a man who had two sons. And the younger of them said to his father, "Father, give me the share of property that is coming to me." And he divided his property between them. Not many days later, the younger son gathered all he had and took a journey into a far country, and there he squandered his property in reckless living. And when he had spent everything, a severe famine arose in that country, and he began to be in need. So he went and hired himself out to one of the citizens of that country, who sent him into his fields to feed pigs. And he was longing to be fed with the pods that the pigs ate, and no one gave him anything. (Luke 15:11–16)

What do we do when we've made a mess of things? Where do we go when we've blown it badly? To what do we turn when we've embittered our child with harsh words, when we've betrayed our spouse with sheer stupidity, when we've alienated a colleague or a classmate with a series of me-first choices, when we've driven a wedge between friends or sown discord among congregants? Where do we go when we've been insensitive, thoughtless, or downright obnoxious? How do we respond when we've drifted away from the faith, compromised the gospel, or turned our back on God?

Grace to You in Galatia

Typically when we sin we like to hide—either our sin or ourselves or both. This is a natural response, hardwired into our genes. We get this instinct from our first parents, the progenitors of the human race, Adam and Eve. When they sinned, they hid (cf. Genesis 3:8–10). And humanity's been hiding ever since.[1]

When Paul's young converts in Galatia first heard his letter of rebuke read aloud, they too, no doubt, wanted to run and hide.[2] As far as Paul was concerned, they'd gone prodigal! They'd turned their faith inside out and upside down; that's what happens when we turn our back on grace and seek to be justified by the Law!

The Apostle Paul is flabbergasted by this dramatic turn of events, though he's not quite speechless. "I am astonished that you are so quickly deserting him who called you in the grace of Christ and are turning to a different gospel" (1:6). "O foolish Galatians! Who has bewitched you?" (3:1). "I am afraid I may have labored over you in vain" (4:11). "You are severed from Christ, you who would be justified by the law; you have fallen away from grace" (5:4).

The Galatians find themselves in a serious situation; in fact, it couldn't be more serious. Paul knows it, and they now know it. Yet notice where this big-hearted apostle leads these wayward young converts. He doesn't take them out behind the shed for a good whipping or banish them to the doghouse for their retribution. Nor does he vent his frustration with them on Facebook or tweet their crime in one hundred and forty characters or less.

Instead the apostle who gave them birth takes them back to where it all began: *grace*. He takes them back to grace. In the middle of the letter's opening paragraph Paul says these easily glided-over but vitally precious words: "*Grace to you* and peace from God our Father and the Lord Jesus Christ" (1:3). Paul's saying, "You've made a mess of things, but all's not lost! Go back to where you began; go back to grace. And there you'll find just what you need—everything you need, the only thing you need. There you'll find grace."

Yet Paul knows the Galatians will have a tough time going back to grace because they've lost confidence in the gospel he preached.

Here's what happened. After Paul left Galatia,[3] his converts came under the influence of certain individuals who discredited his apostleship, called into question the validity of his gospel, and insisted his converts were only half-baked and needed to go all the way and get circumcised, if they were going to shore up their status of children of God.

These "Judaizers," as they're commonly called,[4] were apparently quite effective in persuading the Galatians of the necessity of circumcision, if not the need to embrace the Jewish law as a whole.[5] Of course, they "could have drawn on a powerful battery of arguments to commend the law to the Galatian Christians."[6] In addition, they could have pointed to a number of advantages to circumcision in particular: sharing in the blessing of Abraham (3:6–18), securing their identity as the "sons of God" (3:23–4:7), even finding assistance in the battle against "the desires of the flesh" (5:16).[7]

As a result, Paul's once enthusiastic converts were now ambivalent at best. They'd developed misgivings about whether Paul had told them the whole story and whether his gospel could get them to where they needed to go spiritually. Thus they were suffering from a bad case of buyer's remorse (cf. 4:15, 16), the upshot of which was to turn away from the one who called them in the grace of Christ and turn to a different gospel, the one the Judaizers preached (1:6, 7). So serious, in fact, was their crisis of faith, they were ready to submit to the knife and get circumcised, no small step for them to take given the widespread antipathy toward circumcision among pagans and the inherent undesirability and risks of the procedure for adult males living in the ancient Mediterranean world.[8]

Paul's Message Is Legitimate

Some of us find ourselves in a similar situation to the Galatians. We embraced the gospel with great enthusiasm at first, but we've found that living the Christian life isn't what we expected. As a result, we too wrestle with a bit of buyer's remorse, wondering whether something more is needed to get us to where we want to go in life.

This is just where the Galatians were, which is why Paul's very first word to them is to insist that the message of grace still stands. But, notice, he speaks not about the message but the messenger: "Paul, an apostle—not from men nor through man, but through Jesus Christ and God the Father, who raised him from the dead" (v. 1).

Does he say this because he's insecure about his own credentials? No, but in order to reassert the legitimacy of his gospel! For if Paul himself isn't legitimate, that is, if he's not truly an apostle sent from God, then his gospel isn't legitimate either. It's that simple. This is why Paul insists on his God-given commission here, something he'll go on to do at greater length in this and the next chapter (cf. 1:11—2:10).

This is also why he appeals to the fact that he stands together with a band of fellow gospel workers as he writes to the Galatians—"and all the brothers who are with me" (v. 2).[9] Paul is no lone ranger, a renegade working in isolation from the rest of the early church. The gospel he preaches and the gospel the Galatians first believed is the same gospel preached by Paul's cohorts and many others.

We see, then, Paul insisting that he's a real *agent of grace*. Indeed, this is the point of his apostleship: to extend grace to others on God's behalf! This is also the point of Galatians: *Galatians exists for grace!* That's why Paul writes this letter: he wants to see grace unleashed on a desperate situation.

More importantly, God wants to unleash grace. That's why the church needs not only Galatians but all of Paul's letters, each one of which begins and ends with grace. Indeed, this is why we have the Scriptures as a whole, both Old and New Testaments, because God desires to unleash his grace in our lives through his inspired Word, the Bible!

From Genesis to Revelation the Word of God is a treasure trove of grace. Golden coins of comfort, costly pearls of assurance, precious jewels of promise are all found in the pages of Scripture. In fact, everything that was written in the Bible was written for us, that "through the encouragement of the Scriptures we might have hope" (Romans 15:4).

Therefore, every time we make a mess of things, we must go back to grace by going back to the Word of God. When we blow it, we must not neglect Scripture. Instead of closing our Bible let's open it, read it, look to it, dwell in it! Again, when we sin our tendency is to neglect or even hide, because the Word of God is indeed "living and active . . . discerning the thoughts and intentions of the heart" (Hebrews 4:12). But nowhere else will we find the very thing we need when we make a mess of things. There alone, in God's Word, will we find a message of grace—the gospel. Part of what it means to go back to grace, then, is to go back to the Bible, where the message of grace can be found.

Jesus' Sacrifice Is Sufficient

For Paul it's not enough to reestablish the legitimacy of his gospel. Sure, it may be true, but is it adequate? He therefore needs to demonstrate the sufficiency of the gospel as well. Paul knows he must convince the Galatians that the grace of God, turned loose on the world through the death of Christ, is more than able to meet their spiritual needs.

After Paul left Galatia, the Galatians came under the influence of certain teachers who were promoting the Jewish law as an effective way to advance spiritually (cf. 3:3). In addition, we can assume the Galatians themselves had probably found the Jewish law appealing because of the promise it held out for spiritual help. No doubt they also found themselves frustrated and fatigued with the same thing we often find frustrating and fatiguing: the continuing presence of sin in our lives.

Do we realize we need to be rescued from the dominion of sin? Sin is a lordless power, a godless force. Sin is not merely a one-time thing, an event, an action, something that's over once you've done it. Instead sin has after effects; it lives on! And these aftereffects, in turn, affect us. Is there a way to break free from this sin that so easily entangles?

Paul's answer is a resounding yes! There is. But it's not the path of the Law; it's the cross of Christ. Deliverance from sin and from "the present evil age" comes only one way; indeed, grace itself comes only one way: through the death of the Lord Jesus Christ. "Grace to you and peace from God our Father and the Lord Jesus Christ, *who gave himself for our sins to deliver us from the present evil age*" (vv. 3, 4).

Thus Paul drives the Galatians back to this fundamental fact: *Christ gave himself for our sins*. For the death of Christ alone explains the presence of grace in our lives; and the death of Christ alone opens the wellspring of salvation: justification, sanctification, glorification.

O for a thousand tongues to sing
My great Redeemer's praise,
The glories of my God and King,
The triumphs of His grace!

What are these triumphs of his grace?

He breaks the power of canceled sin,
He sets the prisoner free;
His blood can make the foulest clean,
His blood availed for me.[10]

So, then, when we sin, we don't need to hide from God. When we blow it really badly, we don't have to run away. When we're discouraged with where we are spiritually, we shouldn't flirt with other stuff but instead go back to the cross of Christ, return to the source of grace: the sacrificial self-giving of the Son for our sins.

"Amen" Is All It Takes

But how do we go back to grace? How do we get there? This is a pressing question for some of us because we've blown it big-time. We've all been there. Perhaps we have begun to doubt whether there's any hope for us, any solution. But we've heard that we can go back to grace, and we want to know how.

"Amen" is all it takes!

This is where Paul leads the Galatians: to utter their "Amen" to all that God has done for them in Christ. Notice the truly remarkable way in which he closes this letter's salutation: "[Jesus] gave himself for our sins to deliver us from the present evil age, according to the will of our God and Father, to whom be the glory forever and ever. Amen" (1:4, 5).

This is not a typical way to address a letter, is it? But with this closure Paul ushers the Galatians into the very atmosphere of worship, and by rehearsing what God has done for them in Christ, he invites them to voice their agreement to this great salvation with the confession, "Amen."[11]

You see, the way back to grace couldn't be simpler: we only have to say, "Amen." I'm quite tempted to say that it couldn't be any easier. But I don't want you to think uttering, "Amen" is easy. Because it's not!

In fact, saying "Amen" may be the hardest thing we've ever done. Saying "Amen" is not something we simply do with our head. "Amen" is not "Yep" or "Sure" or "Got it." "Amen" is something we say with our heart.

When we say, "Amen," we're more than observers; we've moved from being spectators to being participants. "Amen" is our way of entering into this divine drama, taking up our part, assuming our role in the story of grace called the death and resurrection of Jesus Christ. Until we do that, we're simply sitting in the audience, out of the action, away from the benefits of grace.

"Amen" is, then, the only entry point into the world of grace. There's no other way in. We can't find grace in any other way because grace is only given to those who have faith; and the voice of faith is expressed in the word "Amen."

A Letter for Prodigals

Galatians is often viewed as a letter for legalists, for those who seek to earn God's favor by their works. And in a sense that is what Galatians is about. But Galatians is also a letter for prodigals—for those who have made a mess of their own lives, who are on the verge of apostasy, almost ready to shipwreck their faith, on the brink of moral or spiritual disaster.

Galatians begins and ends by calling wayward believers back to grace; therefore, it's perfect for prodigals. Galatians never tires of saying to us: the message of grace still stands; the fountain of grace still flows; the way back to grace couldn't be easier—all it takes is a heartfelt "Amen," uttered in response to all that God has done for us in Christ.

This is the good news every prodigal needs to hear! This is the message every profligate son or wayward daughter needs to hear. This is the assurance every drifting church or disillusioned Christian needs to hear. This is the promise every wandering soul in our own prodigal world needs to hear!

But when [the prodigal son] came to himself, he said, "How many of my father's hired servants have more than enough bread, but I perish here with hunger! I will arise and go to my father, and I will say to him, 'Father, I have sinned against heaven and before you. I am no longer worthy to be called your son. Treat me as one of your hired servants.'" And he arose and came to his father. But while he was still a long way off, his father saw him and felt compassion, and ran and embraced him and kissed him. And the son said to him, "Father, I have sinned against heaven and before you. I am no longer worthy to be called your son." But the father said to his servants, "Bring quickly the best robe, and put it on him, and put a ring on his hand, and shoes on his feet. And bring the fattened calf and kill it, and let us eat and celebrate. For this my son was dead, and is alive again; he was lost, and is found." And they began to celebrate. (Luke 15:17–24)

Resolved: Go Back to Grace

Understand, then, this all-important first lesson of Galatians, this first principle of gospel-rooted living: *Go back to grace.* As we strive to move forward in the Christian life, we must remember that we need to go back—again and again and again—to grace. We'll need to go back to grace in order to move forward in life.

I challenge us all to make the following not only a New Year's resolution but a perpetual resolution that we are determined to keep: Every time I blow it, I'll go back to grace. I won't ignore it, play dumb, hide, or try to pass the buck to my spouse or my boss or my mom or my dad or my neighbor or my genes or my personality or my upbringing or my financial situation! Instead I'll look my misstep in the face and then go back to grace—to the cross, that place where Jesus Christ has already taken the blame and condemnation and guilt upon himself.

There, at the foot of the cross, let us resolve to bow down in humble adoration and worship, ascribing glory and honor and praise to the One who gave himself for us "to deliver us from the present evil age, according to the will of our God and Father, to whom be the glory forever and ever. Amen" (1:4, 5).

I am astonished that you are so quickly deserting him who called you in the grace of Christ and are turning to a different gospel—not that there is another one, but there are some who trouble you and want to distort the gospel of Christ. But even if we or an angel from heaven should preach to you a gospel contrary to the one we preached to you, let him be accursed. As we have said before, so now I say again: If anyone is preaching to you a gospel contrary to the one you received, let him be accursed.

1:6–9

2

Apostolic Astonishment!

GALATIANS 1:6–9

IN JUNE 2000 I graduated from The Bethlehem Institute, a pastoral training program of Bethlehem Baptist Church, where John Piper is pastor for preaching and vision. This was the first graduating class. There were only five of us, so our graduation ceremony was held in a cozy restaurant in downtown Minneapolis.

Pastor John, as we affectionately called him, gave the graduation talk. And I'll never forget what he said. We were a small band of aspiring pastors in our early twenties, so he wisely took us to the story of King Solomon.

If you recall Solomon's story from 1 Kings, you know how impressive it is. Solomon is anointed king, is blessed by his father David, establishes his reign, receives an abundance of both wisdom and wealth, builds the temple and a palace, oversees the ark's return to Jerusalem, and establishes the nation of Israel as a major player in the region. All this takes place in the first ten chapters of 1 Kings.

But then you come to 1 Kings 11, which is where Pastor John took us, each with bated breath, anticipating the punch line to the story. Slowly and deliberately, he then read to us how Solomon's story ends.

> Now King Solomon loved many foreign women. . . . And his wives turned away his heart. For when Solomon was old his wives turned away his heart after other gods, and his heart was not wholly true to the Lord his God, as was the heart of David his father. (1 Kings 11:1–4)

Closing his Bible, Pastor John cast his fatherly gaze on each of us and said, "Brothers, finish well! Finish well! O stay the course, and finish well!"

And from there he went on to admonish us to guard our hearts and stay true to our God, the one who'd called us in the grace of our Lord Christ Jesus.

Disbelief over Unbelief

No doubt Paul admonished his young converts in Galatia similarly. He knew eventually he'd have to say good-bye; therefore he made it a point to warn them not to forsake their first love or flirt with any other "gospel" (cf. vv. 6, 7, 8, 9). Surely his plea to these babes in Christ was: Finish well!

Imagine, then, Paul's shock when he learns that the Galatians are turning away from the One who had called them by his grace (1:6). Paul was, of course, no neophyte in ministry; he'd seen it all. Yet what could have prepared him for this heartbreak? With his own blood, sweat, and tears, Paul had established these precious churches (cf. Acts 13:13—14:23), only now to see them abandon the gospel and thus shipwreck their faith!

Unlike Solomon, however, the Galatians aren't being led astray by foreign wives but by *false teachers*. The outcome, however, is the same. Hearts aren't wholly true to the Lord, and affections wander toward other gods and other gospels.

With tears in his eyes, then, Paul composes this letter and sends it posthaste to Galatia. He's compelled to confront his wayward converts with what can only be called *apostolic astonishment*: "I am astonished that you are so quickly deserting him who called you in the grace of Christ and are turning to a different gospel" (1:6). He's incredulous; he can hardly believe their unbelief.

I suspect most of us know someone on the verge of apostasy. Or you yourself may be there. Apostasy can overtake any of us. It's hubris to think it can't happen to us. To the overly confident in Corinth, Paul says, "Let anyone who thinks that he stands take heed lest he fall" (1 Corinthians 10:12). Apostasy is a possibility for us all.

Apostasy Is a Tragedy

But what is apostasy? It's *desertion*. When you desert what you once held dear or turn away from what you once treasured, you commit apostasy. To apostatize is to embrace the Christian faith, then reject it later on.

In the USA apostasy happens every day. In fact, studies show that an alarming number of young adults leave the faith during their time in college. Despite being reared in Christian homes, involved at church, even baptized as teens, when these young adults head off to university, they desert the faith in droves. And statistically speaking high percentages never return.

How do we respond to news of someone forsaking the faith? Does it tear us up inside? Are we overtaken, like Paul, with heartache and astonishment?

Apostasy ought to grieve us deeply. For what could be sadder than for someone to turn his own life-story from gospel triumph to heart-rending tragedy!

Paul is astonished because he knows apostasy is such a tragedy.

Apostasy is tragic because it means that individuals *desert the gospel*. Those who apostatize typically don't see it that way; they often think they're enhancing, rather than abandoning, the gospel. Surely the Galatians didn't think they were abandoning the gospel. But this, Paul says, is precisely what happens when you *add anything to the gospel*. The gospel equation is this: Jesus + Anything Else = Nothing![1] Which is why Paul accuses the Galatians not of adding to the gospel but of turning to "a different gospel" altogether (1:6).

When we apostatize, we also *desert grace*. This is what makes the Galatians' situation so sad: they'd been called "in the grace of Christ" (1:6). But now they're abandoning this place of grace in order to return to a place called bondage (cf. 4:9; 5:1).

But the real tragedy of apostasy is this: we *desert God*. To apostatize is to forsake the living God for a dead idol, a golden calf of our own making. This is what the Israelites did at the base of Mount Sinai; this is what Paul sees the Galatians doing after his departure. Like Israel of old, his converts are "so quickly" (1:6) turning from him who called them.

> When the people saw that Moses delayed to come down from the mountain, the people gathered themselves together to Aaron and said to him, "Up, make us gods who shall go before us. As for this Moses, the man who brought us up out of the land of Egypt, we do not know what has become of him." So Aaron said to them, "Take off the rings of gold that are in the ears of your wives, your sons, and your daughters, and bring them to me." So all the people took off the rings of gold that were in their ears and brought them to Aaron. And he received the gold from their hand and fashioned it with a graving tool and made a golden calf. And they said, "These are your gods, O Israel, who brought you up out of the land of Egypt!" . . . And the LORD said to Moses, "Go down, for your people, whom you brought up out of the land of Egypt, have corrupted themselves. They have turned aside quickly out of the way that I commanded them. They have made for themselves a golden calf and have worshiped it and sacrificed to it and said, 'These are your gods, O Israel, who brought you up out of the land of Egypt!'" (Exodus 32:1–4, 7, 8)

The Apostle Paul, then, like Moses, confronts wilderness apostasy.[2] The Galatians, like the Israelites, are forsaking the God who called them out of Egyptian-like bondage to sin and are turning to a different gospel—a lifeless idol that can neither speak nor save. They think they're improving the gospel, but what they're actually doing is forging a golden calf in the furnace of unbelief. This is the real tragedy of apostasy: we try to improve the gospel, only in the end to find we've abandoned it for an idol made by human hands.

Soul-Trouble and Twisted Truth

Why, then, we may wonder, does anyone commit apostasy? Why do people forsake the Christian faith? Why would anyone in their right mind turn from grace to no grace or from the gospel to that which isn't a gospel at all?

From what we know of the Galatians' own experience, apostasy comes over us when two things happen to us. First, we experience *soul-trouble*— a personal crisis, hardship, tragedy, or loss. And, secondly, we encounter *twisted truth*—some subtle perversion of the truth of Scripture, a slight distortion of the grace of God in the gospel.

Notice what Paul says about the Galatians: they're turning to "a different gospel" (1:6)—"not that there is another one, but there are some who *trouble you* and *want to distort* the gospel of Christ" (1:7). The Galatians were troubled, threatened, scared by these false teachers; they were also being taught a bogus gospel, a distortion of the real one.

This is the twin source of apostasy in every professing Christian's life: soul-trouble and twisted truth. Soul-trouble makes us vulnerable to twisted truth. When we're scared or hurting, discouraged or disillusioned, we're often more open to considering something in addition to the gospel that we first received. We may have found Jesus sufficient up to this point. But given the way things are now, we wonder if it's time to look elsewhere.

Consider Stephen, a freshman at one of the Big Ten schools. After an intense first semester in college, he's glad to be home for Christmas break and enjoy home-cooked meals, time with family and friends, and a respite from his studies. Yet while he's home Stephen's father breaks the news that he and Stephen's mother are getting a divorce.

Stephen's father says "irreconcilable differences" make continuing in marriage an impossibility. Stephen is crushed. But he is also disillusioned: yes, with his parents, but also with everything about his parents and what they've stood for over the years—including their Christian faith, which he came to call his own early in high school.

Stephen returns to college in the throes of deep sadness and anger; he's experiencing soul-trouble, the likes of which he's never tasted. But what he doesn't realize at the time is that his soul-trouble is going to alter his spring semester in a profound way. In fact, his World Religions class—which under other circumstances would have been a useful intellectual exercise—is set to deliver a body-blow to his Christian faith. Now the grace-filled teachings of Buddhism strike Stephen as superior to the hypocritical Christianity he picked up back home and in Sunday school. By the end of the spring semester he no longer attends church; instead he is attending yoga classes with his girlfriend, practicing Transcendental Meditation with his roommate, and reading the writings of the Dali Lama. And by the time Stephen returns home at the end of the school year, he's resigned himself to the fact that he no longer believes in Jesus or calls himself a Christian.[3]

The reality is that one doesn't wake up one morning and decide to forsake the Christian faith. Instead apostasy happens more subtly and slowly. As John Calvin says, "The devil sometimes uses apparently small, subtle issues to distance us from the gospel, without our even perceiving it."[4] This is why forsaking Christ can feel like something that happens to you as much as something you choose to do. Apostasy, in other words, means slowly drifting from the seashore of faith on a raft of doubt, driven by the winds of disappointment and carried by the currents of false teaching.

How to Avoid Apostasy

But how can we avoid drifting? *First, we must hold tenaciously to what we were taught.* Tenacity is what Paul calls for here: "But even if we or an angel from heaven should preach to you a gospel contrary to the one we preached to you, let him be accursed" (1:8). When the Apostle Paul tells you to not listen to him and even to ignore an angel, you know he's calling for tenacity.[5] Charles Spurgeon had the right advice: "Cling tightly with both your hands; when they fail, catch hold with your teeth; and if they give way, hang on by your eyelashes!"[6] Don't let go of the gospel! That's the kind of tenacity we all need if we're going to stay the course and finish the race.

Second, we must let Scripture be our final authority in matters of faith. We must let the Bible rule in our life. Listen to Martin Luther:

> This queen [the Bible] must rule, and everyone must obey, and be subject to, her. The pope, Luther, Augustine, Paul, an angel from heaven—these should not be masters, judges, or arbiters but only witnesses, disciples, and confessors of Scripture. Nor should any doctrine be taught or heard in the church except the pure Word of God. Otherwise, let the teachers and the hearers be accursed along with their doctrine.[7]

We avoid apostasy, thirdly, by heeding Biblical warnings. The Galatians should have done this but obviously failed to do so. Notice, Paul reminds them of what they've already heard: "As we have said before, so now I say again: If anyone is preaching to you a gospel contrary to the one you received, let him be accursed" (1:9).[8]

No one likes to be warned. We often feel like we're being talked down to. Thus our own pride and sense of self-sufficiency strongly resists warnings, even when the warning is the best thing for us. Human beings don't like warnings, whether it's a warning from our parents or a warning in the Bible.

But the reality is this: *warnings save lives*. None of my kids have ever thanked me for hollering, "Get out of the street!" But none of them have been hit by a car either. Warnings work. But they only work when they're heeded. As Christians we must heed the warnings of Scripture in order to stay, as Jesus says, on the hard and narrow way that leads to life (Matthew 7:14).[9]

Respond with Astonishment Ourselves

How do we feel when we learn that someone has abandoned the Christian faith? Does it grieve us little more than would the news that our favorite NFL player has just signed with another team? Does it fill us with no more disappointment than when we learn our favorite restaurant has gone out of business?

When someone abandons the faith, it should strike us with as much astonishment as would our best friend leaving his spouse. In fact, we should respond with *godly jealousy*, the kind Paul has for the Corinthians: "For I feel a divine jealousy for you, since I betrothed you to one husband, to present you as a pure virgin to Christ" (2 Corinthians 11:2).

We must remember, however, that it's not the responsibility of *individual* Christians to call down anathemas on anyone's head. It certainly is the responsibility of all Christians to be Biblically well versed, so they can spot false teaching and encourage others to stay true to the gospel. But pronouncing people apostate isn't our responsibility. It's too sobering a task for any one person; instead it's the responsibility of *the church*, which is to say, it's the responsibility of duly appointed elders, who are entrusted with the task of guarding the moral and theological fidelity of the church (cf. Titus 1:9).

What is, then, our responsibility toward those who are in the process of leaving or who have already left the faith? In Galatians 6 Paul urges the Galatians, or at least some of them, to do for others the very thing Paul is doing for them. Having just explained to them the powerful working of the Holy Spirit within the life of the believer and the believing community, Paul then applies that to them specifically with these words: "Brothers, if anyone is caught in any transgression, you who are spiritual should restore him in a spirit of gentleness" (6:1). This is a call to pursue people: to restore anyone who has been overtaken in any sin, whether it's the sin of lying or the sin of apostasy itself; to plead, to warn, to point that person back to Christ and back to grace.

Apostasy and the Faithfulness of God

Apostasy is a real possibility for each and every one of us. It is a threat to gospel-rooted living because it uproots us from the gospel itself. But let me hasten to add that what is even more real than apostasy is the faithfulness of God.

From what we see in the New Testament, the Apostle Peter was never more than a whisker away from apostasy. There was the time when Jesus needed to rebuke Peter for missing the point of his Messianic mission of suffering. There was the time Peter denied Jesus three times. And there was Peter's great act of hypocrisy in Antioch (cf. Galatians 2:11–14).

Yet here's the good news: Jesus Christ kept him! Left to fend for himself, Peter would have been devoured by the roaring lion (cf. 1 Peter 5:8). But he was never left alone. Jesus stood faithfully by his side, defending, protecting, and keeping him. "Simon, Simon, behold, Satan demanded to have you, that he might sift you like wheat, but I have prayed for you that your faith may not fail" (Luke 22:31, 32).

So, too, God the Father will do for all his children. By his own power God will guard us "through faith for a salvation ready to be revealed in the last time" (1 Peter 1:5). He is more than "able to keep you from stumbling and to present you blameless before the presence of his glory with great joy" (Jude 24). He who "called you to his eternal glory in Christ, will himself restore, confirm, strengthen, and establish you" (1 Peter 5:10). He "will sustain you to the end, guiltless in the day of our Lord Jesus Christ" (1 Corinthians 1:8). Indeed Paul says, "I am sure of this, that he who began a good work in you will bring it to completion at the day of Jesus Christ" (Philippians 1:6). "He who calls you is faithful; he will surely do it" (1 Thessalonians 5:24).

So, then, we must hold tenaciously to what we have been taught, heed the warnings of Scripture, and hope confidently in Jesus. For he says of his followers, "My Father, who has given them to me, is greater than all, and no one is able to snatch them out of the Father's hand" (John 10:29).

We are secure in the Father's hand!

For am I now seeking the approval of man, or of God? Or am I trying to please man? If I were still trying to please man, I would not be a servant of Christ.

1:10

3

People-Pleaser or Servant of Christ?

GALATIANS 1:10

PEOPLE-PLEASER OR SERVANT OF CHRIST? Which are we? People-pleasers have an inordinate desire to please other people; servants of Christ have an all-consuming passion to please God. People-pleasers are motivated by the fear of man; servants of Christ are inspired by the fear of God. People-pleasers pretend to serve God when they really intend to serve themselves; servants of Christ actually intend to serve God by meeting the needs of other people. People-pleasers are anxious for approval from others and distraught when they don't get it; servants of Christ simply love others and leave approval or disapproval to the judgment of God.

So which are we? People-pleasers or servants of Christ? This is the question the Apostle Paul confronts the Galatians with in the opening chapter of the letter. "For am I now seeking the approval of man, or of God? Or am I trying to please man? If I were still trying to please man, I would not be a servant of Christ" (1:10).

Why does he ask this question? Because Paul knows that the crisis in Galatia is not simply a theological crisis but a *moral* one. The Galatians aren't simply confused; they're being people-pleasers rather than servants of Christ. This explains, at least in part, why they're forsaking Paul's gospel. But Paul also knows that the Judaizers are people-pleasers as well. Sure, they've made a good Biblical case for the Galatians to get circumcised, but only so they can, as Paul says, "make a good showing in the flesh" and avoid displeasing those who have power over them (cf. 6:12, 13).

Is it any wonder, then, that Paul injects the theme of people-pleasing into the letter at this point? He must confront people-pleasing head-on because he knows it's a big part of the crisis in Galatia. And what he wants to say to the Galatians—and what I believe God wants to say to each of us—is simply this: *people-pleasers don't make good servants of Christ.*

People-Pleasers Cave under Pressure from Influential People

You see, people-pleasers don't make good servants of Christ because *people-pleasers cave under pressure from influential people.* It is the influential people in our lives, not the insignificant, who tempt us to people-please. No one plays the people-pleaser with someone who's unimportant to them. The homecoming queen at the local high school doesn't play the people-pleaser with any freshman boy. But insecure sophomores sure might try to curry favor with upperclassmen. So, too, we're not likely to people-please with the person who delivers our mail or bags our groceries. But we might be tempted to people-please around our teacher or coach or boss or spouse.

Paul certainly understood the pressure of influential people, how they tempt us to compromise our gospel-rooted principles. In fact, in Galatians 2:1ff. he describes a time when it would have been very easy for him to fudge on his convictions in order to win the approval of those who were influential. He had made a trip to Jerusalem to meet with the leaders of the early church. While there, some exerted tremendous pressure upon him to have his colleague Titus circumcised.

In situations like this people-pleasers give in; they cave under the pressure. They'd rather compromise their Biblical convictions than have the influential people in their lives look on them with disapproval. Perhaps we've found ourselves in a similar situation recently, maybe even this week, at work or at school, talking with a friend between classes or interacting with our supervisor over a project.

People-pleasers yield to pressure. But servants of Christ like Paul stand their ground. To those wielding great pressure to compromise, Paul says, "To them we did not yield in submission even for a moment, so that the truth of the gospel might be preserved for you" (2:5). No doubt this was a costly move for Paul; surely he earned the disapproval of those who were thought influential in Jerusalem. But he knew his compromise at this point would have been even more costly for the Galatians because it would have meant a compromise of the truth of the gospel, which would have meant serving himself and not them with his actions.

People-Pleasers Ignore Harmful Hypocrisy

But that's not all. People-pleasers don't make good servants of Christ because *people-pleasers ignore harmful hypocrisy.* Within the Christian community few things are as corrosive as hypocrisy. When a Christian has a habit of saying one thing and doing another, or denying with his life what he affirms with his lips, he can do all sorts of damage to that community. And it is the responsibility of the servants of Christ within that community to lovingly confront that person in his or her hypocrisy, lest that person's hypocrisy spread like gangrene and harm others.

But people-pleasers don't do confrontation, even loving confrontation, of harmful hypocrisy. Instead they prefer to ignore it, brush it under the carpet, and hope it will just go away. This is because people-pleasers know, as we all do, that by confronting someone we run the risk of his or her being displeased with us rather than pleased. People-pleasers are acutely aware of this danger and therefore steer clear of confrontation, even when they know it's to their own detriment or the detriment of others.

I imagine the Apostle Paul was at least tempted to ignore the harmful hypocrisy he saw developing in the church at Antioch. As we learn from Galatians 2:11–14, when the apostle Peter visited, he and the other Jews freely ate with Gentiles—that is, until a few important individuals from Jerusalem came to town touting a different set of convictions, at which point Peter pulled back. "For before certain men came from James, he was eating with the Gentiles; but when they came he drew back and separated himself, fearing the circumcision party" (2:12). Yet notice how Peter's one act of hypocrisy spread like gangrene and infected the whole church: "And the rest of the Jews acted hypocritically along with him, so that even Barnabas was led astray by their hypocrisy" (2:13). Every last one of them was led astray by Peter's one act of hypocrisy. That's *harmful* hypocrisy, the kind that undermines a whole church.

Every last one of them was led astray, except the converted Pharisee from the city of Tarsus, the Apostle Paul. He didn't ignore or overlook anyone's hypocrisy, not even Peter's. Instead he called Peter on it. Paul confronted Peter's harmful hypocrisy, and did so publicly because of the public nature and consequences of Peter's treachery. "But when I saw that their conduct was not in step with the truth of the gospel, I said to Cephas before them all, 'If you, though a Jew, live like a Gentile and not like a Jew, how can you force the Gentiles to live like Jews?'" (2:14).

Yet how tempting it would have been for Paul to paper over his differences with Peter! How convenient for him to have called this just a little indiscretion and let it slide. How easy it would have been for Paul not to stick his neck on the line or run the risk of alienating himself from the entire church. Yet how much of a people-pleaser he would have been, and not a servant of Christ, if he had had turned a blind eye to Peter's hypocrisy.

We need to realize that the failure to confront harmful hypocrisy within the Body of Christ is one of the reasons why churches remain spiritually anemic and weak. Churches can be breeding grounds for people-pleasers. We might call it by a different name, like passive-aggressive. But at root it is people-pleasing that leads to all kinds of dysfunctions, double standards, failures of leadership, and even hypocrisy itself. Yet instead of engaging in loving confrontation of harmful hypocrisy, we ignore it, then go gossip about it with a spouse or a friend.

Some of us have never lovingly confronted harmful hypocrisy. And the reason is not because we didn't see it; it was right there in front of us. It was because we didn't want to harm ourselves or our own reputation or approval rating in the eyes of others. Though we saw the sin, we didn't say anything. We let harmful hypocrisy slide, and others were harmed by it or had to clean up after us. That's cowardly, not Christlike; that's playing the people-pleaser, not being a servant of Christ.

People-Pleasers Hide from the Shame of the Cross

There is a third reason why people-pleasers don't make good servants of Christ. It's because *people-pleasers hide from the shame of the cross*. No one likes to be embarrassed, least of all people-pleasers. It's death to a people-pleaser to be publicly exposed or humiliated. But to be a servant of Christ you must be willing to take up your cross and follow Jesus. Yet the cross is not just a method of execution—it is a tool of *humiliation* as well.

In the ancient world, death on a cross was the most shameful of deaths. Crucifixion was both painful and gruesome; but it was also public and therefore embarrassing and humiliating. The first-century Jewish historian Josephus called it "the most wretched of deaths."[1] Even the pagan orator Cicero knew it as "so horrible a deed."[2] A man was beaten, stripped naked, then nailed by his hands and feet to a piece of wood, which was then made to stand up in plain daylight, so that every passerby could mock and jeer as he helplessly and hopelessly choked to death.

This is the way Jesus of Nazareth died. He was publicly executed, and in the most embarrassing and humiliating fashion imaginable. "The founder and perfecter of our faith" indeed "endured the cross," but only by "despising the shame" of the cross (Hebrews 12:2). Shameful it was, and shameful it is, and shameful it continues to be in the lives of those who take it up.

No one understood the shame of bearing the cross better than the Apostle Paul. No one suffered more for serving Christ or was more shamefully treated than he. As Christ's servant, Paul insisted upon a circumcision-free gospel for Gentiles. And this infuriated some of his Jewish kinsmen, who took out their frustration on Paul. So he suffered—often and intensely.[3] No doubt this explains his closing challenge to the Galatians: "From now on let no one cause me trouble, for I bear on my body the marks of Jesus" (6:17).

Others, however, tried to sever the relationship between the cross of Christ and being a servant of Christ. In fact, they were the ones stirring up trouble in the churches in Galatia. So in the closing portion of the letter Paul levels with the Galatians about them, and he reveals their real motivation in promoting circumcision. "It is those who want to make a good showing in the flesh who would force you to be circumcised, and only in order that they may not be persecuted for the cross of Christ" (6:12). Their agenda is a people-pleaser's agenda: to keep up appearances and avoid anything difficult or humiliating. And they've come to realize that the only way they're going to be able to do that is by forcing these Gentile converts to get circumcised. So they're advocating for the Galatians to lose their foreskins so they can save their own skin and not be persecuted by their fellow Jews.

Of course, Paul understands how this works. He knows he too could make his life a whole lot easier if he would only fudge a little on the cross of Christ. He knows his persecution would quickly vanish if he would just quietly remove the offense of the cross (cf. 5:11). But as a servant of Christ, he won't do it. Indeed, he can't do it. In fact, just the opposite: he will *not run* from the shame of the cross but rather *boast* in it. "But far be it from me to boast except in the cross of our Lord Jesus Christ, by which the world has been crucified to me, and I to the world" (6:14).

No wonder Paul says with such pathos and emotion earlier in the letter, "I have been crucified with Christ" (2:20). Not in some mystical or glibly sentimental sense, but in a most painfully real and costly sense. He has had to learn the hard way that a servant of Christ cannot avoid the humiliation, cannot run from the shame of the cross.

Less than a week before I was to finish my doctoral thesis and return to the United States, I had dinner with our neighbors in Cambridge, UK. They had invited another friend of theirs, who happened to be a freelance writer—very sophisticated, wealthy, posh, cosmopolitan, bright, quintessentially British. Naturally he was curious as to what I intended to do after graduation.

With a PhD from Cambridge University, he assumed I was headed into a Harvard professorship or something like that.

I told him that I was taking up a pastorate in the Midwest, in a place called Wheaton, Illinois. By the look on his face, I realized I had to explain to him that the Midwest was that big stretch of land between New York and Los Angeles, that place with all the red states and where buffalo still roam freely, and that a pastorate meant working in a thing called a church. But as I was saying all of this, I could see a cheeky grin take shape on his face. It was as if he had all of a sudden discovered what sort of creature he was talking to, and his posture toward me instantly changed. He then peered over the top of his glasses, tilting his head slightly downward toward me, and said, "The pastorate? Hmmm." Then he paused, chuckled, and in a most condescending way said to me with a smirk, "That's a bit anticlimactic from Cambridge, don't you think?"

Now for a people-pleaser like me, that was a pretty painful thing for him to say. I felt remarkably small at that moment. My pride and vanity were instantly ground up like the salt and pepper on the dinner table before me. At the same time I could feel the urge to people-please rise up within me. I wanted to hide from the subtle shame of the moment, the embarrassment of what it meant for me personally to follow Jesus. In fact, just then I felt like I'd gone outside the camp to bear a little of the reproach Jesus himself bore (cf. Hebrews 13:13).

Do you know what the root of the problem with people-pleasers is? *The root of the problem is that people-pleasers are idolaters.* People-pleasers make idols of other people and thus crave their approval as though it were the bread of life. But in idolizing other people and their approval, they ultimately idolize themselves. They make idols of themselves and thus require the approval of others as though it were an offering being given to a god. People-pleasing is a kind of self-worship. It is the antithesis of being a servant of Christ Jesus. Which is why Paul actually puts people-pleasing in direct opposition to serving Christ: "If I were still trying to please man, *I would not be* a servant of Christ" (1:10).

Fighting the People-Pleaser within You

There is a people-pleaser in all of us, one that needs a continual crucifixion if we are going to become the servants of Christ that God wants us to be. But how do we fight and indeed kill the people-pleaser in our own hearts? The same way we fight against any remaining sin in our life: by fighting the fight of faith, by trusting in all that God is for us in Christ.

So if we're going to gain victory in our battle against people-pleasing, we must embrace the fact, first of all, that *Jesus Christ has taken all the judgments against us and nailed them to his cross.* And there they remain, forever! Every judgment that ever stood against us or that ever could stand against us, every harsh or humiliating word uttered by friend or foe, is nailed to the tree. Indeed, on the cross Jesus even dealt with God's own judgment of us—his righteous condemnation of us, the just sentence that stood against us because of our sin. He nailed it all to the cross. "There is therefore now no condemnation for those who are in Christ Jesus" (Romans 8:1).

But if we're going to fight the temptation to people-please, we must also come to really believe that *God's judgment is the only one that counts.* In fact, in light of God's judgment of us, every other judgment ought to be small, even to the point of nonexistent. "But with me it is a very small thing that I should be judged by you or by any human court," Paul tells the Corinthians. "In fact, I do not even judge myself. For I am not aware of anything against myself, but I am not thereby acquitted. It is the Lord who judges me" (1 Corinthians 4:3, 4).

So we must not entrust ourselves to the judgment of others but to the judgment of God. People are fickle, and so are their judgments of us. If we're always working hard to curry favor from other people and to do what they think we should do, we will eventually work ourselves into a state of exhaustion and despair. Remember, God's judgment is far kinder than man's, and God's judgment is also far simpler than man's. It doesn't involve a thousand different and competing expectations of us; God only wants *one* thing from us: "faith working through love" (5:6)—faith in his Son Jesus Christ and love for God and for others born of the Holy Spirit. At the end of the day this is the only thing that counts before God; this is the only thing that will avail at God's judgment (5:5).

Conclusion

People-pleasers don't make good servants of Christ because people-pleasers cave under pressure from influential people, ignore harmful hypocrisy, and run from the shame of the cross. But more than that, people-pleasers live anxious lives, always worrying about whether they'll find approval or disapproval from others; and in so doing they will miss the approval that can come only from God himself.

Bishop Thomas Wolsey once remarked, "If I had served God as faithfully as man, I had been better rewarded, and not forsaken in my distress."[4] There's a lot of wisdom in that statement. Being a servant of Christ is far sweeter than being a slave to man's opinion, and the reward of being a servant of Christ is far, far superior to any reward we can obtain from any man. For only by serving Christ Jesus will we hear on that final day the approval that our hearts so desperately long to hear: "Well done, good and faithful servant!"

*For I would have you know, brothers, that the gospel that
was preached by me is not man's gospel. For I did not receive
it from any man, nor was I taught it, but I received it through
a revelation of Jesus Christ. For you have heard of my former
life in Judaism, how I persecuted the church of God violently
and tried to destroy it. And I was advancing in Judaism
beyond many of my own age among my people, so extremely
zealous was I for the traditions of my fathers. But when he
who had set me apart before I was born, and who called me
by his grace, was pleased to reveal his Son to me, in order that
I might preach him among the Gentiles, I did not immediately
consult with anyone; nor did I go up to Jerusalem to those
who were apostles before me, but I went away into Arabia,
and returned again to Damascus. Then after three years I
went up to Jerusalem to visit Cephas and remained with him
fifteen days. But I saw none of the other apostles except James
the Lord's brother. (In what I am writing to you, before God,
I do not lie!) Then I went into the regions of Syria and Cilicia.
And I was still unknown in person to the churches of Judea
that are in Christ. They only were hearing it said, "He who
used to persecute us is now preaching the faith he once tried
to destroy." And they glorified God because of me.*

1:11–24

4

You Are Your
Best Argument

GALATIANS 1:11–24

IN THE PREVIOUS STUDY we reflected on the theme of people-pleasing. Paul introduces this theme into the letter here in the opening verses. This is a surprising move, until we realize that people-pleasing was a big part of the crisis in Galatia, and thus people-pleasing was a critical issue Paul needed to address. The Galatians had succumbed to the temptation to people-please; so, too, had the Judaizers before them. Evidently the only person who wasn't playing the people-pleaser was Paul, an important point he reiterates again and again throughout the letter (cf. 2:5, 6; 2:11–14; 4:13–18; 6:12–14), beginning with a string of rhetorical questions: "For am I now seeking the approval of man, or of God? Or am I trying to please man? If I were still trying to please man, I would not be a servant of Christ" (1:10).

We see Paul, then, defending his character, and he does so because he knows that the message he preaches is closely tied to the kind of messenger he is. If the messenger can't be trusted, then neither can the message. So he must defend himself in order to defend his gospel. But how? With autobiography, that's how. For Paul, autobiography becomes his argument. He tells his own story not only to vindicate himself, but more importantly to vindicate his gospel. Thus he begins his defense of himself and his gospel this way: "For I would have you know, brothers, that the gospel that was preached by me is not man's gospel" (1:11).[1]

It's as if Paul is saying to the Galatians, "Despite what you might think or what you've been told, the gospel I preach isn't geared for easy consumption by Gentiles; in fact, it's not even the kind of gospel a human being would come up with or invent. My gospel didn't originate in a creative brainstorming session, nor did I pick it up at the mall, see it advertised on television, read it in a book, or buy it online. 'For I did not receive it from any man, nor was I taught it, but I received it through a revelation of Jesus Christ'" (1:12).

However, notice where he goes from there—not to a string of tightly argued proofs from theology, nor to a long series of Biblical proof-texts. Instead Paul simply tells his story: "For you have heard of my former life in Judaism . . ." (1:13). He argues for the divine origin and nature of the gospel by describing the profound change the gospel has made in his life. His autobiography is his best argument. Paul knows his transformed life is the most compelling case he can make for the truth of the gospel.

And it's no different for us. We are our best argument. Our changed life is our best argument for the truth of the gospel. It is our most powerful apologetic. Nothing argues more forcefully for the reality of the gospel. Nothing makes the truth of the gospel more real to others. Nothing brings the power of the gospel closer to others so they can see it and indeed touch it. Our life, changed by the gospel, is our best argument for the truth of the gospel. *We are our best argument!*

Breathing Threats and Murder

We are our best argument for the truth of the gospel, particularly when our lives are changed *against all odds*. It's one thing to believe the gospel and be changed by it when everything in our life seems to point in that direction. It's another thing altogether to be changed by the gospel when everything in our life seems to be working against that ever happening.

That was Paul's situation before he met the Lord Jesus Christ. If ever there was an unlikely candidate to become a Christian, it was Paul. Two things made it highly unlikely, indeed, humanly speaking, completely impossible. First, he was a devout Jew, a Pharisee, in fact. As he says, "And I was advancing in Judaism beyond many of my own age among my people, so extremely zealous was I for the traditions of my fathers" (1:14).

But his Pharisaic beliefs made him, secondly, a persecutor of the Christian faith—not just opposed to the faith, but aggressively opposed, to the point of violence. Paul reminds the Galatians how he "persecuted the church of God violently and tried to destroy it" (1:13). Listen to the way Luke, in the Book of Acts, describes the preconverted Paul, or Saul as he was then called: "But Saul was ravaging the church, and entering house after house, he dragged off men and women and committed them to prison" (8:3). Saul the Pharisee was, as Luke says a bit later, "breathing threats and murder" against the church (9:1). Such was the intensity of his opposition to the faith.

Paul was obviously going to be a tough nut to crack. He was an excellent Pharisee. And excellent Pharisees don't make easy converts, but not because there's anything particularly unique to being a Pharisee, but because excellent Pharisees, like excellent athletes or musicians or academics or mothers or businessmen, have so much to take pride in. And this was Paul's fundamental problem—not primarily his Pharisaism or even his persecution of the church but his *pride*.

> If anyone else thinks he has reason for confidence in the flesh, I have more: circumcised on the eighth day, of the people of Israel, of the tribe of Benjamin, a Hebrew of Hebrews; as to the law, a Pharisee; as to zeal, a persecutor of the church; as to righteousness under the law, blameless. (Philippians 3:4–6)

Pride, or what Paul calls here "confidence in the flesh," is what blinds men and women to their need for Christ; this is what makes it impossible, humanly speaking, for us to come to Christ. When we've put our confidence in our own background or status or achievements, we find it very difficult to come to Christ. This is why Jesus says that unless we receive the kingdom like a little child we cannot enter it (Mark 10:15).

Pride is insurmountable. Left to ourselves, we can't climb over ourselves to get to Christ. But the good news is this: God is sovereign in salvation! And when he transforms our life against all odds, as he did with Paul, it proves to us and to everyone else the truth that Paul himself knew so well: "Christ Jesus came into the world to save sinners."

> I thank him who has given me strength, Christ Jesus our Lord, because he judged me faithful, appointing me to his service, though formerly I was a blasphemer, persecutor, and insolent opponent. But I received mercy because I had acted ignorantly in unbelief, and the grace of our Lord overflowed for me with the faith and love that are in Christ Jesus. The saying is trustworthy and deserving of full acceptance, that *Christ Jesus came into the world to save sinners*, of whom I am the foremost. But I received mercy for this reason, that in me, as the foremost, Jesus Christ might display his perfect patience as an example to those who were to believe in him for eternal life. To the King of ages, immortal, invisible, the only God, be honor and glory forever and ever. Amen. (1 Timothy 1:12–17)

You see, God has a specific strategy when he saves the seemingly unsavable. He wants to show forth his patience. "If he can have mercy on that guy, he can have mercy on anyone, even on me!"

So don't lose confidence in the power of God to change lives. Never give up hope that God can change even the staunchest opponents of the Christian faith. Don't forget that even the most hardened of atheists is never more than a moment away from conversion. Thus should God choose to reveal his Son to, say, a Richard Dawkins or Sam Harris, a Hugh Hefner or Ted Turner, a Charlie Sheen or Lindsay Lohan, a Hugo Chavez or Mahmoud Ahmadinejad, nothing's going to stop him. When it comes to saving souls, God always gets the job done. God is sovereign in salvation!

God can transform lives against all odds. In fact, he loves to do so because it's powerful proof of the truth of the gospel.

A Revelation of Jesus Christ

We are our best argument for the truth of the gospel not only when the change in our life is against all odds, but when the change in our life *comes out of nowhere*. This is how Paul's own transformation came—literally out of nowhere. He was busy advancing in Judaism and wreaking havoc in the church "when he who had set me apart before I was born, and who called me by his grace, was pleased to reveal his Son to me" (1:15). It was like being struck with a burst of light from the sun; in fact, that's precisely what happened. In Paul's own words:

> As I was on my way and drew near to Damascus, about noon a great light from heaven suddenly shone around me. And I fell to the ground and heard a voice saying to me, "Saul, Saul, why are you persecuting me?" And I answered, "Who are you, Lord?" And he said to me, "I am Jesus of Nazareth, whom you are persecuting." Now those who were with me saw the light but did not understand the voice of the one who was speaking to me. And I said, "What shall I do, Lord?" And the Lord said to me, "Rise, and go into Damascus, and there you will be told all that is appointed for you to do." (Acts 22:6–11)

We sometimes talk about finding God. But the truth is that we're found by God. The Apostle Paul didn't find God—God found him and revealed his Son to him. The same was true for the Galatians themselves, as Paul reminds them: "But now that you have come to know God, or rather to be known by God . . ." (4:9). And the same is true for us if we have found Christ and made him Lord of our life. We were found by God. From out of nowhere, as it were, Jesus Christ stepped onto the scene of our life and saved us. Karl Barth, perhaps the twentieth-century's greatest theologian, liked to say that true Christians are the victims of a successful surprise attack by God.[2]

Sometimes God shows up when we least expect him. Out of nowhere, he'll simply appear, like he did Friday afternoon, December 17, 1992. There I was, sitting in the corner booth of the McDonald's at the intersection of 96th and Meridian in my hometown of Carmel, Indiana. It was just an ordinary McDonald's, one we used to bike to as kids in the summer for an ice cream cone. Now I was a young adult, sixteen, a junior in high school, and I found myself sitting across the table from a man I hardly knew. There I was sipping my Diet Coke through a straw, making small talk the best I knew how, when all of a sudden this man drew on his napkin the story of the gospel. And then, out of nowhere, God showed up and I got saved. And my life immediately began to change as though out of nowhere.

When the change in our life comes out of nowhere, it makes it clear to everyone that *it is by the grace of God that we are what we are*. Paul understood this as well as anyone could. He viewed himself as "one untimely born" (1 Corinthians 15:8); he thought of himself as "the least of the apostles, unworthy to be called an apostle, because I persecuted the church of God" (1 Corinthians 15:9). Yet it was his own sense of unworthiness that enabled him to grasp the grace of God for what it truly is and caused him to say, "But by the grace of God I am what I am, and his grace toward me was not in vain. On the contrary, I worked harder than any of them, though it was not I, but the grace of God that is with me" (1 Corinthians 15:10).

By the grace of God, the great Apostle Paul was what he was. And so, too, it is for you and for me: by the grace of God we are what we are. Nothing else explains who we are—or who we're not. Nothing else can make sense of why we are in Christ Jesus and someone else isn't. Only grace makes sense of who we are; only grace explains our life. And the grace of the gospel at work in our life is the most powerful argument we have for the reality of the gospel.

The Persecutor Becomes the Persecuted

We are our best argument for the truth of the gospel, then, not only when our life changes against all odds and from out of nowhere but, thirdly and most importantly, when the change in our life is so real that others see it and say so.

This is what happened in Paul's case, and he's careful to remind the Galatians of it. "I was still unknown in person to the churches in Judea that are in Christ" (1:22). Although many of the believers in and around Jerusalem still didn't know Paul personally, his reputation nevertheless preceded him. In fact, so dramatic was the change in his life and so well-known was it among the early Christians that evidently they had a specific way of talking about Paul. They referred to him as the persecutor turned preacher; in fact, Paul tells the Galatians specifically what was said of him: "They only were hearing it said, 'He who used to persecute us is now preaching the faith he once tried to destroy'" (1:23).

Obviously in Paul's case the reversal was real; it couldn't have been more real. And the change was dramatic, so dramatic, in fact, it was undeniable. Who could argue against the reality of Paul's life?

But more than that, not only were others convinced of the power of the gospel, but they were made to worship because of its power in Paul's own life. "And they glorified God because of me" (1:24). We are our best argument for the truth of the gospel when the change in our lives is so real that others see it and praise God because of us. Our lives are a powerful apologetic for the reality of the gospel when the light of our lives so shines that others see it and glorify our Father who is in heaven (Matthew 5:16).

When the change in our life is so real that others see it and say so, it proves to us and to everyone else that the gospel truly is the power of God for salvation to everyone who believes (Romans 1:16). What else can explain the dramatic reversals in the lives of countless Christians down through the ages? What else can explain the profound transformation in our own life?

Sometimes we domesticate the gospel and forget it is itself the power of God. The gospel is not a flannelgraph illustration to charm children; it's the power of God to transform the life of even the most hardened criminals. The gospel is not a mere formula for how we get saved; it is divine power that actually brings about our salvation from first to last. The gospel is not simply a message about how to get right with God; it's the very presence of Jesus Christ himself enabling us to be right with God and to live rightly before God. The gospel is not a quaint story about who Jesus was and what he did; it's a declaration about who Jesus is even now, an announcement that creates the reality of which it speaks.

The gospel is the power of God for salvation for everyone who believes. We need to treat it as such—in the way we speak about the gospel, in the way we tell our own story of being changed by the gospel, and in the way we live our lives in light of the reality of the gospel.

Conclusion

John Newton, the eighteenth-century pastor, was a man who understood the power of the gospel and the grace of God. He was the author of the timeless hymn "Amazing Grace," whose lyrics seem to tell each of our stories better than we ourselves could. But before John Newton was the great Christian hymn writer, he was a rascal, a slave trader, a rebel.

Yet the mercy of God intervened in his life; the Lord Jesus Christ interposed his grace; Jesus got in Newton's way and ultimately saved Newton from himself. In a letter to a friend, Newton described his own conversion in ways reminiscent of the Apostle Paul's.

> I, though long a ringleader in blasphemy and wickedness, was spared, and though banished into the wilds of Africa, where I was the sport, yea the pity of slaves, I was by a series of providences little less than miraculously recovered from that house of bondage, and at length appointed to preach the faith I had long labored to destroy.[3]

Shortly before his death, Newton composed his own epitaph; it reads like something the Apostle Paul might have written. He wanted it inscribed on plain marble with no other monument or inscription, lest anything distract from the grace of God that made him what he was. It reads:

> John Newton,
> Clerk,
> Once an Infidel and Libertine,
> A Servant of Slaves in Africa,
> was,
> By the rich Mercy of our Lord and Saviour
> Jesus Christ,
> Preserved, Restored, Pardoned,
> and Appointed to Preach the Faith
> He had long laboured to destroy.[4]

John Newton's life was a powerful argument for the truth and power of the gospel!

The single best argument for or against Christianity has always been the same: *Christians*. A superficial, hypocritical life is a strong case against the claim that the gospel saves. But a transformed life, lived to the glory of God, is powerful proof of the truth of the gospel. We are our best argument. May we, therefore, so experience the grace of God in the gospel that others might see our transformed lives and glorify God because of us!

Then after fourteen years I went up again to Jerusalem with Barnabas, taking Titus along with me. I went up because of a revelation and set before them (though privately before those who seemed influential) the gospel that I proclaim among the Gentiles, in order to make sure I was not running or had not run in vain. But even Titus, who was with me, was not forced to be circumcised, though he was a Greek. Yet because of false brothers secretly brought in—who slipped in to spy out our freedom that we have in Christ Jesus, so that they might bring us into slavery—to them we did not yield in submission even for a moment, so that the truth of the gospel might be preserved for you. And from those who seemed to be influential (what they were makes no difference to me; God shows no partiality)—those, I say, who seemed influential added nothing to me. On the contrary, when they saw that I had been entrusted with the gospel to the uncircumcised, just as Peter had been entrusted with the gospel to the circumcised (for he who worked through Peter for his apostolic ministry to the circumcised worked also through me for mine to the Gentiles), and when James and Cephas and John, who seemed to be pillars, perceived the grace that was given to me, they gave the right hand of fellowship to Barnabas and me, that we should go to the Gentiles and they to the circumcised. Only, they asked us to remember the poor, the very thing I was eager to do.

2:1–10

5

Seeing Grace

GALATIANS 2:1–10

WHEN WAS THE LAST TIME YOU SAW GRACE? I don't mean Grace Kelly, the Academy Award winning actress, or Nancy Grace, the CNN commentator, or Mark Grace, the former Cubs and Diamondbacks baseball player. I'm talking about God's grace. When was the last time you saw it?

It's not uncommon to hear people talk about how they need grace. And we often hear people say they're thankful they've received grace. And we all know how fond preachers are of challenging their congregations to believe in grace or get saved by grace. But seldom do we hear anyone talk about seeing grace. When was the last time a friend or a spouse told you they saw the grace of God? Yet when we read the Bible we have to conclude that grace is indeed something we can see.

Seeing grace is the decisive thing in Galatians 2:1–10. Here is Paul's description of an important meeting he'd had with the leaders of the church in Jerusalem. As you see from the first several verses (2:1–6), this was an intense and important meeting; at issue was the controversial question of Gentile circumcision. In fact, some, whom Paul calls "false brothers" (v. 4), were dead-set on seeing Paul's Gentile traveling companion, Titus, undergo circumcision and thus become a Jew (2:3–5).

But Paul stood his ground: "To them we did not yield in submission even for a moment" (2:5). Yet, as he goes on to say, the decisive thing was that the Jerusalem leaders saw grace. In fact, from Paul's perspective seeing grace saved the day. As he explains, when the Jerusalem leadership "saw that I had been entrusted with the gospel to the uncircumcised" (2:7), and when they "perceived the grace that was given to me" (2:9), they concluded that the only right thing would be to partner with Paul by extending to him "the right hand of fellowship" (2:9).

Thus, as Paul explains, the Jerusalem leadership didn't add anything to his gospel (2:6). On the contrary, they affirmed the fact that God was in fact using the gospel to save Gentiles (2:7–9). Therefore, they reached a resolution—all because they saw grace.

Obviously, then, it's essential to be able to see grace. If we want to live a gospel-rooted life, we need to be able to see grace; and if we're going to navigate our way through this complex world, we need to know how to spot grace. The ability to see grace will impact virtually every aspect of our life: how we spend our time, where we invest our money, how we pray, which church we join, how we assess our own spiritual health, how we parent our kids, even how we make difficult decisions or resolve conflicts, as we see in our passage. Seeing grace is an essential life skill for gospel-rooted people.

But how skilled are we at spotting grace? Would we know grace if we saw it? Could we pick grace out of a crowd? Would we recognize grace if it was in our living room or our small group, on our front porch or in the church portico? What should we look for in order to see grace?

Grace in the Advance of the Gospel

The first thing to look for is *gospel advance*. We know we're seeing grace when we see the gospel of Jesus Christ advance in the lives of people. We know it's grace when we find faithful sharing of the gospel met with a believing response to the gospel. We know it's grace when we see a person come under the conviction of sin and put his or her trust in the Savior who died for his or her sins. When these kinds of things are going on, we know we're seeing grace.

Gospel advance is what the Jerusalem leadership saw in Paul. In fact, as Paul tells the Galatians, these leaders recognized that the fruit of Paul's ministry was on a par with the apostle Peter's own: "They saw that I had been entrusted with the gospel to the uncircumcised, just as Peter had been entrusted with the gospel to the circumcised" (2:7). Of course, it wasn't ultimately about Paul; nor, for that matter, was it about Peter. It was about God. He's the one ultimately responsible for gospel advance. Again, as Paul explains, "He who worked through Peter for his apostolic ministry to the circumcised worked also through me for mine to the Gentiles" (2:8). You see, God is the one who works; it's therefore not about Paul or Peter, much less you or me. When it comes to the gospel, we plant and we water, but it is God who gives the growth (cf. 1 Corinthians 3:6). God causes the gospel to advance in people's hearts.

But what precisely was the gospel advance they *saw* in Paul's ministry? No doubt they would have *heard* about Paul's early evangelistic efforts shortly after his conversion and his ministry in Arabia (1:17) and then in Syria and Cilicia (1:21). Surely the pillars of the early church were also hearing what the rest of the churches in Judea had heard: "He who used to persecute us is now preaching the faith he once tried to destroy" (1:23). They were probably even receiving reports of conversions as a result of Paul's gospel ministry, how his preaching came "not only in word, but also in power and in the Holy Spirit and with full conviction" (1 Thessalonians 1:5).

To a certain extent they would have been able to see grace in all these stories. But I suspect they saw grace most clearly and most concretely somewhere else—not in the stories about conversion, but in *the people* who had been converted. And there was one right there in front of them, in their very midst. His name was Titus, and he had made the trip up to Jerusalem along with Paul: "Then after fourteen years I went up again to Jerusalem with Barnabas, *taking Titus along with me*" (2:1). Notice how Paul underscores that it was his decision to take Titus along; you get the sense that Paul knew he would need Titus, not as his luggage boy on a long trip, but as *living proof* of the effect of his gospel ministry.

The well-known Bible teacher Howard Hendricks spoke at a men's retreat I attended on the importance of mentoring. And everything he said was spot-on and helpful. But I did wonder whether this busy seminary professor, writer, and conference speaker knew anything firsthand about mentoring, or was it all just theory for him? Had he ever mentored anyone himself, or could he just wax eloquent about it? He put my suspicion to rest when along the way he took time to introduce a young man who'd joined him on this trip all the way from Dallas. He was one of a half-dozen men whom Dr. Hendricks met with every week at 6:00 A.M. for prayer and accountability and mentoring. He wasn't just talking; he was actually doing it. And the proof was the person he brought with him, the young man standing right there beside him, his Titus.

Do you, like the Apostle Paul, have a Titus? Someone who's proof of the effectiveness of your life as a disciple maker? For some of us, our Titus is our spouse. For others it's a child. For some it's a parent. Still others have a Titus in a neighbor or a classmate or a colleague from work. And some of us are someone else's Titus; we are the proof of another person's gospel-rooted living. That's a wonderful thing. It's good to be able to turn to a Titus in our lives and see the grace of God on display.

When it comes to seeing grace, the proof is in the pudding. But in this case the pudding is people—converted sinners, to be precise. They are the proof of God's grace. Sinners who come to know the Savior—that's the place where you see grace. So if we want to see grace, we can look to those who have come to Christ. We'll find grace in those trophies of grace.

Grace in the Sacrificial Obedience of God's People

We see the grace of God when we see the advance of the gospel. We also see the grace of God when we see *the sacrificial obedience of God's people for the good of others.* When we find Christians laying down their lives to help others and to honor Jesus Christ, we know grace is present. Graceless situations are those in which no one takes up his or her cross and follows Jesus. But grace-filled are those situations in which followers of Christ let goods and kindred go, this mortal life also, in order to glorify their Lord by loving others.

In fact, sacrificial obedience in the service of Christ is the most clear, least ambiguous expression of the grace of God in the world. This is because sacrificial obedience is the most concrete and therefore the most tangible form of grace. Indeed, this is the kind of grace we not only can see, but the kind of grace we can touch and sometimes even handle.

This was the kind of visible grace the leaders of the early church saw when Paul arrived in Jerusalem, for what he brought with him was a bag full of concrete grace. Indeed, it was a bag full of *money.* Do you know why Paul had gone up to Jerusalem in the first place? He tells the Galatians, "I went up because of a revelation" (2:2). But what was this "revelation"? The Book of Acts tells us: it was a prophecy that a famine would hit all of Judea and thus Jerusalem itself.[1] As a result many would be hard-hit and without food.

> Now in these days prophets came down from Jerusalem to Antioch. And one of them named Agabus stood up and foretold by the Spirit that there would be a great famine over all the world (this took place in the days of Claudius). So the disciples determined, every one according to his ability, to send relief to the brothers living in Judea. And they did so, sending it to the elders by the hand of Barnabas and Saul. (Acts 11:27–30)

This explains, then, why Paul was in Jerusalem on this particular occasion. He was there on a ministry of mercy; he was delivering famine relief; he was meeting the needs of the poor saints in Jerusalem. Thus the main reason he went up was to present the leadership of the church with a bag of money, a bag of grace, born of the sacrifices made by the believers in the church in Antioch—not only Jews but Gentiles as well. This, then, like Titus, became another very concrete and compelling proof of the fact that God's grace was at work in Paul's ministry. It made it easy for the pillar apostles to "perceive the grace that was given to me" (2:9).

In February 2009, shortly after the devastating earthquake in Haiti, the disciples of Christ at the church I pastor (Calvary Memorial Church in Oak Park, Illinois) determined, each according to his ability, to send relief to those living in Haiti. We collected over $14,000 and sent it as a relief offering. Many gave sacrificially of their resources to meet the needs of others and thus glorify God. We were able to see grace in that generous act of sacrifice on the part of many, and those who received it were able to see grace as well, concrete grace in the form of disaster relief.

The Jerusalem leadership had an eye for grace, and they clearly saw it in the ministry of the Apostle Paul. But Paul too had a good eye for grace. He was quick to spot it in the lives of others. He told the Corinthians that he saw grace at work in the life of the churches of Macedonia. What was it that he saw?

> We want you to know, brothers, about the grace of God that has been given among the churches of Macedonia, for in a severe test of affliction, their abundance of joy and their extreme poverty have overflowed in a wealth of generosity on their part. For they gave according to their means, as I can testify, and beyond their means, of their own accord, begging us earnestly for the favor of taking part in the relief of the saints—and this, not as we expected, but they gave themselves first to the Lord and then by the will of God to us. (2 Corinthians 8:1–5)

Paul spotted grace in the generosity of the Macedonians. Even though they were financially hard-pressed, they still gave generously to meet the needs of others to the glory of God. And this grace sighting causes the apostle's heart to sing. But it also provides him the perfect opportunity to exhort the Corinthians to do likewise and excel in what he calls an "act of grace":

> Accordingly, we urged Titus that as he had started, so he should complete among you this act of grace. But as you excel in everything—in faith, in speech, in knowledge, in all earnestness, and in our love for you—see that you excel in this act of grace also. (2 Corinthians 8:6, 7)

The quickest way to make grace visible is to excel in the act of grace—that is, to give sacrificially of our resources for the good of others. Generous giving, when it is done to the glory of God, causes grace to appear; indeed, generous giving is itself the grace of God acting in human hearts and human lives.

How are we doing in this respect? How visible is grace in our lives? If the Apostle Paul or the leaders of the church in Jerusalem were to visit our homes or watch our lives, would they see grace? If they were to review how we spend our resources—our time, our treasure, our talents—would grace be what they see? If they were to interview our family or friends or those in our neighborhood or the people with whom we work, would they clearly perceive the grace that was given to us for ministry?

Nothing provides us with a more concrete expression of the grace of God than when believers give of their resources sacrificially to meet the needs of others. You know it's the grace of God when you see someone sacrificially take their own resources and translate them into practical help for other people, whether this involves their time or their treasure or their talents.

Developing Our Ability to See Grace

Seeing grace, then, is about seeing two things: gospel advance in the world and sacrificial obedience for the sake of others. It's about seeing faith born of the gospel and obedience in response to the gospel. Or, even more simply put, we see grace when we see faith and obedience in the lives of God's people.

In order to live a gospel-rooted life, we need to be able to see God's grace in the world around us. This means we need to develop the ability to discern the grace of God when it's there and not look right past it. It's not merely visual perception but *theological insight* that we need.

But how do we develop our ability to see grace? To begin with, we need to know where to look—and where *not* to look. Frankly, some of us have a hard time seeing grace because we don't know where to look.

Seeing grace is not necessarily about looking to the sunny circumstances of our lives. The grace of God isn't like my cat who only likes to curl up and sleep in the warm and sunny spots around the house.

Others think they'll only find grace where there's no personal struggles or battles with sin. That's why we find our own Christian life so discouraging, and that's why we often find churches to be, in our opinion, such graceless situations. Both churches and Christians are works in progress, but we find it much easier to be preoccupied with the nongrace everywhere around us than with the grace.

Grace is everywhere, as much in the difficulties and struggles of our lives as in the good times and the victories, if not more so. As a pastor I have the privilege of seeing grace every single week in the lives of others battling against temptation, struggling to persevere in a difficult marriage, or hanging on to Jesus as an illness sucks the lifeblood out of them. In all this I often see grace.

If we want to develop our ability to see grace, we must let the Bible saturate our mind and our imagination. The grace-filled book of Galatians will enable us to see the grace of God that's all around us; it will give us the categories and the clues we need to spot grace in the world.

We also need to pray because when we pray, we yield our way of looking at the world to God's way of looking at the world. And this will help us see God's gracious ways with the world. Prayer will help us see grace.

Ultimately, however, if we're going to see grace, we need to look to the cross of Christ. In fact, we will never be able to see grace until we've first seen it in the shed blood of Jesus Christ on the cross. But we will need to return to the cross again and again to recalibrate our vision and refocus on the grace of God so perfectly displayed there. "For you know the grace of our Lord Jesus Christ, that though he was rich, yet for your sake he became poor, so that you by his poverty might become rich" (2 Corinthians 8:9).

*Only, they asked us to remember the poor,
the very thing I was eager to do.*

2:10

6

Remember the Poor

GALATIANS 2:10

Only One Request

Occasionally a verse of Scripture is so unexpected or surprising that it causes us to pause and to ponder—and then to want to preach it. This is such a verse: "Only, they asked us to remember the poor, the very thing I was eager to do."

In this passage Paul describes a meeting that took place between him and Barnabas and the leaders of the early church in Jerusalem. It was an important meeting. At issue was whether the gospel Paul preached among Gentiles was sufficient or whether something needed to be added to it. And Paul insists that the Jerusalem leaders had agreed with him that nothing needed to be added to his gospel (2:6). On the contrary, they saw the grace of God given to Paul (2:9) and therefore entered into ministry partnership with him (2:9).

But notice, that's not where this passage ends. Look at 2:10, where Paul hastens to add that they did make one request of him, but only one. And, he says, it was the very thing he was eager to do anyway, so it didn't feel like a request at all, but another confirmation that they shared a common cause in the gospel.

What was that one request? If this were a fill-in-the-blank quiz, how would you answer the following question? *The Jerusalem leadership agreed nothing needed to be added to Paul's gospel; they only asked him to remember what?* Would any of us have answered, *They only asked him to remember the poor?*

Often preachers pass right over this verse because it doesn't seem to fit the context. And Bible commentators find themselves going into contortions trying to explain why this verse is here and what it could possibly mean. One influential evangelical commentator, for example, says, "[The] request was not related to the point at issue and so was immaterial to the conflict stirred up by the Judaizers in Galatia."[1]

And so it's been for many evangelicals. Remembering the poor has been viewed as unrelated to the point at issue in Galatians and immaterial to the conflict. What is the point at issue in Galatia and the point Paul addresses in this letter? It's nothing other than the gospel itself and what it means to live a gospel-rooted life. Yet as this scholar reveals, all too often remembering the poor has been viewed by evangelicals as unrelated to the gospel or immaterial to living a gospel-rooted life.[2]

This is the tragedy of conservative Christianity in the last century. Evangelicals have remembered the gospel but forgotten the poor. We've done well to hold firm to our orthodox beliefs, but we have tended to turn a blind eye to the plight of the poor. We've been faithful to being doctrinally sound, as well we should, but we've been lax about caring for "the least of these" (Matthew 25:45).

The tragedy of liberal Christianity, on the other hand, is that it has remembered the poor but forgotten the gospel! For example, many churches in the town where I pastor are eager to participate in nightly shelters for the homeless, food pantries, or other social services but never speak about the fall of man, the wrath of God, eternal punishment in Hell, substitutionary atonement, or the forgiveness of sins through the blood of Jesus Christ.

But if we're to be holistic and Biblical Christians, and if we're to take the message of Galatians seriously, and if we're to seek to live gospel-rooted lives, we cannot either forget the gospel or the poor. We must remember both; we must hold fast to the gospel and prioritize the poor.

But how does the gospel cause us to prioritize the poor? Why does the good news of Jesus Christ throw the spotlight on the poor? Or why does love for the gospel need to overflow in concern for "the least of these"?

Come, Ye Sinners, Poor and Needy

The gospel causes us to prioritize the poor by enabling us to identify with the poor in our own poverty.

It is very difficult to care for people with whom we have no connection. And most of us, at least on the surface, feel like we have no connection with the poor. Let's face it: most of us aren't poor. We never have been, nor is it likely we ever will be. Most of us have never gone a day without food or a night without a warm bed. In fact, most of us are rich. Indeed, historically and globally speaking most of us are wildly wealthy. And I don't mean only those who make a six-figure income. I simply mean those who make more than ten dollars a day or seventy dollars a week or three hundred dollars a month. If you're in that category, by any historical or global standard you are incredibly wealthy.

But let's also face it: all of us are deeply impoverished because of sin. Because of the fall and because of our own sin, we are all stricken by a more profound kind of poverty than not having enough money. There is a poverty in our relationship with God, with ourselves, with others, and with creation itself, so that while we may not be materially poor, we recognize our own spiritual poverty, the bankruptcy of our lives. This is what the gospel causes us to confront: our own poverty.

The temptation is to see the poor as the problem and the rich as the solution. This engenders pride and in turn leads to all sorts of other attitudinal and practical problems when we try to help those who are materially poor.[3] What they most need is what you and I most need: rescue from spiritual poverty and reconciliation with a loving God. As an old hymn expresses it:

> Come, ye sinners, poor and needy,
> Weak and wounded, sick and sore;
> Jesus ready stands to save you,
> Full of pity, love and power.

This is the invitation of the gospel; this is the way the gospel speaks to each and every one of us without exception: "Come, ye sinners, poor and needy." We cannot come to Jesus until we first recognize we are poor and needy. Jesus won't save those who think they're rich and strong. Nor can we live for Jesus unless we heed the invitation on a daily basis to come to him in repentance as poor and needy sinners. Realize, therefore, that if this gospel is truly at work in our lives on a daily basis, then we are on a daily basis coming to terms with our own poverty.

What I Do Have I Give to You

So the gospel causes us to prioritize the poor by enabling us to identify with the poor in our own poverty. But, secondly, the gospel causes us to prioritize the poor *by emboldening us to share with the poor out of our abundance.*

Jesus' earliest disciples certainly weren't rich. Yet they were emboldened to share with the poor because they understood the abundance they had in Christ. They realized:

- Each Galatian believer was "no longer a slave, but a son, and if a son, then an heir" (Galatians 4:7).
- They had "every spiritual blessing in the heavenly places" in Christ (Ephesians 1:3).
- They had been "born again to a living hope" (1 Peter 1:3).

- They had been born again into God's family with all the rights of sons (John 1:12, 13).
- They were "qualified . . . to share in the inheritance of the saints in light" (Colossians 1:12).
- They were "fellow heirs with Christ," and all that is his was now theirs (Romans 8:17).
- They were promised the kingdom by the "good pleasure" of the Father (Luke 12:32).
- They were heirs of the whole world (Romans 4:13).

Perhaps you've felt at times like Peter and John, when a poor man outside the temple gate in Jerusalem asked them for money. Notice Peter's response: "I have no silver and gold, but what I do have I give to you. In the name of Jesus Christ of Nazareth, rise up and walk!" (Acts 3:6). Although Peter had nothing materially to give, what he had was an abundance! He had nothing, yet he possessed everything. So he gave out of his abundance.

The gospel doesn't challenge us to give to others what we ourselves don't have. It challenges us to give to others what we've already been given in abundance. The gospel calls us to say with Peter, "What I do have I give to you." Regardless of our financial situation or the money in our wallet or purse or the change in our pocket, we always have *the name of Jesus to give away*, generously and freely, to whomever asks, even to those who don't ask but need Jesus to heal their souls.

So the next time someone asks you if you can spare some change for bus fare or a train ticket or some food, first acknowledge that person's presence by looking him or her in the eye, perhaps even reaching out your hand to shake or touch his or hers; and regardless of whether you share your money, don't hesitate to share with him or her the most valuable thing you have: *the name of Jesus Christ*!

The Son of Man Has Nowhere to Lay His Head

We see, then, how the gospel enables us to identify with the poor in our poverty and to share out of our abundance in Christ. But the gospel, thirdly, causes us to prioritize the poor *by calling us to follow Jesus in his pursuit of the poor*. The gospel calls us to a life of discipleship; it calls us to take up our cross and follow Jesus. But if we faithfully follow Jesus, where will he lead us sooner or later?

One thing is crystal clear about the life and ministry of Jesus: he pursued the poor. *He pursued the poor, first of all, by becoming poor himself.* "For you know the grace of our Lord Jesus Christ, that though he was rich, yet for your sake he became poor, so that you by his poverty might become rich" (2 Corinthians 8:9).

Poverty was an essential part of Jesus' earthly identity. He wasn't rich. He wasn't even middle-class. He wasn't college educated. He didn't own a home. He had no retirement savings. He didn't own a car, much less two or three. As far as we know, he never went on vacation, save a trip to Egypt as a boy to avoid being murdered. Our Lord was poor, and he had no illusions or misgivings about it. Nor did he want his followers to have any illusions or misgivings about it either. This is why he said to any would-be followers, "Foxes have holes, and birds of the air have nests, but the Son of Man has nowhere to lay his head" (Matthew 8:20).

Secondly, Jesus pursued the poor by proclaiming good news to them. In fact, that was central to his own proclamation of the kingdom of God. The Gospel writer Luke tells us that Jesus marked the beginning of his public ministry by going into the synagogue in his hometown of Nazareth on the Sabbath, opening the Isaiah scroll and finding the place where the prophet says, "The Spirit of the Lord is upon me, because he has anointed me to proclaim good news to the poor. He has sent me to proclaim liberty to the captives and recovering of sight to the blind, to set at liberty those who are oppressed, to proclaim the year of the Lord's favor" (Luke 4:18, 19).

And, thirdly, Jesus pursued the poor by promising a great reversal of fortunes for the poor one day. The good news Jesus both preached and embodied goes beyond souls getting saved and going to Heaven. It's certainly not less than that, but it's definitely more than that. The good news Jesus proclaimed was the good news of *God's kingdom coming to earth.* And this kingdom is going to include a great reversal of fortunes for the poor by Christ. In a word, those who oppress the poor shall be put down. The last shall be first, the humble shall be exalted, and the meek shall inherit the earth.

"Jesus has come as the Poor One for the poor."[4] And all who would follow after him must go and do likewise. If you truly love the gospel and the Savior, then you will follow Jesus in his pursuit of the poor because in so doing you will be pursuing Christ himself.

The Very Thing I Was Eager To Do

The early church, Paul himself included, was committed to remembering the poor. In fact, as Paul says, this was "the very thing I was eager to do" (2:10). "Eager" is a strong word. It affirms a clear resolve and willingness to do whatever it takes to prioritize the poor.

How eager are we to remember the poor? Not just their financial plight, but their plight as persons made in the image of God. Perhaps we'd like to cultivate eagerness for remembering the poor, but we're wondering how to go about it. Here are a few things to consider.

First, we should focus on gratitude rather than feeling guilty for what we have. Many of us have been given so much. The tendency is to feel guilty because of what we have when we see how much those around us don't have. Resist that temptation. Guilt is not a good or God-honoring motivation. Instead cultivate thankfulness for all that God has given us because thankfulness paradoxically frees us from having to hang on tightly to what we have. When we take our eyes off the gift and fix them on the Giver, we realize that gifts aren't the source of lasting joy, God is.

Second, we should open our eyes to the plight of the poor. We should simply stop and see the plight of the poor in our community and in our city and in our country and in our world. Grapple with what Dr. Martin Luther King Jr. meant when he said, "The violence of poverty and humiliation hurts as intensely as the violence of the club."[5] Open your mind and heart to what a single mother, who's lived her whole life on the poverty line, means when she says, "In part [poverty] is about having no money, but there is more to poverty than that. It is about being isolated, unsupported, uneducated and unwanted. Poor people want to be included and not just judged and 'rescued' at times of crisis."[6] Most of us have no idea what that means, and thus we are far removed from remembering the poor in their plight.

Third, we should open our lives, as well as our homes, to the poor and invite them in. Jesus had been invited to dine at the home of a wealthy and influential Pharisee. He took the occasion to challenge the one who had invited him with this parable:

> When you give a dinner or a banquet, do not invite your friends or your brothers or your relatives or rich neighbors, lest they also invite you in return and you be repaid. But when you give a feast, invite the poor, the crippled, the lame, the blind, and you will be blessed, because they cannot repay you. For you will be repaid at the resurrection of the just. (Luke 14:12–14)

Fourth, we should take the next step in following Jesus in pursuit of the poor. For some of us this will mean wrestling with the gospel itself. For others this will mean adjusting our attitude toward our wealth or toward the poor. For others this will mean reaching out in their neighborhood, serving in a soup kitchen or social service ministry, or perhaps even exploring international adoption. Each of us needs to take the next step.

Finally, this passage speaks directly to those who are in fact poor. We can ask them to help us pursue Jesus by letting us into their lives. We can encourage them not to hide their life or their poverty from us but instead to open their lives to us and to help us learn how to open our lives to them.

Speaking candidly but I trust not condescendingly, we need those who are poor to help us understand who we ourselves are and how we can better pursue Jesus.

Conclusion

If we're going to live a gospel-rooted life, we must remember the poor. And if our churches are going to be gospel-rooted churches, we must remember the poor. To forget the poor is to drift from the gospel. No matter how orthodox our theology, or how white-hot our worship services, or how vibrant our youth ministry, or how meaningful our family ministries, or how large our budget or our attendance, if we neglect the poor, we miss what it means to truly be a gospel-rooted church.

But if we prioritize the poor in our hearts and in our ministry, then God Almighty will cause us to be a city on a hill whose light shines into the darkness of this dark world. If we share our bread with the hungry and bring the homeless poor into our homes, if we see the naked and cover them, then the Lord promises through the prophet Isaiah that our light shall break forth like the dawn, and our healing shall spring up speedily; our righteousness shall go before us, and the glory of the Lord shall be our rear guard (cf. Isaiah 58:6–8).

But when Cephas came to Antioch, I opposed him to his face, because he stood condemned. For before certain men came from James, he was eating with the Gentiles; but when they came he drew back and separated himself, fearing the circumcision party. And the rest of the Jews acted hypocritically along with him, so that even Barnabas was led astray by their hypocrisy. But when I saw that their conduct was not in step with the truth of the gospel, I said to Cephas before them all, "If you, though a Jew, live like a Gentile and not like a Jew, how can you force the Gentiles to live like Jews?"

2:11–14

7

Staying in Step with the
Truth of the Gospel

GALATIANS 2:11–14

GALATIANS IS ABOUT GOSPEL-ROOTED LIVING. The ultimate question the letter seeks to answer is, how should we live in light of the good news that Jesus Christ has died and been raised? This is what Paul wants to unpack in this letter, and this is what we're seeking to unpack: gospel-rooted living.

Of course, Paul doesn't hesitate to expound the truth of the gospel—what the gospel is and what the gospel isn't. But his purpose goes beyond mere exposition; his goal is to ensure that the Galatians actually live the truth of the gospel; or, to use a phrase from today's passage, Paul wants to call them back to conduct that is "in step with the truth of the gospel" (cf. 2:14).

In this passage Paul throws the spotlight on what it means to stay "in step with the truth of the gospel." But he does so not by telling us two or three ways in which we stay in step with the truth of the gospel; that comes a little later in chapters 5, 6. Instead in this passage we see the converse: how one falls out of step with the truth of the gospel.

These verses describe a tragic situation that developed in Paul's home church in Antioch, where he and his colleague Barnabas had spent much time ministering together. In short, an entire part of the church, in fact the majority, fell out of step with the truth of the gospel by falling headlong into hypocrisy.

This is the great threat to staying "in step with the truth of the gospel": hypocrisy. Our fidelity to the truth of the gospel is constantly under threat from hypocrisy. Most often when we fail to live out the truth of the gospel, we've veered off into hypocrisy. So in order to stay faithful to the gospel, you and I must be vigilant in our fight against hypocrisy's menacing presence.

Hypocrisy as Playacting

But what is hypocrisy? We certainly hear the word tossed around like a grenade these days, usually aimed at one's political opponents. And from the way the word is often used on the evening news or political talk shows, you get the impression that a hypocrite is anyone who fails to live up to his or her ideals. It's someone who fails to practice what he or she preaches. But in that case I'm a chronic hypocrite because I never live up to my own ideals, and I suspect you don't either.

When it comes to understanding hypocrisy, we're actually helped by the etymology of the word. In antiquity a hypocrite was an actor, someone who would put on a mask and play a part in a performance. Thus the word came to connote "the concealing of one's true character, thoughts, or feelings under a guise implying something quite different."[1] When you act hypocritically, you mask your true convictions and play a part that's not really yours.

Playacting is what Paul sees Peter and the rest of the Jews doing in Antioch. They've put on a mask to cover up what they truly believe about the gospel. Because of a delegation that came down from Jerusalem—"men from James," Paul tell us (2:12)—Peter changed the way he interacted with the Gentile believers in Antioch. Prior to that point, Peter and the rest of the Jews were enjoying the freedom purchased by the gospel; they were freely eating with Gentiles, even sharing in the Lord's Table together as one body in Christ. Paul says, "For *before* certain men came from James, he was eating with the Gentiles; *but when* they came he drew back and separated himself" (2:12). Thus Peter played the hypocrite, and the rest of the Jews with him.

Hypocrisy, then, isn't simply failing to live up to what you believe. That's sin, to be sure. But it's not the particular sin of hypocrisy. Nor is it what Paul accuses Peter and the other Jews of doing. When we live out our gospel convictions in one situation but then cover them up in another—that's hypocrisy.

Hypocrisy is when a believer plays the part of a nonbeliever. It's like playing the part in a play in which the gospel isn't real or doesn't count. It's assuming a role in a drama in which the story isn't defined by the gospel. It's when a Christian acts the part of the non-Christian. It's what Peter did in Antioch by choosing to cover up with his behavior his true convictions about the gospel.

We all understand, of course, that we can affirm something to be true and yet fail to live up to it. This is what it means to deal with our own sin and struggles. But we must understand as well that we can affirm something to be true and yet intentionally live in a way that covers that up and makes it look like we don't believe it to be true. This is the kind of playacting the Bible calls hypocrisy. It's a kind of treachery, like a husband who removes his wedding ring so he can play the part of a single man. It's an act of dishonesty and disloyalty.

In what situations are we tempted to playact, to cover up what we believe by how we live? In what situations do we find that we're putting on a mask that conceals our true convictions about the gospel or who Jesus is?

The Sources of Hypocrisy

Certain kinds of situations will tempt us to play the hypocrite. Consider Peter's situation. Why did he mask his own convictions? Because it was expedient; it was quite advantageous for him personally. There was strong social pressure to do so. But it was more than peer pressure. Fear of reprisals was a motivating factor. In fact, it was the unhappy prospect of suffering that caused Peter to playact in Antioch. Notice what Paul sees in Peter's underlying motive: "He drew back and separated himself, fearing the circumcision party" (2:12).

Peter slid into hypocrisy because of fear. He feared the so-called "circumcision party," who would have taken great offense at his free interactions with Gentiles. Peter feared them because they had the ability to punish Peter for moving beyond the bounds of what was lawful for a Jew to do. Thus Peter drew back and separated himself from the Gentiles because he didn't want to suffer crucifixion with Christ for the sake of the Gentiles.

Hypocrisy is Peter's crime. But just underneath the mask of hypocrisy lurks an inordinate desire to people-please. In Galatians 1:10 we learn that people-pleasers don't make good servants of Christ. As we consider Galatians 2:11–14, we confront a variation of this same truth: people-pleasers do make very good playactors. While not good servants of Christ, they're adept at playing the part of the non-Christian, should circumstances require it.

Hypocrisy is how people-pleasers navigate their way through difficult situations where competing social pressures are in play. They resort to putting on a mask in order to make it through an otherwise awkward situation. When we fear social ostracism, we're tempted to play the hypocrite. We're tempted to reach for the mask to cover up our true convictions when we're worried about what others might think of us if they know who we truly are. Recognize as well that the more willing we are to be crucified with Christ, the less likely we are to playact around others.

Hypocrisy's Harm

We see, then, how serious hypocrisy is. It's an act of treachery. And thus it's often extremely harmful. It is harmful to the hypocrite himself. In fact, notice what Paul says of Peter because of his hypocrisy: "He stood condemned" (2:11). Peter was liable to God's judgment, should he not repent of his hypocrisy. That's how harmful hypocrisy is to a hypocrite.

But hypocrisy is harmful to others as well. All of us probably have a sad story or two to tell about how we've been hurt by someone else's hypocrisy. For some of us it's a mom or a dad; for others it's a youth group leader or a pastor. Religious hypocrisy is the worst kind of hypocrisy; it's the most damaging because it's the least expected and the hardest to get over.

We can think of hypocrisy as a virus. It needs human interaction to survive; indeed it spreads and thrives on contact. And when it finds the right environment, hypocrisy can go viral and infect a whole community. This is what happened in Antioch. Notice the impact of Peter's hypocrisy: "And the rest of the Jews acted hypocritically along with him, so that even Barnabas was led astray by their hypocrisy" (2:13).

Most people are easily infected by hypocrisy. Most of us, like the rest of the Jews in Antioch, need just a bit of exposure and the virus will spread. However, some have built up a stronger resistance to hypocrisy; these are people like Barnabas, who wasn't the first to be infected with the hypocrisy spreading through the church in Antioch. But at the end of the day even Barnabas, as Paul laments, couldn't withstand the contagion.[2] Even if Barnabas was not personally infected with hypocrisy, he was nevertheless impacted by it. He was, as Paul says, "led astray," carried away by the strong undertow of hypocrisy at work in the church in Antioch.

Notice then the spread of hypocrisy—first Peter, then the rest of the Jewish believers, then even Barnabas. But recognize as well that hypocrisy's impact wouldn't have stopped there; it not only harmed the Jewish believers, but it would have doubtless also impacted the Gentiles. In fact, as Paul says, Peter's hypocrisy was so powerful that it was in effect forcing Gentiles "to live like Jews" (2:14).

We must realize, then, the power of our hypocrisy to harm others. Playing the hypocrite is doing more than setting a bad example; your hypocrisy and mine can actually compel others to stray from the truth of the gospel.

There's a sobering challenge in all of this for parents. Moms and dads, you are the key influencers in your homes. So beware of playing the hypocrite there. Although no one from work or church will see your playacting, your children certainly will. And they may even feel compelled to do what they ought not to do because of your hypocrisy.

There's also a sobering challenge here for everyone who names the name of Christ. When you and I play the hypocrite and act like there's no gospel, not only can we infect other Christians and cause them to do the same, we can also impact non-Christians and cause them to miss out on the gospel.

Staying in Step with the Truth of the Gospel

Think of the truth of the gospel as a balance beam. Our task is to stay on it. But the world outside us, the people around us, and the sin within us are constantly pulling at us, tempting us to lean in one direction or another and thus fall out of step with the truth of the gospel. How, then, can we keep our balance and stay in step with the truth of the gospel?

First, look straight ahead. Don't look down. That will only cause your mind to think about falling rather than staying on. Don't anxiously worry about falling into hypocrisy. Instead we must fix our gaze straight ahead, upon that single point right in front of us. And that point is Jesus Christ. We must not look around from side to side, checking out who's in the audience, what expressions they have on their faces, whether they're smiling or frowning at us. That will only mess us up and cause us to lose our balance. Instead we must fix our gaze intently on the one whose smile we truly long to see. We should seek to be pleasing to him rather than being a pleaser of everyone else.

Second, hold out your arms. This is how we stay balanced. But when it comes to staying in step with the truth of the gospel, we must hold out our arms not just for balance but for help. Remember this was the way we first learned to walk the balance beam. We had a buddy on the right and left holding our hands, helping us stay in step with the beam itself. Staying in step with the truth of the gospel is like that. We need each other. Sometimes we need another brother or sister to grab us and keep us from falling headlong into hypocrisy. Most of the time we need others who know us to speak truth into our lives. As we hold out our arms to maintain our balance, do we have people like that?

Third, trust that you'll stay on. Fixating on how narrow the balance beam is only sets us up for failure. The worst thing an Olympic gymnast could do would be to take a tape measure to the balance beam before the competition. The truth of the gospel is not a narrow, behavioral sliver we need to anxiously worry about staying on. Once we're on it, we realize it's both broad and wide. We need to walk in step with the truth of the gospel, confident God's grace will indeed keep us.

Conclusion

But what if we fall? What should we do if we lose our balance, step away from the truth of the gospel, and stumble into hypocrisy like Peter did? What can we do when we realize our conduct isn't in step with the truth of the gospel?

In those moments we must *return to the truth of the gospel*. We should say with the Apostle Paul, as he told Peter, "We know that a person is not justified by works of the law but through faith in Jesus Christ" (2:16). God freely justifies the ungodly by faith. This is the glorious truth of the gospel. Go back to it, again and again.

Interestingly, Martin Luther actually viewed this passage and the example of Peter as a great comfort to believers. "For it is a great comfort for us to hear that even such great saints sin—a comfort which those who say that saints cannot sin would take away from us." He continues:

> Samson, David, and many other celebrated men who were full of the Holy Spirit fell into huge sins. Job (3:3ff.) and Jeremiah (20:14) curse the day of their birth. Elijah (1 Kings 19:4) and Jonah (4:8) grow tired of life and pray for death. Such errors and sins of the saints are set forth in order that those who are troubled and desperate may find comfort and that those who are proud may be afraid. No man has ever fallen so grievously that he could not have stood up again. On the other hand, no one has such a sure footing that he cannot fall. If Peter fell, I, too, may fall; if he stood up again, so can I.[3]

This teaches us about true gospel-rooted living. We are feeble and frail, even the best and most godly among us; we are never more than a hair's breadth away from hypocrisy ourselves. Who among us is stronger or has greater resolve than the Apostle Peter?

So, too, we see that our own steadfastness or inherent holiness is never in itself enough. As Luther says, "Our inherent holiness is not enough. Therefore Christ is our entire holiness; where this inherent holiness is not enough, Christ is."[4]

*We ourselves are Jews by birth and not Gentile sinners; yet
we know that a person is not justified by works of the law
but through faith in Jesus Christ, so we also have believed
in Christ Jesus, in order to be justified by faith in Christ and
not by works of the law, because by works of the law no one
will be justified.*

2:15, 16

8

The Truth of the Gospel

GALATIANS 2:15, 16

PETER'S HYPOCRISY IN ANTIOCH called for open rebuke because his conduct was out of step with the truth of the gospel (2:11–14). But the situation in Antioch, as well as the crisis in Galatia, required that Paul expound the truth of the gospel with clarity, so that no one could possibly miss it. And that is what he does in this passage.

These two verses form a single sentence in the original. Thus what we have here is a one-sentence summary of the truth of the gospel; what we have here is the Bible's teaching on justification in a nutshell. It's a single sentence that therefore captures the heart and soul of the Christian faith, for these two verses answer the question of how unworthy sinners like you and me find right standing before a holy God.

This is no doubt what Paul said to Peter in Antioch. But this is also what Paul wants *the Galatians themselves* to hear, so he includes it in this letter. Yet the truth of these verses is something we all need to hear! For this is the sum of the whole matter, the source of life and joy and peace and an endless string of happy tomorrows with the living God.

Do we revel in the truth of these verses? Is this the foundation of our hope for the future? Is it to this truth—the truth of the gospel—that we turn when we've blown it? Do we approach the trials and tests in our lives steadied by the reality in these verses? Does this truth inform how we deal with our own sin? Does this truth shape how we think about other religions? Does it shape our outlook on the world and people and eternity?

The truth of the gospel in these two verses is perhaps best unpacked with three simple questions. But these questions are intended to probe the depth to which the truth of the gospel has penetrated our own hearts. That's what we all need to do: ask ourselves how firm is our handle on the truth of the gospel.

"Jews by Birth and Not Gentile Sinners" (2:15)

The first question is very simple and straightforward. It's not intended to be a trick question, even though people often find it rather tricky to sort out. The question is this: *Are we relying upon who we are or what we've done for our right standing with God?* This is where the truth of the gospel must first probe. What are we relying upon or trusting in for our standing before God?

In Antioch Paul had to confront this issue head-on because of the clear implications of Peter's hypocritical behavior. By withdrawing from table fellowship with Gentiles, Peter was sending a clear message about what counts: reliance upon the Law and its works to secure favor with God, rather than trust in God's provision in Christ alone.

Frankly, it was natural for Jews to presume upon God's favor because of who they were or what they'd done. The temptation for Jews has always been to presume upon God's grace because they possess God's Law (cf. Romans 2:17–24). Thus Jews have always been able to say what Peter and the others were saying in Antioch: "We ourselves are Jews by birth and not Gentile sinners" (2:15).

John the Baptist confronted a similar kind of presumption on the banks of the Jordan. As many of the pious Jews of the day were coming to him to be baptized, he no doubt caught them off guard when he said, "You brood of vipers! Who warned you to flee from the wrath to come? Bear fruit in keeping with repentance. And do not presume to say to yourselves, 'We have Abraham as our father,' for I tell you, God is able from these stones to raise up children for Abraham" (Matthew 3:7–9). These forceful words were intended to drive a spear through Jewish presumption.

However, we need to understand that Jewish presumption is only *an expression of human presumption.* The tendency to presume upon the grace of God is not unique to the Jewish faith; it's endemic to fallen humanity. This is how sinful creatures cope with the reality of their sin: they deceive themselves into thinking everything's actually okay with who they are. This kind of human presumption is perhaps best captured in the title of that best-selling self-help book *I'm OK—You're OK.*[1] This is the deceit of fallen humanity: to assume that I'm okay and thus to presume that God's okay with me just as I am.

But because presumption is a human tendency, it can also be a Christian tendency rearing its ugly head even within Christian circles. There is such a thing as Christian presumption: presuming upon the grace of God because we've taken part in some practice of the Christian faith. Perhaps the most obvious is baptism. It is a precious Biblical practice, but baptism has also been the source of presumption for who knows how many countless thousands, even millions, of people. I can't tell you the number of funerals I've been to where the officiating minister or priest offered hope for the deceased because of the person's baptism as an infant. The minister or priest can't say much about the individual's trust in Christ, so he resorts to the person's sharing in the rite of baptism, just as Jews have done with circumcision. It's as though the minister is saying, "We ourselves are Christians by baptism; we are not non-Christian sinners."

I know very few evangelical Christians who would place that much stock in baptism. But an interesting variation of presumption has cropped up in evangelical circles—the tendency to presume upon God's grace and love because of our own inherent lovability. You see, as evangelicals we tend to explain the truth of the gospel with reference to the love of God for the world. That's right and good and Biblical, but sometimes we do so in a way that can sound as though God is *obligated* to love us because, well, we're so lovable. We say things like, "God loved you so much and wanted to be in a relationship with you so badly that he gave his own Son for you, so you could be with him forever." We sometimes make it sound as if the inherent lovability of the person is what drives God to save; it's as though God would be crazy to have not saved us because of how lovable we all are. But this actually inverts the truth of the gospel and leads to a peculiar form of Christian presumption. We've inadvertently lost sight of the fact that God shows his love for us in this: "While we were still *sinners*, Christ died for us" (Romans 5:8).

This is why we do well to remind ourselves of who we are in ourselves. Paul had to remind the Corinthian believers of who they were apart from Christ. After having warned them that "neither the sexually immoral, nor idolaters, nor adulterers, nor men who practice homosexuality, nor thieves, nor the greedy, nor drunkards, nor revilers, nor swindlers will inherit the kingdom of God," he hastens to add, "And such were some of you" (1 Corinthians 6:9–11). It's good to remind ourselves of who we are in ourselves, apart from Christ, and especially good for those who are, in a sense, Christians by birth. It's good for us to not lose sight of the fact that we are by nature children of wrath, not children of God.

Thus, just as the truth of the gospel will poke a hole in our presumption, so too it will let the air out of our own self-righteousness. Self-righteousness feeds itself on having a leg up on others because of our background or experiences or some other distinguishing quality. But the truth of the gospel levels all of that and undermines whatever basis we might think we have for smug self-satisfaction.

In fact, our Lord Jesus Christ had some rather sharp things to say to those who rested upon their own righteousness. The Gospel writer Luke tells us that Jesus told a parable about a Pharisee and a tax collector "to some who trusted in themselves that they were righteous, and treated others with contempt" (Luke 18:9). Perhaps you know the punch line to that parable: the tax collector went home justified, while the self-righteous Pharisee did not.

"The Faithfulness of Jesus Christ" (2:16a)

Once we've come to terms with the first question about presumption, a second question confronts us. And the second question is this: *Are we convinced that Christ's death is the only reliable basis of our right standing before God?*

Despite the fact that Paul himself is a Jew by birth and not a Gentile sinner, he nevertheless has come to recognize that there is only one reliable basis for one's right standing with God. And it's not Paul's Jewish heritage or his observance of the Law; in fact, it has nothing to do with anything Paul himself has done. Instead it has everything to do with what Jesus Christ has done. This is what Paul says in 2:16a: "Yet we know that a person is not justified by works of the law but through faith in Jesus Christ."

I prefer a variant translation of the second part of that verse: "through the faithfulness of Jesus Christ." The English Standard Version rightly, in my view, acknowledges in the footnote that this is a viable alternative translation of the original Greek expression. I go with this variation simply because I think what Paul has in mind here is the *basis* of justification, not the *means* of justification. He will speak to the means of justification in the very next clause ("so we also have believed in Christ Jesus . . ."). But right now he wants to contrast two competing bases for our justification: on the one hand, the provision of the Law with its works; on the other hand, the provision of Jesus Christ and his death.[2]

Through his encounter with the risen Christ, Paul had come to realize that righteousness or justification cannot come through the Law (cf. 2:21).[3] Why not? For the same reason the writer to the Hebrews recognized: "For it is impossible for the blood of bulls and goats to take away sins" (10:4). The provisions of the Law cannot deal with the problem of sin. There's only one way to effectively deal with the problem of sin, whether in the world or in our lives: the death of Jesus Christ. "What can wash away my sin? Nothing but the blood of Jesus. What can make me whole again? Nothing but the blood of Jesus." Everything else is at best a Band-Aid, leaving us hemorrhaging all over inside.

"We Also Have Believed" (2:16b)

Because there is only one provision that counts, there is only one response that makes sense, and that's the response of faith. This leads, then, to our third question: *Are we trusting in Jesus Christ alone for our right standing before God?*

Notice the logic of Paul's train of thought in this verse. Because he knows the only provision that counts is the faithfulness of God's Son unto death, "So," he says, "we also *have believed* in Christ Jesus," in order to be justified by the provision of Christ and not by the provision of the Law. Rather than relying upon the Law with its works, Paul has fled to Christ Jesus for salvation from sin and condemnation.

I've quite intentionally framed this third question in terms of trusting in Christ Jesus rather than simply believing or having faith in Christ Jesus. Of course, trust and faith can be synonymous. But the problem is that "faith" is widely misunderstood as referring to something you do with your head rather than with your whole person. I've often heard people say they "believe in Jesus" or "have faith in Jesus," yet there's very little evidence in their lives that they're actually trusting in Jesus, relying upon him, clinging to him.

But there's another problem with the word "faith" in its popular usage. It's easy to start thinking that faith is a onetime thing. It's easy to slip into thinking that you come to believe in Christ Jesus for justification, but once you've gotten that over and done with, you then move on to something else. After you believe, you then get on with the rest of the business of the Christian life.[4]

It is easy to become confused on this point. The Galatians were quite muddled. In fact, Paul has to upbraid them for losing sight of the fact that the way they began is the way they continue. Listen to how Paul chastises them:

> O foolish Galatians! Who has bewitched you? It was before your eyes that Jesus Christ was publicly portrayed as crucified. Let me ask you only this: Did you receive the Spirit by works of the law or by hearing with faith? Are you so foolish? Having begun by the Spirit, are you now being perfected by the flesh? (3:1–3)

These poor Galatians had done what so many Christians do: they'd gotten off to an excellent start but wound up changing their whole strategy after just a couple of laps. Yet when this happens, what's easily lost is the fact that believing in Christ Jesus isn't only how you start the Christian life, it's also how you continue in the Christian life.

Here's the good news. The truth of the gospel is the truth of the gospel whether you're a non-Christian or a new Christian or a seasoned Christian.

The call of the gospel is always and forever the same: trusting in Christ alone. But the temptation is also always and forever the same: to try to finish the Christian race differently than how we began it. This is why Scripture's advice is consistent.

> Therefore, as you received Christ Jesus the Lord, so walk in him, rooted and built up in him and established in the faith, just as you were taught, abounding in thanksgiving. (Colossians 2:6, 7)

In other words, we must not only embrace the truth of the gospel, we must also live in light of the truth of the gospel. We must continue to return to the truth of the gospel again and again. We need to feed upon it each and every day. We must never veer off onto some other truth but instead bask in the glorious truth of what Jesus Christ has done for us.

A Shocking Gospel

This is the gospel in a nutshell, a single-sentence summary of the truth of the gospel, the heart and soul of the Christian faith. "This was the truth of the gospel in Christ Jesus: the misery of the sinner and the mercy of God."[5] It's the kind of good news that's so good, it's shocking. Or at least it ought to be. It ought to shock us because it's so foreign to our way of thinking about the world much of the time. For it's not ultimately about us; it's ultimately all about God's provision in Jesus Christ—his blood and righteousness.

> Jesus, Thy blood and righteousness
> My beauty are, my glorious dress;
> 'Midst flaming worlds, in these arrayed,
> With joy shall I lift up my head.
>
> Bold shall I stand in Thy great Day;
> For who aught to my charge shall lay?
> Fully absolved through these I am
> From sin and fear, from guilt and shame.
>
> The holy, meek, unspotted Lamb,
> Who from the Father's bosom came,
> Who died for me, e'en me to atone,
> Now for my Lord and God I own.
>
> Lord, I believe Thy precious blood,
> Which, at the mercy seat of God,
> Forever doth for sinners plead,
> For me, e'en for my soul, was shed.

Lord, I believe were sinners more
Than sands upon the ocean shore,
Thou hast for all a ransom paid,
For all a full atonement made.

Were sinners more than the sands upon the ocean shore, even then God's provision in the death of his Son Jesus Christ would be sufficient. Even then a satisfying ransom would be paid, even then a full atonement made.

But if, in our endeavor to be justified in Christ, we too were found to be sinners, is Christ then a servant of sin? Certainly not! For if I rebuild what I tore down, I prove myself to be a transgressor. For through the law I died to the law, so that I might live to God. I have been crucified with Christ. It is no longer I who live, but Christ who lives in me. And the life I now live in the flesh I live by faith in the Son of God, who loved me and gave himself for me. I do not nullify the grace of God, for if righteousness were through the law, then Christ died for no purpose.

2:17–21

9

Cruciformity: The Shape of Gospel- Rooted Living

GALATIANS 2:17–21

IN OUR JOURNEY THROUGH GALATIANS we've grappled with different aspects of what a gospel-rooted life looks like. But this passage takes us to the very heart of gospel-rooted living. In these verses Paul defines for us the essence of what it means to live a life rooted in the saving work of Jesus Christ.

The apostle Peter's unfortunate hypocrisy in Antioch called for open rebuke from the Apostle Paul (2:11–14). But it also called for clarification of the truth of the gospel; this Paul provides in 2:15, 16, in all likelihood a continuation of his words of rebuke to Peter. But Paul doesn't stop there. Instead he goes on in 2:17–21 to offer *a positive example* of what it means to live out the truth of the gospel. And the positive example is his own example (cf. 4:12). Paul is the paradigm of gospel-rooted living.

These verses do not merely contain a bunch of interesting theological ideas; instead they offer a provocative description of a gospel-rooted way of life. What Paul describes here is the shape the gospel takes in his own life. And that shape is the shape of the cross: "I have been crucified with Christ" (2:20). Thus, at the heart of gospel-rooted living is *cruciformity*.[1] Life in Christ is all about being crucified with Christ.

Galatians is littered with references to the crucifixion (cf. 2:19, 20, 21; 3:1, 13; 5:11, 24; 6:12, 14, 17; cf. 1:4; 4:4, 5). In fact, the cross serves as the Christological center of gravity in the letter, so that Christ stands forth as the Crucified One, whose death was itself an example par excellence of suffering-persecution. This in turn shapes Paul's view of his own suffering-persecution, as well as the way in which he speaks about it in Galatians.

Cruciformity like Paul experienced comes from taking gospel risks for the good of others. If your life is truly rooted in the gospel, then cruciformity will be the shape of your life as you give yourself for the good of others. If the gospel's taken root in your life, God won't let you be conformed to the pattern of this world. Instead he will transform you into the image of his Son so that your life increasingly looks like his (Romans 12:2). But this means your life will look more and more like a crucifixion: sacrificially giving yourself for the sake of others. Cruciformity is the form it will take—conformity to the cross of Christ.

Christ Is Not a Servant of Sin (2:17, 18)

Cruciformity is the shape of Paul's life as he pursues gospel ministry. Why? Because he is driven by a desire—indeed, a calling—to reach Gentiles with the good news of Jesus Christ. But in order to proclaim the gospel effectively to them, he must live among them and interact with them. "To those outside the law," Paul says, "I became as one outside the law . . . that I might win those outside the law" (1 Corinthians 9:21). And this means sharing meals together and sharing lives with one another.

Yet Paul's approach to winning Gentiles makes some Jews nervous. In fact, Jews of a stricter persuasion are convinced Paul is going too far. He relates to Gentiles in ways that are simply unacceptable—even unlawful. "When you're with Gentiles, Paul, you act just like a Gentile. There's hardly any difference between you and them. But don't you realize, Paul, that this makes your Messiah and ours an accomplice to their sin?"[2]

No doubt Paul confronts these kinds of accusations regularly. In fact, we hear him respond to this sort of charge in 2:17: "But if, in our endeavor to be justified in Christ, we too were found to be sinners, is Christ then a servant of sin?" Notice what's implied in this rhetorical question. Paul acknowledges that from a strict law-observant Jewish standpoint, he could be judged a "sinner." This is because in his attempt to reach Gentiles, he does indeed "live like a Gentile and not like a Jew" (2:14) in order to reach Gentiles. Thus Paul would appear to the stricter types to be little different than "Gentile sinners" (2:15). Paul doesn't disagree with this point. Nor does he try to avoid this charge against him.

What Paul rejects entirely, however, is the implication that his behavior makes Christ "a servant of sin" (2:17). God forbid, Paul asserts. "For if I rebuild what I tore down, [only then would] I prove myself to be a transgressor" (2:18). Paul transgresses God's will only if he does what Peter did in Antioch. If Paul would have withdrawn from table fellowship with Gentiles, he would in effect have rebuilt what Jesus Christ died to tear down—namely, "the dividing wall of hostility" between Jews and Gentiles (cf. Ephesians 2:14). Therefore, call Paul what you want—a miscreant, a sinner, an apostate—he doesn't violate God's will or nullify God's grace; in fact, in his ministry to Gentiles he magnifies it (2:21).

The Price to Be Paid for Ministry among Gentiles (2:19, 20a)

But by admitting that he can be judged to be a sinner, Paul acknowledges that there is a price to be paid for his ministry to Gentiles. He knows as a Jew there is a price he will have to pay in order to maintain his mission to Gentiles, for it leaves him constantly exposed to the charge that he is in violation of the expectations for one who claims to be a faithful Jew.

From Paul's own testimony, we know that he continued to be not only accused of being in violation of the Law but punished because of it. Thus, when he would visit synagogues, he'd be brought up on charges and then often flogged with a whip or a stick. "Five times I received at the hands of the Jews the forty lashes less one. Three times I was beaten with rods. Once I was stoned" (2 Corinthians 11:24, 25).[3] And to think of the bellyaching I'm prone to do when I'm only slightly inconvenienced in the service of Christ!

No wonder Paul talks about his relationship to the Law as one marked *by death*. "For through the law I died to the law" (2:19). He had to pay the price for ministry among Gentile sinners, and that price was the death-dealing *curse* of the Law. Thus, through the curse of the Law he died to the curse of the Law. By routinely coming under the discipline of the Law, the Law's intimidating curse no longer had a hold on his heart, he no longer feared its judgment. In Antioch Peter withdrew from table fellowship with Gentiles because he was afraid of "the circumcision party" and what they would do to him if he continued to act that way: forty lashes less one! But Paul stood his ground there in Antioch and elsewhere. He was willing to pay the price for continued ministry among Gentiles, even if it meant more sacrifice, increased suffering, another hostile crowd, or another round of beatings![4]

So this tattered apostle can say with tremendous gospel-rooted conviction and resignation, "I have been crucified with Christ" (2:20). That's the kind of life he lives—crucified with Christ. He too has been put on trial, brought up on false charges, and, like Jesus, punished as a transgressor of the Law (2:19; cf. 3:13). Truly he has learned that a disciple is not above his teacher, nor a servant above his master (Matthew 10:24). Cruciformity is his way of life.[5]

But so too is it for every follower of Christ. So we shouldn't be surprised if we suffer a little mistreatment in the service of the gospel. There's a price to be paid for gospel ministry. And if we're not willing to pay that price, then we're unlikely to see the gospel advance through our lives. But if we want to see the gospel go forward, it's going to require of us cruciformity. We will be conformed to the cross.

God works powerfully through cruciform people. In fact, he's used cruciform people to renew whole countries. This happened in eighteenth-century Britain, where God raised up a generation of valiant early Methodist evangelists—including Howell Harris, George Whitefield, and Charles and John Wesley—who embraced cruciformity with Christ for the sake of the gospel. Listen to how one historian of this period explains the link between their willingness to embrace cruciformity and the salvation of many souls.

> If Methodism had not come into contact with the mob it would never have reached the section of the English people which most needed salvation. The "Religious Societies" shut up in their rooms, would never have reformed the country.
>
> It was necessary that a race of heroic men should arise, who would dare to confront the wildest and most brutal men, and tell them the meaning of sin, and show them the Christ of the Cross and of the Judgment Throne.
>
> The incessant assaults of the mob on the Methodist preachers showed they had reached the masses. With a superb courage, rarely, if ever, equaled on the battlefield, the Methodist preachers went again and again, to the places from which they had been driven by violence, until their persistence wore down the antagonism of their assailants. Then, out of the once furious crowd, men and women were gathered whose hearts the Lord had touched.[6]

Resurrection Living (2:20, 21)

Like these great eighteenth-century evangelists, the Apostle Paul is fearless before the threat of the crowds. He isn't intimidated by the opinions or accusations of others; their disapproval doesn't impede the gospel ministry to which God has called him. He doesn't even fear the accusations of the Law, for he knows that his own Master, the Lord Jesus Christ, has already endured the curse of the Law when he hung on a tree, the cross (cf. Galatians 3:13; Deuteronomy 21:23). And what was the upshot of that for Jesus—banishment from God as one who is accursed or vindication from God as one who is righteous?

Cruciformity in the cause of Christ never ends with the curse of death. It always leads to the glorious dawn of the resurrection from the dead. "I have been crucified with Christ," Paul says. But he doesn't stop there, with death. He goes on to speak of the resurrection life he now lives: "It is no longer I who live, but Christ who lives in me" (2:20). Paul is tried like Jesus, executed like Jesus, raised like Jesus, and thus now he, like Jesus, lives to God. His life is continually marked by cruciformity. But so too is it continually sustained by resurrection power!

Realize, then, that a gospel-rooted life inevitably leads to a crucified life. If we're truly rooted in the saving work of Jesus Christ, we will experience an ongoing kind of death, a continual crucifixion with Christ. We cannot be firmly rooted in the gospel and not experience a kind of sacrifice and suffering that we might very well call death. If there's no death in our life, there's probably no gospel either.

However, we should have great confidence in the fact that resurrection awaits us on the other side of every experience of crucifixion. "I have been crucified with Christ." But that doesn't mean we stop living. That only means Christ lives in us. His resurrection life takes over our earthly life. So while we may end up dying to what we hold dear in this life, we will nevertheless live to God, for the same one who raised Jesus from the grave will raise us up as we give up our life in service for him.

This is why, then, we can only live this cruciform way of life in one way—namely, by faith. Without faith not only is it impossible to please God (Hebrews 11:6), it's impossible to live a cruciform, gospel-rooted life. But this faith that marks our new resurrection way of life is not faith in something abstract or obtuse. It is faith in the crucified Christ, the one "who loved me and gave himself for me" (2:20).

If we truly wrap our life around the life of Christ, if Jesus truly lives within us, then the Christ who is in us will do what Christ did in his earthly life: he loved others and gave himself for others. So, too, this life in us will cause us to do the same. Cruciformity is, then, *conformity to the self-giving action of the Son of God*. What shape did Jesus' own loving and giving take? It took on the shape of the cross. That's where he demonstrated his love for us and gave himself for us.

Conclusion

We see, then, the shape that the gospel took in the life of the Apostle Paul. But what shape has it taken in ours? When people get a good look at who we are, do they see the cross of Christ? Is our life conformed to the pattern of the cross? Is cruciformity the shape of our life?

Cruciformity is the shape of gospel-rooted living—conformity not to the pattern of this world, but to the cross of Christ. This is our Christian calling, as well as the challenge of discipleship: not to be enslaved to the self-protective ways of this world, but to walk in step with the truth of the gospel. "If anyone would come after me," our Lord declares, "let him deny himself and take up his cross daily and follow me" (Luke 9:23).

If we want others to see Jesus Christ, then we must consider what sort of radical gospel-oriented sacrifice we can make for the good of other people, so they can see the cross of Christ in our lives. May we each live a gospel-rooted life—a cruciform life—to the glory of God!

O foolish Galatians! Who has bewitched you? It was before your eyes that Jesus Christ was publicly portrayed as cruci- fied. Let me ask you only this: Did you receive the Spirit by works of the law or by hearing with faith? Are you so foolish? Having begun by the Spirit, are you now being perfected by the flesh? Did you suffer so many things in vain—if indeed it was in vain? Does he who supplies the Spirit to you and works miracles among you do so by works of the law, or by hearing with faith . . . ?

3:1–5

10

There's Only One
Way to Finish

GALATIANS 3:1–5

HUMAN BEINGS have a remarkably high capacity for foolishness. My favorite is the story of a man who woke one morning in the dead of a Minnesota winter to find that the engine of his car had frozen. His solution? Pour hot gasoline into his car. So he put some into a pot and warmed it on his kitchen stove. As you can guess, that didn't go so well.

Or there's the story of two truck drivers who stopped before a low-hanging overpass to decide whether their eighteen-wheeler could go under it. The driver pointed out that the overpass only had a clearance of thirteen feet, one inch, yet their truck required at least fourteen feet. But his colleague had an even more astute observation. There weren't any cops around, so they should just go for it. And they did. Again it didn't go so well.

The only way you could top this kind of folly would be to try *to finish the Christian life in your own strength*. That's not a good idea; in fact, it's foolish. Yet how prone we are to do this very thing!

The Christians in Galatia are trying to finish the Christian race in their own strength.[1] And Paul is beside himself as a result. He can't believe it; surely some devilry is at work in Galatia, prompting such madness. Hence Paul peppers them with a string of rhetorical questions:

> O foolish Galatians! Who has bewitched you? It was before your eyes that Jesus Christ was publicly portrayed as crucified. Let me ask you only this: Did you receive the Spirit by works of the law or by hearing with faith? Are you so foolish? Having begun by the Spirit, are you now being perfected by

the flesh? Did you suffer so many things in vain—if indeed it was in vain? Does he who supplies the Spirit to you and works miracles among you do so by works of the law, or by hearing with faith . . . ? (3:1–5)

This isn't Paul's first, or only, rebuke of these "foolish" Galatians. The letter's opening salvo is similarly chiding (cf. 1:6–9). But here Paul doesn't simply repeat his earlier rebuke; he further clarifies the issues at stake. The Galatians are attempting to do the unthinkable: they're contemplating circumcision and thus trying to finish the Christian race by the flesh rather than by the Spirit (3:3).

But why would adult male converts to Christ, living in the ancient world, want to get circumcised? There was no doubt some social pressure, given their precarious identity. But ultimately they'd become convinced that circumcision was the key to finishing the race, crossing the finish line, and finding success with God on the Last Day.

Presumably they'd been told by the agitators, the Judaizers, that no matter how well they'd started, they wouldn't find success at the finish without undergoing circumcision. Or to put it in theological terms, the Galatians had become convinced that they needed circumcision in order to be saved. No doubt what was being touted in Antioch was also being promulgated in Galatia. Certain men were telling these believers, "Unless you are circumcised according to the custom of Moses, you cannot be saved" (Acts 15:1). And evidently the Galatians were buying it.

Thus Paul is distraught over his wayward flock, for their behavior implies nothing less than a departure from the gospel.[2] And a departure from the gospel, in turn, jeopardizes their entire future. Paul fears he's labored over them in vain (4:11). Though they were "running well," they're not any longer (5:7). Indeed, they appear to have "fallen away from grace" (5:4), having turned away from the One who "called [them] in the grace of Christ" (1:6). And if they don't finish the race by grace, they can't possibly receive the prize. It's that simple. To go to circumcision is to leave Christ; but leaving Christ will only leave them utterly exposed on the Day of Judgment. Christ will be of no help to them on that day.[3]

So what's Paul's response? In short, he pleads with the Galatians not to look to the Law but instead to stick with the Spirit. If they want to finish their race, they must rely on the Spirit's empowering presence. The Law, with its works, won't lift a finger to help. The Spirit alone is able to grant them success in their race.

The question for the Galatians, then, is a crucial one for you and me as well. How can we promote the presence of the Spirit? Or more accurately, by what means does God pour the Spirit into our lives? Paul says God is the one "who supplies the Spirit to you" (3:5). But our question is, how? This paragraph of Galatians is designed to answer that question and to get the Galatians back on track, to finish the race by the Spirit and not by the flesh.

God Supplies the Spirit through the Cross of Christ (3:1)

But before Paul points the Galatians to the key issue, he takes them back to how they began their life in the Spirit. He reminds them how it all began with something they saw, indeed, with something they encountered. "It was before your eyes that Jesus Christ was publicly portrayed as crucified" (3:1). The Galatians began life in the Spirit when they saw Jesus Christ crucified.

Notice that Paul emphasizes how visible this sight of Christ was: "It was *before your eyes* that Jesus Christ was publicly portrayed as crucified" (3:1). This is an allusion to more than vivid, imaginative preaching. Paul wants them to recall how he *physically embodied* the cross of Christ. The Galatians thus saw the crucified Christ in the crucified Paul.

How? Through, Paul says, his own apostolic suffering. As a result of his many trials and tribulations, he has indeed been "crucified with Christ" (2:20). And in the flesh-and-blood of his very real suffering—the gash across his forehead, the welts on his arm, the black-and-blue around his eyes, the scars down his back—the Galatians see the crucified Christ publicly portrayed.[4]

But Paul reminds them of how they saw the crucified Christ to reinforce the fact that the Spirit comes only *through* the cross of Christ. That is to say, God only supplies us with the Spirit if our sins have been forgiven because of the death of Jesus Christ. Unless our sins have been washed away by the blood of Christ, the Holy Spirit cannot enter our lives. Apart from having our sins forgiven, the *Holy* Spirit would destroy, not sanctify us.

Paul's point, then, is that the Spirit comes through the cross of Christ and only through the cross of Christ. The Spirit never does an end run around the cross. It all begins with the forgiveness of sins God accomplishes in the death of Jesus. This is the door through which the Spirit travels; the door is opened by the death of Christ.

But this is also where we must return, again and again, as we continue to struggle with sin. Every day we must pray, "Forgive us our debts, as we also have forgiven our debtors" (Matthew 6:12). While a true believer cannot lose his *union* with the Spirit, he can interrupt his *communion* with the Spirit.[5] And sin is the great disruption to communion with God. Like unplugging the cord to your computer, sin cuts us off from the source of power.

This is why confession of sin ought to be a regular part of our Christian life. "Confess your sins to one another," James tells us (5:16). Have you ever noticed how almost instantly we feel stronger when we've confessed sin? How do we explain this empowerment? Confession takes us back to the cross, where we see the crucified Christ. And there we gaze afresh at God's forgiveness and there receive a fresh outpouring of God's Spirit. "Repent therefore, and turn back, that your sins may be blotted out, that times of refreshing may come from the presence of the Lord" (Acts 3:19, 20).

God Supplies the Spirit in Response to the Hearing of Faith (3:2, 5)

But if the cross of Christ and the forgiveness of sins is the door *God* opens to enter into our sinful lives, then what's the door *we* open to allow God to enter? Paul points the way with a rhetorical question intended to cut to the chase: "Let me ask you only this: Did you receive the Spirit by works of the law or by hearing with faith?" (3:2).

Of course, the Galatians know they didn't receive the Spirit by getting circumcised or by doing any of the other works of the Law. When Peter preached in Joppa to Cornelius and those of his household, the Holy Spirit simply came upon them as Peter was speaking to them. "And the believers from among the circumcised who had come with Peter were amazed, because the gift of the Holy Spirit was poured out even on the Gentiles" (Acts 10:45). How did the Spirit come upon these Gentiles or those in Galatia? As Paul says, not by "works of the law" but by "hearing with faith."

But the giving of the Spirit isn't a onetime thing. As Paul adds, the Spirit *continues to come into their lives* in response to that same responsive faith: "Does he who supplies the Spirit to you and works miracles among you do so by works of the law, or by hearing with faith?" (3:5). The Galatians began their Christian life with the hearing of faith; so, too, this is how they must continue in the Christian life. And, indeed, this is how they must complete the Christian life—by the hearing of faith.

God pours his Spirit into our lives when we are *responsive* to the word of the gospel. But we must recognize that there are two ways to hear: there's hearing with the ear, and there's hearing with faith. Only the latter kind of hearing opens the door to the Spirit's presence.

Realize, then, that religious activities *in themselves* do not mediate the presence of the Spirit. We can engage in all sorts of church activities, but if the hearing of faith isn't undergirding it, then all we have is lots of activity. We may be busy, but we'll lack the empowering presence of the Spirit.

This insight ought to motivate us to give top priority to *the Word of God* in everything we do. If we desire the Spirit's presence, we must be Bible people; we need to be Word-driven in our approach to ministry and to life because God's presence comes as we respond to God's Word with faith.

God the Father loves to honor God the Son by supplying us with God the Spirit in response to our responsiveness to his Word. For as God says through the prophet Isaiah, "This is the one to whom I will look: he who is humble and contrite in spirit and trembles at my word" (66:2). God looks to the one who hears his Word with faith; God pours out his very presence into the life of just that kind of person.

God Supplies the Spirit in the Midst of Suffering (3:4)

So the cross of Christ and the hearing of faith are the two doors through which God's Spirit travels in order to enter into our lives. But there's a third way in which God supplies his Spirit to us.

Did you notice Paul's curious mention of the Galatians' suffering in this passage? "Did you suffer so many things in vain—if indeed it was in vain?" (3:4).[6] Why would Paul remind them of their suffering at this point? Why warn them that their suffering will go to waste if they continue down the path they're on? Is Paul only adding insult to injury?

Paul wants them to realize this: *God supplies his Spirit generously in times of great difficulty.* The Galatians remember that when they came to Christ, they began to experience various challenges and hardships because of their new faith. But they also recall that God wasn't hindered by this; in fact, these were the very circumstances in which God through his Spirit moved with great power in their lives. Like the Thessalonians, the Galatians "received the word in much affliction, with the joy of the Holy Spirit" (1 Thessalonians 1:6).

Some of us only like to invite guests into our home when we have everything clean and in its place. We've mopped the kitchen floor, taken out the trash, vacuumed the carpets, washed the windows, dusted the lampshades and bookshelves, stocked the refrigerator, bought freshly cut flowers, even given the kids a bath. Of course, it's tempting to think of the Holy Spirit in a similar way, as though he only likes to show up when everything in our lives is as it should be, when we've passed through the rough patches and dispensed with the difficulties.

But the experience of countless Christians points in a different direction. In fact, many seasoned believers will tell you they never experience greater or sweeter supplies of God's Spirit than when they're in the midst of suffering. This certainly was Paul's experience. He'd learned to be content in the most difficult times, times of "weaknesses, insults, hardships, persecutions, and calamities" (2 Corinthians 12:10). How did he do it? He'd come to know this glorious truth: "When I am weak, then I am strong" (2 Corinthians 12:10). Indeed, he'd heard the Lord Jesus say to him in those very circumstances, "My grace is sufficient for you, for my power is made perfect in weakness" (2 Corinthians 12:9).

Have you ever been around someone who is experiencing great suffering and loss and yet, at the same time, great faith in God? There's a beautiful radiance to such a person. The Holy Spirit appears to rest quite tangibly on him or her. Recently at a funeral I spoke with a man in his forties who'd lost his wife to cancer. He was understandably heartbroken, and yet he was radiant. His soul was saturated with a joy and peace clearly born of the Holy Spirit (cf. Romans 15:13). God's presence was palpable. You could see the Lord's sustaining presence in his eyes, watch it in his demeanor, hear it in his voice and in the words he spoke. Clearly God was pouring out his Spirit into this grieving and yet faith-filled heart.

God loves to show forth his power in the midst of our weakness. Suffering is thus not a hindrance to experiencing more of God; rather it's often the ideal situation in which to receive fresh empowerment from on high.

So we shouldn't begrudge the difficulties in our life, whether big or little. Instead let's view them as God's loving design for us, to give us more of himself through his Holy Spirit. Indeed, we can embrace suffering—respond to it with the hearing of faith—as a God-given opportunity to experience more of God. Such opportunities are the very things we need to keep us moving toward the finish line.

Of course, this isn't easy to do. But when we live by faith in the Son of God who loved us and gave himself for us in the midst of our hardships, we will find that God will be pleased to supply us with an abundance of his Spirit; we will find Christ living in us.

Conclusion

What challenges do we face? Where do we need the empowering presence of the Holy Spirit to help us persevere to the end? And how will we find that power or strength to get us from where we are to where we need to be? It is God who supplies the Spirit to us. And he does so through the cross of Christ, in response to the hearing of faith, and often in the midst of difficulty.

As Christians we need a fresh supply of the Spirit every single day. We live the Christian life only by the Spirit, in reliance upon the presence and power of the Holy Spirit. Some of us have been trying to live the Christian life in our own strength; that's why we find it so taxing and even tedious. We're trying to live for God apart from the empowering presence of God. But that simply won't work. The only way to live to God is to no longer live in ourselves but to find Christ living in us (cf. 2:19, 20).

Let's go back, then, to the cross of Christ, look to the Word of God, and not begrudge the suffering God sends our way, for these are the very means by which God supplies his Spirit to us. This is what we need to keep us running the race!

. . . just as Abraham "believed God, and it was counted to him as righteousness"? Know then that it is those of faith who are the sons of Abraham. And the Scripture, foreseeing that God would justify the Gentiles by faith, preached the gospel beforehand to Abraham, saying, "In you shall all the nations be blessed." So then, those who are of faith are blessed along with Abraham, the man of faith.

3:6–9

11

Abraham's Blessing

GALATIANS 3:6–9

THIS PASSAGE CONTAINS some very good news. Here God tells us that anyone can share in the blessing he's given to Abraham. Regardless of our race or class or gender, irrespective of our ethnicity or age or nationality, no matter our personal history or credit score or dumb decisions of the past, we can each become the beneficiary of Abraham's blessing. This is the main point of this passage: "So then, those who are of faith are blessed along with Abraham, the man of faith" (3:9). This is better news than a tax refund or a pay raise or any other windfall we can imagine.

Now for some this may sound quaint but not altogether exciting. If we were raised in the church, perhaps there's a certain fascination with Abraham. He's that mysterious Bedouin character of Sunday school stories and songs: "Father Abraham had many sons . . ." But if we weren't raised in the church, we'll likely have trouble seeing any relevance in receiving Abraham's blessing. We'd much rather find a way to get in on the good graces of Facebook founder Mark Zuckerberg, who recently pledged $100 million in Facebook stock to the Newark, NJ, school district.[1] That's something to get excited about, right?

The Christ-followers in Galatia were certainly interested in Abraham's blessing. In fact, that's what all the fuss was about. Paul wrote this most intense and heated of his letters in order to sort out the issue of who can receive Abraham's blessing. There was no more relevant question for Paul or the Galatians. And it would have doubtless been of interest to the Judaizers who were stirring up trouble in Galatia.[2]

But interest in Abraham's blessing isn't simply an antique interest, fascinating like collecting rare stamps is fascinating. Actually it couldn't be more relevant today—perhaps especially today, in our post-9/11 world. The three great monotheistic religions of the world—Judaism, Christianity, and Islam—all trace their start to God's promise of blessing to Abraham. More than half the world's population, over three billion people, have a vested interest in this issue, or at least they ought to if they rightly understand their own faith tradition.

We will find most things about which the Bible speaks more relevant as we understand better what they are. This is certainly the case with Abraham's blessing. When we understand what it is, we'll realize how highly relevant it is to each one of us. And when we understand how we can share in it, we'll no doubt hear it as very good news indeed.

The Reverse of the Curse

So what is the blessing of Abraham to which Paul refers in this passage? Perhaps the simplest way to define it is this: *Abraham's blessing is God's solution to the world's problems.* What are the world's problems? Well, the world's problems begin inside each one of us, with the evil in every human heart. But our problems don't end there; the world's problems include all the strife and violence that exists between people and communities and even countries. Think of those constants of human history—domestic abuse, racism, genocide, and so on.

Yet what vexes the world can't be confined to human beings; it includes the chaos and disintegration of the creation itself. We see and feel creation's "groaning" (cf. Romans 8:22) in things like earthquakes that bury the unsuspecting under tall piles of rubble or tsunamis that wash away entire villages without even asking or molecules that mutate for the worst by becoming another case of pancreatic cancer or miscarriages that break a hopeful mother's heart and leave her without any explanation as to why.

But Abraham's blessing is *God's way of reversing the effects of the curse.* If you look at the story line of Scripture, you find that God called Abraham and promised to extend the divine blessing through him (Genesis 12). But this chapter comes not only on the heels of Genesis 3—11, which describes the fall and its aftereffects, but comes as *a direct response* to what we see in those chapters. And what do we see in that portion of Scripture that describes the fall and its aftereffects?

> Genesis 3–11 shows how every dimension of life is tragically adrift from the original goodness of God's purpose. The earth lies under the sentence of God's curse because of human sin. Human beings are adding to their

catalogue of evil as the generations roll past—jealousy, anger, murder, vengeance, violence, corruption, drunkenness, sexual disorder, arrogance. . . . Women enjoy the gift of childbirth along with suffering and pain. Men find fulfillment in subduing the earth, but with sweat and frustration. Both enjoy sexual complementarity and intimacy, but along with lust and domination. Every inclination of human hearts is shot through with evil. Technology and culture are advancing, but the skill that can craft instruments for music and agriculture can also forge weapons of violent death. Nations experience the richness of their ethnic, linguistic and geographical diversity along with confusion, scattering and strife.[3]

Abraham's blessing is, then, God's solution to each and every one of these problems. Thus nothing could be more relevant to us than Abraham's blessing, whether we live in Chicago or Tripoli or Tokyo. Abraham's blessing is God's way of reversing the horrific effects of the curse upon the whole creation.

Think about Abraham's blessing this way. Consider the horrific video footage of the devastation wrought by the tsunami that struck Japan in March 2011. Picture in your mind's eye the twenty-second clip of the ocean literally coming ashore and rolling over the tops of villages, consuming everything in its path—houses, schools, hospitals, cars, children, the elderly, the unaware. Sheer and unrestrained devastation.

Now imagine Abraham's blessing as that tape played *in reverse*. Imagine it as God's reversing and thus *undoing* all that senseless devastation and destruction, turning it all back, restoring it to its original state, bringing his *shalom*-peace out of utter chaos and desolation. Then imagine that great reversal not just for Japan but for the entire creation—indeed the entire cosmos!

That is what the Bible understands to be Abraham's blessing. This is why God blessed Abraham and called him to be a blessing to the nations, to the world: the promise of a new creation, free from sickness and sin and death. This is the ultimate solution to all our problems; this is the answer to every one of our dilemmas; this is the antidote to every disease, the resolution of every conflict. This is what every one of us needs; this is what each one of us wants. This is the blessing God promised to Abraham and to those who are blessed along with Abraham.

In Abraham by Faith

So how do we share in Abraham's blessing? To put it simply, *we share in Abraham's blessing by joining Abraham's family.* This is the whole thrust of this passage. In particular, in verse 8 Paul quotes the key passage from Genesis

12, where God says to Abraham, "In you shall all the nations be blessed." God's blessing of Abraham is extended to others only through Abraham. "*In you* shall all the nations be blessed." Not in Mohammed or Buddha or Oprah Winfrey or the President of the United States or your 401K or your church or your pastor—we can share in God's blessing only in Abraham.

But in order to share in Abraham's blessing we must become children of Abraham; we must each become his son or daughter. We all understand that a person's benefits (i.e., "blessings") get passed down to that person's descendants, not randomly distributed to complete strangers. Periodically we see in the news a brouhaha over some fabulously wealthy person's estate—who are the rightly heirs of that person's wealth? I don't join in those fights, even though I wouldn't mind a bit of that blessing. But I recognize that I have no claim to it. I'm not a part of that family, not even close. And so it is with Abraham and sharing in his blessing. Only if you are Abraham's offspring are you an heir to Abraham's inheritance (cf. 3:29).

So the next logical question is, how do we become a son or daughter of Abraham? Here's where things became controversial for Paul and indeed for early Christianity. It was quite natural for the Jews in Paul's day to assume that the only way to become a part of Abraham's family was to become circumcised and thus become a Jew. After all, the Lord God did say explicitly to Abraham, "This is my covenant, which you shall keep, between me and you and your offspring after you: Every male among you shall be circumcised" (Genesis 17:10).[4]

Yet what Paul understands from Scripture itself is that God had *already* declared his intention to bless the nations apart from their becoming Jews. Thus Paul can say a most remarkable thing: "And the Scripture, foreseeing that God would justify the Gentiles by faith, preached the *gospel* beforehand to Abraham, saying, 'In you shall all the nations be blessed'" (3:8).[5] Because God always intended to justify sinners by faith, God could tell Abraham many hundreds of years before Christ that through him God's blessing would extend to all nations and indeed to the whole creation.

Inclusion in Abraham's family was thus never going to be tied to circumcision; it was always going to be about faith—"Just as Abraham 'believed God, and it was counted to him as righteousness'" (3:6; cf. Genesis 15:6). God had always intended to enfold Gentiles as Gentiles into the family of Abraham. God had always intended to reckon people a part of Abraham's family by faith, and not by works of the Law.

Therefore, Paul can draw the conclusion, "Know then that it is those of faith who are the sons of Abraham" (3:7). Those who are of the same faith as

Abraham share in the same blessing promised to Abraham. We must, then, be *Abraham look-alikes*; we must live our lives just like Abraham did his—that is, by faith, for Abraham was "the man of faith" (3:9).

An Abraham Look-Alike

But what does an Abraham look-alike look like? What does it mean to be a man or woman of faith like Abraham? It means, first of all, that we have *a Christ-focused faith*. Genesis 15:6 says Abraham "believed the LORD." But it would be a mistake to take this to mean that Abraham simply had some vague notion of a divine being or higher power. What it meant for Abraham was to believe in the God who had spoken a very specific word to him, a word of promise. But now, in these last days, God has spoken to us through his Son (cf. Hebrews 1:2). Jesus Christ is the one who has died and been raised and now sits at the right hand of God and will one day return to judge the living and the dead; and it is this Jesus in whom all the promises of God are both Yes and Amen. And so to be a man or woman of faith, and thus a child of Abraham, is to live a life of faith that is focused upon all that God has promised to do for us and for the world in his Son, Jesus Christ.

But to be of the same faith as Abraham also means that this faith of ours is *an obedient faith*. While Abraham is indeed the *model* of faith, his faith was no mere intellectual assent. His was a living and active kind of faith, not a dead one. His faith was what led him to follow God even when he had no idea where God was going to take him (Hebrews 11:8). His was a faith that enabled him to offer up his own son Isaac (Genesis 22; Hebrews 11:17, 18; James 2:21). "You see that faith was active along with his works," the book of James reminds us, "and faith was completed by his works; and the Scripture was fulfilled that says, 'Abraham believed God, and it was counted to him as righteousness'" (2:22, 23).

Yet Abraham's obedient faith wasn't a perfect faith; a quick perusal of his life story makes that perfectly clear. But Abraham's faith was *a persevering faith*. And so too is ours if we are like Abraham, "the man of faith." This means not waffling in unbelief and thus wavering concerning the promises of God. This also means not staying down when we fall down, but getting back up, dusting ourselves off with repentance, refocusing our life with faith, and setting out again in the strength of the Holy Spirit.

A persevering faith means growing increasingly strong in faith over a lifetime, just like Abraham did, and thus growing in our capacity to give God glory by being increasingly convinced that God is able to do for us what he has promised (cf. Romans 4:20, 21). This was the trajectory of Abraham's life.

That is why, as Paul says, "His faith was 'counted to him as righteousness'" (Romans 4:22). "But the words 'it was counted to him' were not written for his sake alone, but for ours also" (Romans 4:23, 24).

Conclusion

Practically speaking, to live our life as an Abraham look-alike will mean that we'll need to go, we'll need to leave, and we'll need to seek. God's first word to Abraham was "Go." So, too, if we follow in his footsteps, we'll need to go; we'll need to go out from the world in order to be set apart for God, no longer conformed to the pattern of this world (Romans 12:2).

Just like Abraham, we'll also need to leave; we'll need to say good-bye to the life we perhaps imagined for ourselves—the comforts, the perks, the benefits. Instead it will mean going with Jesus outside the camp to bear the reproach he himself bore (Hebrews 13:13).

But we'll only truly go and leave if we, like Abraham, are seeking a better future from God. It is said of Abraham that he lived his life as a nomad because he was "looking forward to the city that has foundations, whose designer and builder is God" (Hebrews 11:10). So, too, you and I, like Abraham, need to have our hearts set on pilgrimage, not on settling down as though this place were lasting. "For here we have no lasting city, but we seek the city that is to come" (Hebrews 13:14).

A "city that is to come"—that is the Christian hope! Not simply going to Heaven when we die but inhabiting a real city that will be the fulfillment of God's blessing to Abraham. It will also be the consummation of everything God has been doing from the beginning—all because of Christ and through Christ.

> Then I saw a new heaven and a new earth, for the first heaven and the first earth had passed away, and the sea was no more. And I saw the holy city, new Jerusalem, coming down out of heaven from God, prepared as a bride adorned for her husband. And I heard a loud voice from the throne saying, "Behold, the dwelling place of God is with man. He will dwell with them, and they will be his people, and God himself will be with them as their God. He will wipe away every tear from their eyes, and death shall be no more, neither shall there be mourning, nor crying, nor pain anymore, for the former things have passed away."
>
> And he who was seated on the throne said, "Behold, I am making all things new." Also he said, "Write this down, for these words are trustworthy and true." And he said to me, "It is done! I am the Alpha and the Omega, the beginning and the end. To the thirsty I will give from the spring of the water of life without payment. The one who conquers will have this heritage, and I will be his God and he will be my son. . . ."

Then the angel showed me the river of the water of life, bright as crystal, flowing from the throne of God and of the Lamb through the middle of the street of the city; also, on either side of the river, the tree of life with its twelve kinds of fruit, yielding its fruit each month. The leaves of the tree were for the healing of the nations. No longer will there be anything accursed, but the throne of God and of the Lamb will be in it, and his servants will worship him. They will see his face, and his name will be on their foreheads. And night will be no more. They will need no light of lamp or sun, for the Lord God will be their light, and they will reign forever and ever. . . .

The Spirit and the Bride say, "Come." And let the one who hears say, "Come." And let the one who is thirsty come; let the one who desires take the water of life without price. . . .

He who testifies to these things says, "Surely I am coming soon." Amen. Come, Lord Jesus! (Revelation 21:1–7 ; 22:1–5 , 17, 20)

For all who rely on works of the law are under a curse; for it is written, "Cursed be everyone who does not abide by all things written in the Book of the Law, and do them." Now it is evident that no one is justified before God by the law, for "The righteous shall live by faith." But the law is not of faith, rather "The one who does them shall live by them." Christ redeemed us from the curse of the law by becoming a curse for us—for it is written, "Cursed is everyone who is hanged on a tree"—so that in Christ Jesus the blessing of Abraham might come to the Gentiles, so that we might receive the promised Spirit through faith.

3:10–14

12

Clearing the Way for God's Blessing

GALATIANS 3:10–14

MY FATHER-IN-LAW spent his life operating on hearts. He was a thoracic surgeon in Indianapolis for thirty years. He retired several years ago. But before he hung up his stethoscope and put away his scalpel, I figured I should go in and watch him operate.

So I did, and I learned a valuable lesson from doing so. Watching my father-in-law perform open heart surgery, it was crystal-clear to me that you may have a strong heart, but if you have a blocked artery, you're as good as dead. One blocked artery can so hinder the flow of blood to the heart, and thus to the rest of the body, that it can be, and often is, fatal. Which is where heart surgeons come in: they deal with the blockage that hinders the life-giving flow of blood so a person can go on living.

In a way that is what God did by sending his Son, Jesus Christ, into the world. The mission of the Son into our sin-torn world was a massive operation, vastly more so than even open heart surgery. But if God's life-giving blessing was going to flow into the lives of people, it was necessary.

Just as surely as the heart pumps blood, so too it's God's desire to pump blessing into the world. But something has gotten in the way of God's blessing—human sin and, in response to human sin, God's curse.

This first happened when Adam and Eve sinned. As a result God cursed the creation. But it happened again with God's own redeemed people, the people of Israel, who were to be the agents of God's reversal of the curse for the whole world. Yet they too sinned and as a result came under God's curse; only this time it was *the curse of the Law*.

This is, in a nutshell, what Paul says in this passage: *The Law's curse blocks God's blessing.* But Christ's death has removed the Law's curse, so that now in Christ Jesus God's blessing can once again freely flow to the world.

God has cleared the way for his blessing to flow to the nations, to people of every language and tribe and nationality and race, even to you and me. Through the cross of Christ he cleared the way. He sent his Son, our Savior, into the world. Jesus Christ thus came as an obedient Son to make his blessings flow "far as the curse is found," as the Christmas carol puts it.

The Law's Curse Blocks God's Blessing (3:10–12)

In the immediately preceding passage (3:6–9) we see that Abraham's blessing goes to those who live their lives by faith along with Abraham, the man of faith. From the beginning God always intended to extend Abraham's blessing to the nations. Genesis 12:3, which Paul quotes in 3:8, says this very thing: "In you shall all the nations be blessed."

But, of course, the Biblical story doesn't simply go from Abraham in Genesis 12 to the Great Commission and the nations in Matthew 28. It's not as if God leap-frogs over the top of the Jewish people, the nation of Israel.[1] There are many, many chapters in between. and those chapters tell the story of the people of Israel, Abraham's physical offspring. This is the story of the Old Testament. And it's a rich and colorful one.

But from a human perspective it's also sad. It's a story of grace and redemption, yes; but it's also a story of rebellion and sin, eventually leading to Israel herself receiving the curse of the Law for failing to keep the Law. This is Paul's point in 3:10: "For all who rely on works of the law are under a curse; for it is written, 'Cursed be everyone who does not abide by all things written in the Book of the Law, and do them'" (cf. Deuteronomy 27:26).[2]

Paul, then, goes on to reinforce this point in the next two verses, with two more pithy statements and two more Old Testament citations (3:11, 12). If the Law's not the path to blessing, and if it's not the route to justification, then what is? We experience God's blessing and find justification before him only by living a life of faith: "Now it is evident that no one is justified before God by the law" (3:11a). In fact, this is what the prophet Habakkuk himself learned many hundreds of years before Christ: "The righteous shall live by his faith" (Habakkuk 2:4).

Lest there be any misunderstanding, Paul drives home this point with a second pithy statement and another quote from the Old Testament. Why can't God's blessing be found in the Law? Because, as Paul says, "The law is not of faith, rather 'The one who does them shall live by them'" (3:12). In order for the Law to bless, the Law must be kept. But this is where Israel fell short. She did not keep the Law. If she would have, as Leviticus 18:5 says, then, to be sure, she would have found life through the Law.[3] But she didn't; so she received the curse of the Law and thus *death* through the Law. And this eventuated in her being exiled out of the land of promise and scattered among the nations.

The main point of these three verses, then, is simply this: Israel is under the curse of the Law; and so too are all who depend on the works of the Law. Yet this is not only a statement of historical fact; it's also a warning to anyone who, like the Galatians, thinks that the Law itself is the pathway to blessing or the way to life.[4]

What we learn from the whole Old Testament, as well as from this passage, is that God has posted a gigantic "Dead End" sign over the path of the Law. The Law *cannot* give life (3:21). Apart from the grace of God, the Law of God will only stir up the sin within you, ultimately choking you to death.[5]

What folly, then, to try to sail the ship of morality all the way to Heaven. It's been tried many times, but it simply won't work. Listen to how Charles Spurgeon grapples with the dead end of the Law as the pathway to God's blessing:

> The law seemed also to blight all my hopes with its stern sentence, 'Cursed is everyone that continueth not in all things which are written in the book of the law to do them.' Only too well did I know that I had not continued in all those things, so I saw myself accursed, turn which way I might. If I had not committed one sin, that made no difference if I had committed another; I was under the curse. What if I had never blasphemed God with my tongue? Yet, if I had coveted, I had broken the law. He who breaks a chain might say, 'I did not break that link, and the other link.' No, but if you break one link, you have broken the chain. Ah, me, how I seemed shut up then! I had offended against the justice of God; I was impure and polluted, and I used to say, 'If God does not send me to hell, He ought to do it.' I sat in judgment upon myself, and pronounced the sentence that I felt would be just. . . . So the law worried and troubled me at all points; it shut me up as in an iron cage, and every way of escape was effectually blocked up.[6]

Perhaps some to whom we minister are still locked up in that iron cage. They've tried every way of escape but found them all to be blocked. They've tried moral reform, allegiance to the right Christian causes, even church membership. Yet they've never truly come to Christ by faith in brokenness and repentance, in need of grace and mercy. And so they're still shut up in an iron cage, still trying to convince themselves that the one who keeps the Law's demands shall live by them.

Christ's Death Redeems from the Law's Curse (3:13)

Shut up in an iron cage with no way of escape—that's a fit description of the life of everyone apart from the grace of God. It is a good description of Israel of old. The whole nation was shut up in an iron cage with no way of escape. In fact, the Old Testament ends with the entire nation scattered among the nations of the world. And the only thing they can do is wait for God to show up and do something about their desperate situation. Thus they sing (in the words of the later hymn), "O come, O come, Emmanuel, and ransom captive Israel, that mourns in lonely exile here, until the Son of God appear."

And after many hundreds of years Immanuel did indeed come. "When the fullness of time had come, God sent forth his Son, born of woman, born under the law, that he might redeem those who were under the law" (4:4, 5). Or as Paul triumphantly declares in this passage, "Christ redeemed us from the curse of the law" (3:13).

I love the strength of this verse. Notice it does not say Christ *tried* to redeem us from the curse of the Law; nor does it say Christ *made it possible* for us to be redeemed from the curse of the Law. His statement is much heartier and full blooded. Paul was convinced that Christ accomplished something *definitive* on the cross. His death was *entirely effective*; he accomplished precisely what he wanted to accomplish: he redeemed his people from the curse of the Law.[7]

But how did Christ redeem us from the curse of the Law? He did it in a way that was, in the words of one of the twentieth century's most famous theologians, "almost unbearably severe."[8] He accomplished redemption by doing the unthinkable: "by becoming a curse for us" (3:13). Now for a pious Jew like Paul this would have been a horrific thought, blasphemous even. Jesus had been nailed to a tree that we now call the cross. And the Law clearly states, "Cursed is everyone who is hanged on a tree" (3:13b; cf. Deuteronomy 21:23).

He who knew no sin became sin, "so that in him we might become the righteousness of God" (cf. 2 Corinthians 5:21). What a remarkable twist to the story! It's like a heart surgeon who realizes the only way his patient will survive is with a heart transplant; so the surgeon voluntarily gives his own heart, his very own life, to save his dying patient.

This is what our Lord did at Calvary. Let us, then, in the words of the hymn "I Stand Amazed,"

. . . stand amazed in the presence
Of Jesus the Nazarene.
And wonder how he could love me,
A sinner, condemned, unclean.

He took my sins and my sorrows,
He made them His very own;
He bore the burden to Calvary,
And suffered and died alone.

O how marvelous! O how wonderful!
And my song shall ever be:
O how marvelous! O how wonderful!
Is my Savior's love for me!

When life is difficult and we begin to feel like we're under God's curse, we can run to the cross of Christ and find that the curse has indeed been lifted from us.

In Christ Jesus God's Blessing Now Flows (3:14)

Because of the cross of Christ, the curse of the Law has been lifted. That which blocked the flow of God's blessing has now been removed. God's blessing can flow to the nation of Israel and even to all the nations of the earth. This is the upshot of what Paul wants to say in this passage: in Christ Jesus the blessing of Abraham now flows not only to Israel but to the Gentiles of the nations (3:14).

When people from among the nations of the earth turn from sin and trust in Christ, they receive forgiveness and reconciliation and thus stand in the channel of God's promised blessing. This is the great impulse behind the outreach and mission of the church: to extend God's blessing to the nations.[9]

But also, Paul says, Christ's death opens the pathway for God's blessing to flow to the nation of Israel. The promised Spirit now flows to the remnant of Israel. They experience renewal through the Spirit as they embrace their own Messiah by faith. Christ's absorbing the curse of the Law allows God to pour out his promised Holy Spirit upon his people through faith (3:14b).

This is what Israel's prophets had envisioned would one day take place. God would restore the nation of Israel by removing her sin and sending his Spirit. And this pouring out of God's Spirit upon the people of Israel happened on the Day of Pentecost (Acts 2). Speaking to the crowd of Jews in Jerusalem at that time, the Apostle Peter tells them:

This Jesus God raised up, and of that we all are witnesses. Being therefore exalted at the right hand of God, and having received from the Father the promise of the Holy Spirit, he has poured out this that you yourselves are seeing and hearing. (Acts 2:32, 33)

But the renewal of Israel is not yet complete. It's only partial. Indeed, a day is coming when all Israel shall be saved; right now this is not the case. Two thousand years ago Paul recognized that "a partial hardening has come upon Israel" (Romans 11:25). And it remains to this very day. But as Paul goes on to say, one day this hardening will be removed, and then "all Israel will be saved" (Romans 11:26a). "'The Deliverer will come from Zion, he will banish ungodliness from Jacob'; 'and this will be my covenant with them when I take away their sins'" (Romans 11:26b, 27; Isaiah 59:20, 21).

Yet when Israel is at last fully renewed, this will mean, as Paul says, even greater blessing for the nations! Israel's partial renewal has already meant great things for the nations. But what, then, will Israel's complete renewal mean for the nations of the earth? It will mean a massive enfolding of people from every tongue and tribe and language and people (cf. Romans 11:11–16).[10]

Conclusion: Clearing the Channel of Our Lives

The coming of Christ Jesus into the world, dying in our place upon the cross, taking upon himself the dreaded curse of the Law, has enabled God's blessing to flow freely. God has cleared the way for his blessing. And he's done so because of Christ and only in Christ—in Christ *alone*. So we must exhort those who have not already done so to flee to Christ and hide themselves in him as their only hope!

What must happen for us to be effective channels of God's blessing to flow into the lives of others? We need the mind of Christ our Savior, our minds conformed to his, our hearts saturated with his Word, his peace ruling our lives in everything, his love filling us as the waters cover the sea. His humility must be ours, so that we exalt him and gladly abase ourselves; his strength and courage must be ours as we run the race set before us, looking onward and upward, only to Jesus; and his beauty must rest upon us as we seek the lost to win, so that forgetting the channel, they may only see him.[11]

To give a human example, brothers: even with a man-made covenant, no one annuls it or adds to it once it has been ratified. Now the promises were made to Abraham and to his offspring. It does not say, "And to offsprings," referring to many, but referring to one, "And to your offspring," who is Christ. This is what I mean: the law, which came 430 years afterward, does not annul a covenant previously ratified by God, so as to make the promise void. For if the inheritance comes by the law, it no longer comes by promise; but God gave it to Abraham by a promise. Why then the law? It was added because of transgressions, until the offspring should come to whom the promise had been made, and it was put in place through angels by an intermediary. Now an intermediary implies more than one, but God is one. Is the law then contrary to the promises of God? Certainly not! For if a law had been given that could give life, then righteousness would indeed be by the law. But the Scripture imprisoned everything under sin, so that the promise by faith in Jesus Christ might be given to those who believe.

3:15–22

13

Why Then the Law?

GALATIANS 3:15–22

WHEN I VISIT PEOPLE'S HOMES, I always enjoy seeing what's on their refrigerator: family photos, school calendars, grocery lists, the latest art project, a wedding invitation, magnets, bumper stickers, baby announcements, a reminder about a doctor's appointment—just about anything and everything!

My wife and I have one or two pictures on ours. But in the center, prominently displayed so they can't be missed, are our three Wilson family rules. These are three simple, commonsense rules we consistently encourage our children to follow.

#1: No talking back.
#2: No interrupting.
#3: Obey the first time.

But do you know what we've found with our kids? Posting rules on the refrigerator doesn't create the desirable behavior in their lives! This doesn't mean posting our rules is pointless. They reveal what's important to us as parents, set clear expectations for our kids, provide them with boundaries for appropriate behavior, and communicate how we want them to interact with us and each other. But at the end of the day we realize that these rules don't create the obedience they command.

Rules are like that. They guide behavior but don't create it. Every parent knows this. But so, too, does every police officer. In the United States today seven million people are in jail or prison or on parole or probation; yet as a society we've never had more laws on the books. Obviously, laws don't create compliance.

Sadly, this is true even of God's Law. On Mount Sinai Moses receives God's Law. It calls for righteousness. But it cannot create righteousness. This is the basic weakness of the Law: it cannot create within us the desire to do the very thing it demands of us. It can guide right desire, but it cannot give right desire. Or as Paul puts it in this passage, the Law cannot give *life*.

The Law's inability to give life is the thrust of what Paul says about the Law in Galatians.[1] The Law cannot do the most important thing: *make us alive*! Only the Father, who gave life to his Son by raising him from the dead, can give us life through the presence of his Holy Spirit, the kind of life we need to live the new life God desires for us.

We live in a world of laws and rules and ordinances and policies. Everywhere we look, we find someone laying down the law for us. Indeed, each one of us is, at any given moment, under many more laws than the ancient Israelite ever was. And yet, like the Israelites, we're prone to think we can find life from the law, whether God's Law or man's. As fallen creatures, this is one of our fundamental mistakes: looking to rules to find life.[2]

If you're wondering whether that's true, consider children. How easily they fixate on rules, as though the rules were the source of life. But perhaps our kids develop this mind-set by watching their parents. Don't we as parents easily assume and thus act as though rules are the means of giving life? If we will take an honest look at our own hearts, we'll see how quickly we go to the rules or the expectations or the law and there try to derive some power for living. Indeed, this may be most tempting for Christians themselves, for those who take God's Law and thus human laws quite seriously.

Law and Promise (3:15–18)

For those of us addicted to seeking life in the Law, this passage provides sweet medicine. But first let's remind ourselves of where we've been and what we've seen. Long ago God promised to bless the world through Abraham (3:6–9). Yet the Law that God gave to Abraham's offspring blocked the flow of this blessing (3:10–14). Thus what God promised to Abraham has not, and indeed cannot, come through the Law. It is just the opposite in fact. Israel is under the Law's curse rather than enjoying God's blessing.

Here in 3:15–18, then, Paul no doubt feels compelled to deal with how God's Law relates to God's promise. More specifically, how does the Law that God gave Moses on Mount Sinai relate to the promise that God made to Abraham when he said, "In you shall all the nations be blessed" (3:8)?

If we simply follow the story line of Scripture, we'd have every reason to think that the Law God gave to Moses *directs the flow* of God's promise to the nations. First came the promise to Abraham; then, 430 years later, came the Law to Moses. Presumably then that which came later (i.e., the Law) would direct the flow of that which came first (i.e., the blessing).

In this scenario the Law is like a funnel into which God pours his promised blessing. This is how first-century Jews, like those stirring up trouble in Galatia, would have viewed things. It's also how some twenty-first-century Jews view things. If you want the blessing promised to Abraham, you must go to the Law to get it. To be blessed with Abraham, you need to become a child of Abraham, one of his offspring to whom the promise was given. And this means you must become Jewish, embracing the Law with its works and way of life.

If you spend any time on the Internet, you come across pop-up advertisements, boxes that show up on your screen in bright, flashing colors and offer you something fantastic, like a new iPad or an all-expenses-paid trip to Maui. And, amazingly, all you need to do, they tell you, is click on the button at the bottom of the screen.

If you've ever been suckered into one of these too-good-to-be-true offers, you're now wise as to how they work. While they wow you with a great promise, you soon realize it's not nearly that simple. You realize you only receive the promised gift once you've done something far more involved and a lot more complicated!

Paul, however, says that God's promise and Law don't relate to each other in that way. The Law doesn't modify or complicate the promise or the original terms of the covenant that God made with Abraham. As Paul says, "To give a human example, brothers: even with a man-made covenant, no one annuls it or adds to it once it has been ratified" (3:15).

More importantly, Paul clarifies the identity of the recipient of God's promise to Abraham. Ultimately, he says, the recipient isn't Israel, nor is it even the Church. According to this passage, the true recipient of God's promise to Abraham is God's single seed, Christ. "Now the promises were made to Abraham and to his offspring. It does not say, 'And to offsprings,' referring to many, but referring to one, 'And to your offspring,' who is Christ" (3:16).

Here, then, is the key point about God's promises: *Christ Jesus is the one true beneficiary of all of God's promises.* God has given everything to Christ. Every blessing God wants to give to the world, and to you and me, has already been given to Jesus. Thus every blessing we seek, every good thing in the world, is to be found in Christ. "For all the promises of God find their Yes in him" (2 Corinthians 1:20).

We share in these promises, therefore, by coming to Christ and being found in him. "In you shall all the nations be blessed," God said to Abraham. But how do we get into Abraham? Not by getting into Israel through the Law, but by coming to Christ by faith. As Paul will say a little later on, "In Christ Jesus you are all sons of God, through faith. For as many of you as were baptized into Christ have put on Christ. . . . And if you are Christ's, then you are Abraham's offspring, heirs according to promise" (3:26, 27, 29).

Christ is at the center of all that God is doing in the world. Indeed, Christ is the center of all that God wants to do *for* the world—and for you and me. So don't make the mistake the Galatians were making. Don't look anywhere for God's blessing other than to Christ. It can only be found in him.

Law and Sin (3:19, 20)

Paul, then, summarizing the message of the Old Testament and the experience of the Jewish people, says that the Law that God gave to Moses did not serve to bring about the promise. So what, then, is the purpose of the Law? Or as Paul goes on to ask, "Why then the law?" (3:19).

That's a good question, and Paul has a good answer. It's a profound answer, but it's also a provocative one. "It was added," he says, "because of transgressions, until the offspring should come to whom the promise had been made" (3:19). God gave the Law because of sin, until he could definitely deal with sin through the death of his Son.

Think about that. God gave the Law because of sin. So, too, societies write laws because of sin. Villages issue ordinances because of sin; parents make rules because of sin; teachers post classroom guidelines because of sin; employers have company policies because of sin.

Of course, if children were always obedient, there'd be no need for rules, much less timeouts or spankings. And if students were always honest, there'd be no need for rules about cheating, much less reasons for suspensions. And if citizens were always upstanding, there'd be no need for laws, much less policemen or prisons. And if the people of God were perfectly sinless, there'd be no need for the Law of God, much less its curses and judgment.

Yes, God's Law, like our household rules, reveals to God's children something of who he is. But his Law is primarily intended to curb sin and keep it from escalating. That's the point of what Paul is saying here.

Ironically, however, the Law has another effect on God's people, as it did on the people of Israel. The Israelites realized that in its attempt to curb sin, the Law actually exposed sin. The Law revealed not only the character of Israel's holy God but also the insidious nature of sin—its power to control and confuse, to dominate and deceive.

We need to be clear on the purpose of the Law; otherwise we'll get sideways. Everything God created has a purpose and as such is a good thing. But as we know, even good things can become bad, when we use them for something they were never intended to do. Charles Spurgeon had a nice way of capturing this thought. He liked to say, "A handsaw is a good thing, but not to shave with." A handsaw's good for cutting wood, but not facial hair. And if you put your handsaw to that sort of use, you'll wind up losing more than hair!

"There's sense in choosing your tools," Spurgeon says, "for a pig's tail will never make a good arrow, nor will his ear make a silk purse. A good thing is not good out of its place."[3] And if that's true with a handsaw or a pig's tail, how much more God's Law! The purpose of the Law is to restrain sin; yet in so doing it reveals sin's subtlety and power.

How true this is in our own experience! How creative we are at tiptoeing around God's Law to get it to serve our own purpose. We know how the Law animates sin within us. We hardly need the lesson book of the Old Testament to teach us that. We see it everywhere in our own lives.

Law and Life (3:21, 22)

Paul, then, seems to be saying that the Law's purpose is largely a negative one: it's intended to restrain sin and thus reveal sin. But this could easily imply to some that the Law itself is against the promises; the Law seems to have hindered rather than helped God's purposes. No wonder Paul asks, "Is the law then contrary to the promises of God?" (v. 21).

My kids, of course, wouldn't like it if I told them our three Wilson rules were only going to help them get in trouble rather than walk in obedience or earn an extra dessert. No doubt one of our older children would connect the dots and complain, "C'mon, Dad, that's not fair! Are these rules out to get us?"

This is the kind of response Paul anticipates to his statements about the Law. But his answer to his own question is quite to the point: "Certainly not!" (v. 21). But why not? Note what he says: "For if a law had been given that could give life, then righteousness would indeed be by the law" (v. 21).

The Law cannot give life. This is Paul's fundamental insight into God's Law. But this same insight applies equally as well to all laws, rules, ordinances, commands, and requirements. While they have a purpose, their purpose isn't to give life. And when they're looked to for that purpose, they bring about just the opposite: death.

What does that mean? It means that the Law cannot provide you with the *motivation* to do what the Law calls you to do. It can certainly guide you in doing God's will, but it cannot motivate you to want to do God's will. It can tell you how to channel your desires in a way that honors God, but it cannot give you God-honoring desires.

Understand, then, that it's not the Law's fault that you can't keep the Law; nor is it the Lawgiver's fault. Instead the fault rests entirely with you and me. God's good Law is unfortunately weakened by our flesh, our fallen human nature, our sin—something we've all inherited from Adam, something we only find deliverance from in Christ. When our first parents fell into sin in the garden, we fell with them, into the enslaving pit of sin from which we cannot escape on our own, no matter what we do or how hard we try. This is a dramatic conclusion to which to come, but it's exactly where Paul leads us: "But the Scripture imprisoned everything under sin" (3:22).[4]

This was true even for the children of Israel. And this explains why their own history as a nation was marked by sin and ultimately by judgment. Even though the nation was redeemed from slavery in Egypt, the people themselves, as a whole, were not redeemed from *slavery to sin*. Although God had delivered the nation physically, he chose not to deliver them *spiritually*—at least not the vast majority of them.

Thus when this redeemed-yet-unredeemed people received the Law at Sinai, it didn't go so well. God provided them the right circumstances to obey his Law, but he had not given them *a heart* to obey his Law (cf. Deuteronomy 30:6; Jeremiah 4:4). They were still spiritually dead; they'd not been made alive. Therefore, the gift of God's Law, tragically, led to their undoing. It brought a curse rather than a blessing.[5]

This would then readily explain the metaphor of a pedagogue, which Paul uses to describe Israel's relationship to the Law. What does it mean, historically speaking, for Israel to possess the Law and yet be imprisoned "under sin" and thus "held captive under the law" (3:22, 23)? Paul explains by way of a metaphor: As a result of being kept under the curse of the Law (3:23), "the law was our guardian [pedagogue] until Christ came" (3:24). Here Paul employs the metaphor of the pedagogue to describe the peculiar function of the Law prior to the coming of Christ. While there has been considerable debate over the precise import of this analogy,[6] perhaps Paul's main point is that Israel's confinement under the curse of the Law means that the Law is not a mediator of the promise but a mere pedagogue, a household slave whose presence reminds the trustee that he is still a minor and thus unable to have access to his inheritance (cf. 4:1–3). Insofar as the Law curses Israel while Israel is "under sin," the Law serves as a token of Israel's continued estrangement from the inheritance.[7]

But here's the good news of the gospel, and here's the message of hope to those who are in Christ Jesus by faith:

There is therefore now no condemnation for those who are in Christ Jesus. For the law of the Spirit of life has set you free in Christ Jesus from the law of sin and death. For God has done what the law, weakened by the flesh, could not do. By sending his own Son in the likeness of sinful flesh and for sin, he condemned sin in the flesh, in order that the righteous requirement of the law might be fulfilled in us, who walk not according to the flesh but according to the Spirit. (Romans 8:1–4)

Christ Jesus died in order to deal with our sin and every transgression we've committed against God's Law and will for our life. But more than that, because Christ Jesus was raised from the dead, he now *gives life* through his Spirit, whom he pours out in the lives of his people. If we're in Christ Jesus, we "wait for the hope of righteousness," not through the Law but "through the Spirit, by faith" (5:5). And we live this life of faith focused on the promises of God and depending upon the Spirit for strength and power.

We live by the Spirit, not by the Law. It is God's Holy Spirit who gives life to our souls and causes us to love God and the things of God. So if we live by the Spirit, let us, as Paul says, also "*walk* by the Spirit" (5:16). Let us follow the leading of the Spirit (5:18), "keep in step with the Spirit" (5:25), and bear "the fruit of the Spirit" (5:22, 23). For the Law does not threaten a curse but offers a blessing to the ones who bear the fruit of the Spirit (5:23).[8]

The Law and Us

This dense and admittedly complex passage has invited us to grapple with God's Law and its purpose in God's plan of salvation. We've wrestled with the Law and promise, the Law and sin, and the Law and life. The only thing left to do is to take up the question of the Law and us. How does God's Law relate to our lives? What can we glean, if anything, from our understanding of the role of God's Law in God's plan to bless the nations?[9]

First, remember that the Law has an important but limited role in our lives. The Law's purpose is not to give us life but to help guide us in living out the life we already have. When we need motivation, we must look to the person and work of Jesus Christ and trust in his promises to us. We must seek to live the life God would have us live *by faith* and not by the Law, looking to God's gracious provision in Christ rather than to God's sober demands in his Law. We must not ignore the Law but let it guide us. We must not seek to derive life from it.

Therefore, secondly, we must root our lives in God's promises, not in God's Law. This is what it means to be gospel rooted. People who root their lives in the Law rather than in the gospel tend to be cold, prickly, sharp, and brittle. They're not pleasant to be around, at least not up close. They're spiritual porcupines. So we must not root our lives in God's Law but instead root our lives in the sustaining soil of the gospel. And as we do that, our lives will be filled with the lush, happy fruit of obedience.

Thirdly, we must rely upon the Holy Spirit by faith for the motivation we need to live. Motivation to live to the glory of God and in accord with God's will comes in two ways: by treasuring God's promises in his Word and by experiencing God's presence through his Holy Spirit.[10] And these two, Word and Spirit, always go hand in hand. The Spirit of God likes to walk lockstep with the Word of God, for the Spirit of God loves to honor the Son of God, who is the Word of God.

As we look to the Bible to find the strength we need, treasuring all that God promises to be for us in Christ Jesus, we can trust that the Spirit will take our little spark of intention and turn it into a flame of gospel-rooted motivation—to the glory of God!

Now before faith came, we were held captive under the law, imprisoned until the coming faith would be revealed. So then, the law was our guardian until Christ came, in order that we might be justified by faith. But now that faith has come, we are no longer under a guardian, for in Christ Jesus you are all sons of God, through faith. For as many of you as were baptized into Christ have put on Christ. There is neither Jew nor Greek, there is neither slave nor free, there is no male and female, for you are all one in Christ Jesus. And if you are Christ's, then you are Abraham's offspring, heirs according to promise.

3:23–29

14

Heirs According
to Promise

GALATIANS 3:23–29

ON FRIDAY, APRIL 29, 2011 the world paused to watch the royal wedding of
Ms. Kate Middleton to Prince William (to be more precise, William Arthur
Philip Louis, son of the heir to the thrones of the sixteen Commonwealth
realms).

It was a splendid sight to behold. In fact, it was in many ways quite moving. I found it especially charming to see the good number of people Kate
Middleton had invited from her village of Bucklebury in Berkshire. She and
the prince wanted a "people's wedding." So they invited the village postman,
the local pub owner, and a shopkeeper and his wife.

But this modest touch only underscored the remarkable thing that was
happening. On Thursday, April 28 she was just Kate Middleton. Yet a day
later she has been enfolded into the Royal Family. She's taken on a new identity. No longer is she Kate Middleton of Bucklebury. She is now the Duchess
of Cambridge. And by virtue of her marriage to the future king, she herself
has become heir to the throne as well.

An heir is one who can claim a legal right to an inheritance. And that's
what we become by faith in Christ, which is the high point of this passage:
"And if you are Christ's, then you are Abraham's offspring, heirs according
to promise" (3:29). Those who belong to Christ are "heirs according to promise." They now stand in line to receive the inheritance that God is preparing
for his children.

Granted, this doesn't make them heirs of the Crown, like Kate Middleton.
But actually theirs is an inheritance infinitely more splendid! For what God has

promised to his heirs is this: "the kingdom of God" (5:21), "eternal life" (6:8), "a new creation" (6:15). In Romans Paul says believers will inherit "the world" (4:13). In the book of Hebrews the inheritance is referred to as "the city that is to come" (13:14), "a kingdom that cannot be shaken" (12:28), and "a better country, that is, a heavenly one" (11:16). But it is the book of Revelation that brings this Biblical promise to a crescendo with its vision of "a new heaven and a new earth" (21:1), "the holy city, new Jerusalem, coming down out of heaven from God, prepared as a bride adorned for her husband" (21:2).

This is what God long ago promised to Abraham and to his seed: the reverse of the curse, the restoration of fallen humanity, the renewal of the whole creation. But how do we become "heirs according to promise"? This passage says we must become Christ's. We must belong to him. We come to possess these "precious and very great promises" (2 Peter 1:4) only by being ourselves *possessed by Christ*. Christ must own us. He must become ours, and we his. It's like a royal wedding!

Imprisonment before Christ (vv. 23–25)

But Paul begins with an example of the situation apart from Christ. And his example is the people of Israel, God's people under the old covenant, the people we read about in the Old Testament. Israel is God's lesson book for the nations.

This passage paints the bleak picture of life apart from Christ as imprisonment. Israel is imprisoned, and so too is the rest of humanity. This imprisonment came as a result of sin's entrance into the world through the fall. Paul alludes to this in the previous passage: "The Scripture imprisoned everything under sin" (3:22). This is likely a reference to Genesis 3, where in response to human sin God places a curse not just upon humanity but upon the whole creation.[1] Everything is under the controlling power of sin and therefore is powerless to free itself from sin.[2]

For Israel, being imprisoned by sin has been more complicated than for the rest of the nations. Why? Because they were given God's Law. But because they were under the power of sin when they received God's Law, the Law didn't bless but cursed them. Thus they've not only lived under sin, like the rest of the nations, but they've had the added experience of being "held captive under the law" (3:23). That is, they were under the *curse of the Law*.[3] And because of this the Law's curse blocked the promise. As a result, as Paul says, "The law was our guardian until Christ came" (3:24). The Law, with its curse, served as a constant reminder to Israel as a nation that they did not have access to God's inheritance, the one promised to Abraham.

Recently I was challenged by a comment I read about the plight of African-Americans in our society.[4] This person expressed deep frustration over the feeling of being held captive by powers bigger than himself, imprisoned in circumstances from which he could not escape, no matter how hard he tried, and therefore facing the desperate feeling of being denied access to the blessing of opportunity. This is analogous to Israel's experience under the old covenant before the coming of faith; and this is the kind of experience we have if we're not Christ's through faith. Apart from him we are held captive and imprisoned and are denied access to God's glorious inheritance.

Incorporation into Christ

But God didn't intend this situation to go on forever. Instead he put Israel behind bars, under lock and key, "until the coming faith would be revealed" (3:23b). The great turning point in human history is the dawning of faith with the advent of Christ: "But now that faith has come, we are no longer under a guardian" (3:25).

Thus, with the coming of Christ everything changes. Jews who place their faith in Jesus the Christ, their Messiah, come out from under the curse of the Law. And Gentiles, who were up to that point "separated from Christ, alienated from the commonwealth of Israel and strangers to the covenants of promise, having no hope and without God in the world" (Ephesians 2:12), now, by the grace of God, can become "sons of God, through faith" (3:26).

But how? By becoming "in Christ Jesus" (3:26), or to use a more theologically robust expression, by being *incorporated into Christ*. Incorporation into Christ is at the heart of these verses. It means being included into something, like when you show up at the gym and are incorporated into a pickup game, or when you join a few friends for dinner and are incorporated into the conversation, or when you marry the prince and become a part of the Royal Family. You're incorporated when you're included.

A person becomes a son or daughter of God—incorporated into Christ—*through faith*. Faith is what unites us to Christ and all of his saving benefits for us. But notice how Paul makes this wonderful reality of incorporation concrete by pointing to a very concrete Christian practice—*baptism*. "For as many of you as were baptized into Christ have put on Christ" (3:27).

I don't think he says this because he believes going into the waters of baptism has saving significance or somehow unites us to Christ. Instead he says this because for him, and for the earliest Christians, repentance and faith and conversion and baptism were often experienced as a *single event*, a package deal if you will.[5]

Unlike many Christians today, the earliest Christians didn't view baptism as something you did months or even years after your profession of faith, long after you'd become part of a church. Baptism was the rite of *initiation into the church*. It was the principal way in which you *professed* your faith in Christ.

As evangelical Protestants we've been very careful to avoid the error of thinking that baptism somehow saves a person. But in our desire to safeguard against that particular misunderstanding, we've inadvertently fallen into another misunderstanding. Nowadays many evangelicals treat baptism as though it were an optional part of the Christian life, treating it like a baby announcement we send to family and friends, sharing the good news that we have become a Christian.

There's a good challenge here for many pastors and churches. We need to take a hard look at the robust significance of baptism we find in the New Testament. But there's also a good challenge here for many individual Christians. Perhaps some of us have been professing Christians for a while, yet have never been baptized. Let this serve as an exhortation to take this step of faith and obedience.

New Identity in Christ (v. 28)

If we have been baptized into Christ, we have "put on Christ" (3:27). He is now our new adornment. We've laid aside our old self—our old identity, our old way of life—and have put on a new person, Jesus Christ, who is now our new identity and our new way of life.

Notice, then, how this passage moves from incorporation into Christ through faith to receiving a new identity because of Christ. Hence Paul says, "There is neither Jew nor Greek, there is neither slave nor free, there is no male and female, for you are all one in Christ Jesus" (3:28).

Whatever excluded us from the promise under the old covenant is now removed with the dawning of the new. These age-old distinctions are no longer barriers to sharing in Christ and becoming part of his people, his Body, and his Church.

It is not that these distinctions are erased in Christ. This isn't a prooftext, for example, for unisex bathrooms! Instead the point is that these distinctions are radically subordinated to who we now are in Christ. Christ is the decisive thing about us, not that we are Jewish or Greek, slave or free, even male or female.[6]

Our adopted twin boys, Addis and Rager, have a different identity than ours ethnically, racially, and socially. They're black and African and Ethiopian and were formerly orphans. Yet when they became ours, all of this was *radically subordinated* to their new identity as our children. None of it was erased; they're still black and African and Ethiopian. But none of that is now the main thing or the determinative thing about them.

New identity in Christ is significant not only for us as individuals but for the church as a new community. In fact, incorporation into Christ provides the basis for this new community; indeed it's the only place on earth where age-old distinctions no longer determine how we ought to relate to one another. Whatever tends to divide communities is now done away with in Christ: "You are all one in Christ Jesus" (v. 28).

Race, class, gender—these three human distinctions have bedeviled the human race for centuries. The strife and suffering caused by differences in race, class, or gender is incalculable. Only in Christ Jesus do we find the reconciliation of these differences, and thus the resultant unity among those of a different race, class, or gender.

Regrettably, on this score the church has more work to do. Eleven A.M. on a Sunday morning is still the most segregated hour of the week.[7] It doesn't require great powers of observation to see that most local churches tend to call together one social class or another. Furthermore, there is still work to be done in helping the genders better honor and serve one another within the one Body of Christ.

All of this is daunting. But each of us can begin on the local level by resisting the temptation to allow the church to be a place for cliques, a breeding ground for folks of a similar background or income or gender. In fact, if our church experience has largely been with people very much like us, we might well be missing out on all that the Body of Christ is meant to be. And perhaps it's time for us to mix it up!

Share in the Inheritance with Christ (v. 29)

By being incorporated into Christ, we not only take on a new identity in Christ—we also stand in line to share in the inheritance with Christ. By being joined to Christ, we become coheirs with him. "And if you are Christ's, then you are Abraham's offspring, heirs according to promise" (3:29).

Again notice the flow of thought. Through faith, and by being baptized into Christ, we become Christ's. We relinquish ownership of ourselves and give ourselves to the ownership of another, namely, Christ.

This is the paradoxical principle of losing our life and so to find it, giving up our rights and so to be given the right to become children of God, laying down all that we have and so to receive all we could ever want, letting go of mastery of ourselves so we can be mastered by another—Christ!

But incorporation into Christ qualifies us to be Abraham's offspring. And as a result the promise God made to Abraham and to his seed is now good for all who come to Christ through faith. Indeed, everything God promised to Abraham's offspring is offered to us if we come to Christ. Whether we are a Jew or Greek, slave or free, male or female, white-collar or blue-collar, Democrat or Republican doesn't matter. What matters is whether we are Christ's.

How good of God to design it this way! How generous of Christ to share his inheritance with poor and needy sinners like us! How gracious of him to let us have a piece of what is rightfully his! And how merciful of him to make the only condition not the color of our skin or the size of our bank account or whether we have two X chromosomes rather than one but whether we trust in Christ!

If You Are Christ's

There is nothing more relevant or more practical than this new identity, new community, new inheritance.

If we are Christ's, then we have nothing to fear, even in these uncertain times, because we know "it is your Father's good pleasure to give you the kingdom" (Luke 12:32).

If we are Christ's, then we ought to take heart and find strength to endure whatever it is God has for us because we know that "when you have done the will of God you may receive what is promised" (Hebrews 10:36).

And if we are Christ's, then we ought to walk by faith, living a truly countercultural life for the cause of Christ, because we know that here we have no lasting city. Instead we are "looking forward to the city that has foundations, whose designer and builder is God" (Hebrews 11:10).

I mean that the heir, as long as he is a child, is no different from a slave, though he is the owner of everything, but he is under guardians and managers until the date set by his father. In the same way we also, when we were children, were enslaved to the elementary principles of the world. But when the fullness of time had come, God sent forth his Son, born of woman, born under the law, to redeem those who were under the law, so that we might receive adoption as sons. And because you are sons, God has sent the Spirit of his Son into our hearts, crying, "Abba! Father!" So you are no longer a slave, but a son, and if a son, then an heir through God.

4:1–7

15

Adoption as Sons

GALATIANS 4:1–7

DID YOU KNOW a baby's cry matches its mother's language? A newborn child, just two or three days old, cries in a distinctive way, mimicking the sound of the child's mother. Researchers recently studied sixty healthy newborn children from both French and German families. What they found was fascinating: each newborn baby has its own "cry melody," a specific pattern of sounds that is unique to his or her cry. But more than that, they found that babies will match their cry to the sounds and intonations of their mother's voice.[1]

I suspect, however, that very few mothers need a study like this to tell them something so obvious. From day one mothers know this to be true. That's why they can hear their baby's faint cry seemingly from miles away and even pick out the sound of their baby crying amidst a chorus of other crying infants.

But did you realize this is true of God's children? They too have their own distinctive cry, and this passage tells us what it sounds like: "Abba! Father!" This is the unique cry of the children of God.

This is also one of the great privileges of being children of God. When God adopts us as sons or daughters, he sends his Spirit into our heart, causing us to cry, "Abba! Father!" (4:6). And this cry identifies who we belong to, who our Father is. But it also clarifies for us, and for others who hear our cry, whether we are children of God.

Paul realizes the Galatians have begun to doubt their status as God's children and thus are doubtful about whether they'll receive God's inheritance, eternal life. So Paul points to this distinctive cry as a way for them to confirm their status as sons of God. As he reminds them, "If a son, then an heir through God" (4:7).

The Period of Enslavement (4:1–3)

Of course, the phrase "*if* a son" (4:7) implies that not everyone *is* a son. Not every expression of human distress makes this particular sound. If you're not a child of God, you won't make this sound. You'll cry, but because God isn't your Father, or you his child, your cry will sound quite different.

In fact, at the beginning of this passage Paul describes what it's like for us to be not in God's family but in the orphanage of the world. Prior to being adopted by God, we're in a state of enslavement. And as his example Paul points to the children of Israel, not unlike what he did in the previous passage (3:23–25).

In particular Paul recalls Israel's enslavement in Egypt. His point is: as long as the children of Israel are enslaved, they are no different than slaves—that is, they are no different than any other nation or people. In that state they have no more access to God's inheritance than anyone else. "I mean that the heir, as long as he is a child, is no different from a slave, though he is the owner of everything, but he is under guardians and managers until the date set by his father" (4:1, 2).

But notice what Paul goes on to say, for it is both remarkable and provocative: "In the same way we also, when we were children, were enslaved to the elementary principles of the world" (4:3). What is he saying? Israel's period of enslavement didn't stop at the exodus. *Instead the concept of enslavement describes their entire history as a nation.* Although the exodus redeemed them from Egyptian slavery, they stayed enslaved to something far worse, what Paul calls "the elementary principles of the world."

This is an intriguing phrase and has proven endlessly puzzling to students of Galatians. Paul appears to be referring to the basic elements of the created order, the primordial powers at work in the world, which fallen human beings turn into idols and worship as gods. What are those basic elements of the created order? Let me give you three, and you'll have a better understanding of what Paul is talking about: money, sex, and power. These "elementary principles of the world" are all around us all the time. We cannot avoid them. But more than that, they're incredibly powerful, so powerful, in fact, that sinful creatures like you and me are constantly tempted to turn them into idols and then worship them as gods.[2]

This is the Bible's verdict upon fallen humanity apart from the redeeming work of Christ and adoption into God's family: we're enslaved to powers beyond our own control. We see this to be true in the life of Israel, even when she was redeemed from Egyptian slavery. But we also see this among all the peoples of the earth. Listen to what Paul says of the Galatians because it's true of each one of us apart from Christ: "Formerly, when you did not know God, you were *enslaved* to those that by nature are not gods" (4:8). Enslavement to non-gods that we treat like gods—that's the state of every single person apart from being adopted by God.

The Process of Adoption (4:4, 5)

But thankfully it wasn't God's desire to leave sinful humanity in a state of enslavement. The Father wasn't content to let humanity forever languish in the orphanage of the world. Instead his heart was set on adoption. "But when the fullness of time had come, God sent forth his Son, born of woman, born under the law, to redeem those who were under the law, so that we might receive adoption as sons" (4:4, 5). You see, God was eager to create one new family out of the myriad of families on the earth and to forge a single family through the act of adoption.

Human adoption is often an extensive and intensive and even expensive process. An adoption for starters entails a mountain of paperwork. It's also not something you rush into; the timing must be right. Your motives need to be right as well. You have to be both mentally and emotionally prepared for the lengthy and taxing process it often is. And in the case of international adoption, you have to be prepared to travel to the country of origin, stay there for a period of time, see the process to completion, and transport your adopted child home. Adoption, then, like pregnancy itself, isn't for the faint of heart!

Yet we need to understand that the process God went through to adopt his sons and daughters was even more extensive and intensive and expensive than this. Vastly more so! God waited patiently for, not many months, but many hundreds of years; only then was it just the right time, "the fullness of time" (4:4). And only then did he initiate the adoption process.

But notice *how* the Father initiated the process: "God sent forth his Son" (4:4). And here's why: the heavenly Father is a holy God and therefore could not simply take sinful creatures to himself and call them his own, without first dealing with their sin. This is why the Son had to be "born of woman, born under the law" (4:4). He not only had to take on human flesh—he had to submit himself to the *curse* of the Law.[3] You see, in order to adopt sinful creatures like you and me, the Son not only had to become *incarnate*, he had to be *crucified* and on the cross become a curse for us (cf. 3:13).[4]

When my wife and I adopted twins from Ethiopia, it was an extensive and intensive and indeed expensive process. And we had to travel a remarkably long way to Addis Ababa, the capital of Ethiopia, where our boys lived. Once in that country, we still had more work to do, and it wasn't always easy or straightforward. But imagine if my wife and I would have sent our firstborn son, Ezra, to Ethiopia to adopt our twins for us. And just imagine if we knew the only way we were going to be able to adopt Addis and Rager was to let Ezra be publicly executed while in Ethiopia. What if the only way to adopt our twins was to sacrifice our firstborn? Yet that's precisely what the Father did in sending the Son into the world and onto the cross, "so that we might receive adoption as sons" (4:5).

If we're God's sons or daughters, we enjoy that privilege only because of adoption. God went to great lengths to secure our adoption; he spared absolutely no expense. In fact, he paid the highest price by giving his Son so we could be made right with him and become his children by faith. Recognizing this, is it any wonder Scripture says, "See what kind of love the Father has given to us, that we should be called children of God" (1 John 3:1).

The Privilege of Sonship (4:6)

To receive adoption as sons—what a remarkable privilege! This fact alone ought to thrill our hearts, and all the more as we further understand the privilege of being adopted into God's family. Which is where Paul takes us in the very next verse; in fact, he points to two privileges: "And because you are sons, God has sent the Spirit of his Son into our hearts, crying, 'Abba! Father!'" (v. 6).

One privilege of divine adoption is *the change of a child's nature*. Human adoptions are of course very special, but they don't change a child's nature. The change is only legal and relational; there's no *inner transformation* of the child. But when God adopts a person into his family, he changes who he or she is from the inside out. In Christ we become new creatures! We receive new spiritual DNA, God's own in fact.

How does that happen? God changes our nature by sending the Spirit of his Son into our hearts. And there, in the very core of our being, his Spirit remains and resides. He never departs. But more than that, he transforms us, starting from the inside and steadily working his way out, over time consuming the whole of who we are.

This leads to a second privilege of divine adoption: *a change of disposition*. Those with new DNA through the Spirit of God express that changed nature in a changed disposition, toward both God and the circumstances of their lives. From the moment of their new birth they begin to cry like newborn babies. However, theirs is a distinctive cry because it flows from this new

Spirit-given nature and disposition. It is a cry of intimacy and dependence, and this is what it sounds like: "Abba! Father!"

But what kind of cry is this? Well, the only other person who cries this way is Jesus. In fact this is the cry he uttered in the garden of Gethsemane. His final hour had come. He was staring death in the face. No doubt he was also coming to terms with the suffering he was about to endure on the cross. His soul was in utter anguish. And at precisely that moment he voiced this cry: "Abba, Father, all things are possible for you. Remove this cup from me. Yet not what I will, but what you will" (Mark 14:36; cf. Matthew 26:39; Luke 22:42).

The cry "Abba! Father!" is the Son's cry of distress to his loving heavenly Father. It's his way of addressing his Father in his time of greatest need. Yes, this is a cry of intimacy and dependence. But it is even more fundamentally a *cry*—a response to pain, something one utters in the face of suffering or in the midst of hardship.

Because God sends the Spirit of Christ into the hearts of every one of his adopted children, they learn to cry this same cry when they're in a time of need. Adopted sons and daughters cry out to their heavenly Father in the same way God's one and only Son did. In fact, the cry of an adopted child of God is the cry of the Son himself, uttering his cry to God in them and for them through his Spirit (cf. Romans 8:15–17).[5]

God's adopted children have, then, a very distinctive cry; they have a distinctive way of responding to life's challenges. The distinctive thing is not that God's children have fewer challenges. Nor is it that God's children don't grieve or experience disappointment. Instead the distinctive thing about God's children is this: when they cry they make a different sound than those who aren't God's children. When faced with suffering, whether great or small, God's children turn to their heavenly Father and cry out to him, "Abba! Father!" And by faith they expect their heavenly Father to hear and respond to their cry.

Have you listened to yourself cry lately? What do you sound like when you are faced with difficulties or hardships or suffering or setbacks? If we heard a recording of your response to some recent difficulty in your life, what would we hear? Would we hear the sound, "Abba! Father!"? Or would we hear something else entirely, perhaps the sound of grumbling or even the gnashing of teeth?

All too often the children of God get into difficulties in life and start to cry, as well they should, but it's not the distinctive cry of his adopted sons and daughters. Instead it sounds like the cry of those who don't know God as their Father. It's not the cry of intimacy and dependence; instead it's the cry of indignation and desperation—"What am I going to do!" or "How can God do this to me!"

God's children who are walking with the Lord don't gnash their teeth at their heavenly Father. Even when they receive a heavy blow in life, they don't curse the day they were born, much less curse the God who made them. Nor do they cry the way the world does—blaming themselves or others or God, suffocating under a sense of guilt and shame, or redoubling their efforts to work harder to get themselves out of their mess. God's children look to their heavenly Father in faith and cry out to him, "Abba! Father!"

The Promise of Heirs (4:7)

Notice, finally, then, how this passage concludes. Paul brings this passage, indeed this whole section of Galatians (3:1—4:7), to a climax here in this final verse. Here he affirms the very point he's been working so hard to establish throughout the letter, the heart of what the Galatians need to become convinced of again: "So you are no longer a slave, but a son, and if a son, then an heir through God" (4:7).

These Gentile converts in Galatia are not slaves despite what they may have been told. They're sons of God—the God of Abraham, Isaac, and Jacob, the God of Israel, the God of the nations! And they themselves ought to know it because God has sent the Spirit of his Son into their hearts, and they now respond to the challenges in their lives in a distinctive way. They have a distinct cry, and it is this distinctive cry that confirms they are indeed God's children. And if they are God's children, then they are heirs through God.

Note the wonderful way in which God connects suffering and sonship. *We're assured of our sonship by how we respond to our suffering.* So we shouldn't begrudge the suffering God brings into our lives—whether large or small—because those are God-ordained occasions to confirm our adoption as sons of God. "It is for discipline that you have to endure. God is treating you as sons. For what son is there whom his father does not discipline? If you are left without discipline, in which all have participated, then you are illegitimate children and not sons" (Hebrews 12:7, 8).

Of course, no one likes discipline at the time. This isn't a call to be happy in the midst of our hardships. But it is a call to walk by faith in the midst of them, knowing that discipline will later on yield "the peaceful fruit of righteousness to those who have been trained by it" (Hebrews 12:11).

Are we struggling right now? Are we heavy-laden with hardship or difficulty? Perhaps it's the Father's loving discipline—not to pay us back for being naughty children but to cultivate greater holiness in our hearts as his beloved sons or daughters.

So we shouldn't begrudge the suffering God sends us. Instead we can rejoice in the very core of our being that we're indeed sons or daughters of the heavenly Father and see the hardship as an occasion through which God will *increase* our confidence in being his heirs.

Conclusion

Every newborn baby has its own distinctive cry. So, too, do the children of God. And we know we're children of God when we cry in a certain way. We know we've been adopted into God's family when we respond to the circumstances in our lives with the cries of intimacy and dependence. We know we are sons or daughters of God when we look to our heavenly Father in time of need with confidence and trust. We know we're his children when we find ourselves crying out, "Abba! Father!"

This isn't something we manufacture in our own strength; this distinctive cry of the children of God is something God himself causes to well up within us by his Spirit—the Spirit of his Son—whom he sends into our heart when he adopts us as his children. This is how we know we've been adopted; this is how we know we are children of God. And if we are children of God, then we are heirs through God.

Formerly, when you did not know God, you were enslaved to those that by nature are not gods. But now that you have come to know God, or rather to be known by God, how can you turn back again to the weak and worthless elementary principles of the world, whose slaves you want to be once more? You observe days and months and seasons and years! I am afraid I may have labored over you in vain.

4:8–11

16

Turning Back Isn't the Way Forward

GALATIANS 4:8–11

WE HAVE ALL probably at some point come to a place in life where the way forward was so hard that we wanted to turn around and go back.

Perhaps we've tried to make strides in our career or a relationship or our walk with Christ, yet in doing so things got harder, not easier. Then it dawned on us. To go any further would require more of us than we wanted to give. So we glanced over our shoulder at the past and concluded it would be easier simply to turn around and head back rather than continue moving forward in the face of the difficulties.

This is where the Galatians are. They find themselves in a tough spot; the way forward doesn't look either obvious or easy. So they decide to turn back to what's familiar—specifically to their own preconversion pagan practices, as Paul laments: "You observe days and months and seasons and years" (4:10).[1]

As a result Paul believes the Galatians are deserting the one who has called them. They're defecting from the faith by turning to the idolatrous practices of their former way of life. Indeed they're relapsing into their former state of slavery, that time of ignorance when they neither knew God nor were known by him.

The steadfast Apostle Paul, of course, finds this as ridiculous as the Israelites wanting to return to Egypt. Having been liberated from Egyptian bondage, the Israelites confronted a difficult wilderness transition and then wanted to turn back. "Would that we were in Egypt; we want to go back; it's too difficult out here in the wilderness."

You may recall how they responded to the report of the spies. When they heard of "giants" in the land, they were so distraught and even indignant, they decided to appoint a replacement for Moses, one who would lead them back to Egypt:

> And all the people of Israel grumbled against Moses and Aaron. The whole congregation said to them, "Would that we had died in the land of Egypt! Or would that we had died in this wilderness! Why is the LORD bringing us into this land, to fall by the sword? Our wives and our little ones will become a prey. Would it not be better for us to go back to Egypt?" And they said to one another, "Let us choose a leader and go back to Egypt." (Numbers 14:2–4)

Yet this is in effect just what Paul hears the Galatians saying. Astonishingly, like the Israelites of old, the Galatians *want* to return to slavery![2]

Now you would think it would be obvious to us that turning back isn't the way forward. And yet we, like the Israelites or the Galatians, often do this very thing.

But why? Usually because we see the past as more promising than the future. When the way forward is hard, we have to walk by faith, not by sight, if we're going to walk at all. And that's precisely why going back is often so much easier. We've been there and done that. Traveling in that direction requires little, if any, faith; it's familiar territory.

But when it comes to living the gospel-rooted life, *turning back isn't the way forward*. In fact, turning back is first-class folly. Paul gets this. But the Galatians evidently don't. So Paul must once again warn and even rebuke them, to keep them from plunging any further into madness.

Powerless to Move Forward

Turning back is first-rate folly, first of all, because turning back leaves us *powerless to move forward*. Why? Because when we return to our former way of life, we find it doesn't actually provide us with greater strength and freedom to help us move forward. In fact, it's just the opposite: we find we're back in bondage to what once held us captive.

This is what Paul wants the Galatians to see. If they turn back to their old way of life with its outlook and practices, they'll yield their lives to that which is *powerless* to get them to where they need to go. But more than that, they'll also give themselves to that which will only *re-enslave* them, the very thing Paul, with stinging irony, says they *want* to do. "But now that you have come to know God, or rather to be known by God, how can you turn back again to the weak and worthless elementary principles of the world, whose slaves you want to be once more?" (4:9).

Yet I think we all know how tremendously enticing our preconversion practices can be. Saint Augustine certainly did. His old habits had a stranglehold on him, so that he found it practically impossible to break free. He wanted to move forward in the Christian life, yet found it nearly impossible to part company with his sinful, enslaving past.

> I was held back by mere trifles, the most paltry inanities, all my old attachments. They plucked at my garment of flesh and whispered, "Are you going to dismiss us? From this moment we shall never be with you again, for ever and ever. From this moment you will never again be allowed to do this thing or that, for evermore." What was it, my God, that they meant when they whispered, "this thing or that?" Things so sordid and so shameful that I beg you in your mercy to keep the soul of your servant free from them! These voices, as I heard them, seemed less than half as loud as they had been before. They no longer barred my way, blatantly contradictory, but their mutterings seemed to reach me from behind, as though they were stealthily plucking at my back, trying to make me turn my head when I wanted to go forward. Yet, in my state of indecision, they kept me from tearing myself away, from shaking myself free of them and leaping across the barrier to the other side, where you were calling me. Habit was too strong for me when it asked, "Do you think you can live without these things?"[3]

When the way forward is hard, we're tempted to turn back. And in that moment of temptation we'll find, like Augustine, that all our old attachments—those paltry inanities and mere trifles, those seemingly innocent little habits and God-belittling attitudes—call out to us, beckoning us not to depart, pleading with us to return, promising life and joy and peace. "Are you going to dismiss us?" they'll ask. "From this moment forward we'll never be with you again," we'll be reminded. "Can you really live without us?"

Whenever progress with Christ proves difficult, we'll hear voices clamoring for us to come back. And if we listen, we'll find our minds flooded with the memories of how good life used to be. But we must not listen to those hollow sounds or look to those mirage-memories. They're just our old attachments razzing us; give them only a deaf ear and a blind eye.

Turning Your Back on the One Who Truly Knows You

When we turn back to our preconversion past, we inevitably find not more freedom but more bondage. And if that were not disincentive enough, there's something even worse. *By turning back we turn our back on the only one who truly knows us.*

This, Paul says, is what the Galatians are doing. Formerly, when they served "those that by nature are not gods," they were completely ignorant of God (4:8). But now they've come to know God; or rather, as Paul hastens to remind the Galatians, they've in fact come "to be known by God" (4:9).

Knowing God is the essence of the Christian life. "And this is eternal life, that they know you the only true God, and Jesus Christ whom you have sent" (John 17:3). But this is the essence of what it means to know God: *being known by God*.

> What matters supremely, therefore, is not in the last analysis the fact that I know God, but the larger fact which underlies it—the fact that *he knows me*. I am graven on the palms of his hand. I am never out of his mind. . . . He knows me as a friend, one who loves me; and there is no moment when his eye is off me, or his attention distracted from me, and no moment, therefore, when his care falters.[4]

To be known by God, to have been chosen in Christ Jesus before the foundation of the world (Ephesians 1:4), to be kept as the apple of his eye, hidden under the shadow of his wing (Psalm 17:8), to have our name written in the Book of Life (Revelation 20:15), to know it's our Father's good pleasure to give us the kingdom (Luke 12:32)—what utter insanity it would be to turn our back on so generous a God!

Squandering Everything Others Have Invested in You

While Paul has exposed the core of the Galatians' foolishness in turning back, he's not said everything he wants to say. There is one further reason why their turning back is so crazy, and for Paul it's a highly personal one. It's implied in his closing, pathos-filled comment: "I am afraid I may have labored over you in vain" (4:11).

At first glance Paul's remark might strike us as a bit too self-referential to be appropriate at this point, like a father who tells his son who's just fallen off his bike and broken his arm, "Well, son, it looks like I've just wasted my time teaching you how to ride that bike!"

What we need to understand in order for this comment to be more than a sentimental appeal is this: *as an apostle to the Gentiles, Paul's life and ministry were inextricably tied to his converts.*

By virtue of his unique calling, Paul can't simply separate his success from his converts, as we might. Instead only if his converts stand fast does he truly live; only if they continue in the faith can he ultimately rejoice. And if they fall short of faithfulness, he's more than a little disappointed. It's a strike against his very identity and sense of eschatological hope. Or at least this is what Paul himself seems to think, as he confesses to the Thessalonians: "For what is our hope or joy or crown of boasting before our Lord Jesus at his coming? Is it not you? For you are our glory and joy" (1 Thessalonians 2:19, 20).

Paul's personal investment in his converts is remarkable, perhaps even startling for some. It's like what a mother must feel for her firstborn son who has gone astray. And in fact this is just the image Paul conjures up for the Galatians. His anguish is so acute, he's like a woman in labor, prepared to give birth to them all over again: ". . . My little children, for whom I am again in the anguish of childbirth until Christ is formed in you!" (4:19).[5]

Toward the end of my senior year in high school, a year after I'd come to Christ, I did something really idiotic. My parents were out of town, and I threw a big party at my house. The whole thing ended terribly. The party got busted. Parents had to come get their sons and daughters. I had to tell my parents. And just as bad, if not worse, I had to tell my girlfriend's parents, her father in particular.

Now my girlfriend then is my wife now, and her father is of course now my father-in-law. But he also was the one who had led me to Christ twelve months earlier and had been meeting with me on a regular basis for prayer and Bible reading. It was to this particular person—my spiritual father in the faith—that I knew I had to confess.

I'll never forget his disappointment when I told him what I'd done. He didn't get angry or shout, chastise, or criticize. That may, in some sense, have been easier. Instead he simply expressed his deep disappointment with me. How could I have turned back, he asked, to those "weak and worthless" things (4:9) I'd been set free from when I came to Christ?

His was a supremely gentle, fatherly rebuke. Yet it hit me like a ton of bricks. The grief was indescribable, crushing really. All I could do was stare at the floor in shame. And when the conversation ended and forgiveness was extended and received, I remember weeping bitterly, like penitent Peter, over the foolish thing I'd done, but even more so because I'd turned away from the one who'd already invested so much in me.

Paul no doubt shed his own tears over the Galatians, not out of regret but distress. Like a mother he'd given them birth, and like a father he'd invested so much in them. Yet now they were prepared to throw that all away as they turned their backs on him and his gospel. His final appeal is thus that they not break his heart, nor squander everything he's done and indeed suffered for them.

It's fitting for us as pastors to address children, teenagers, and young adults. We do well to ask them questions such as: Do you realize or appreciate how many people have invested in you over the years, how significant have been the sacrifices for your sake, how numerous have been the prayers made for you, how steady the support and encouragement? Should you eventually abandon the faith, you will in effect waste all this investment in you. You'll not only break hearts, you'll squander who knows how much spiritual labor undertaken on your behalf. If you forsake Christ, it will all be in vain—for you and others. On the other hand, realize that for those who have poured themselves into your life for the sake of Christ, they have no greater joy than to see you walking in the truth (3 John 4). If you stand fast in the Lord, then they will truly live (1 Thessalonians 3:8).

We all need to hear the message, don't turn back; that's folly, and that's not the way forward!

Conclusion

The Galatians, like the Israelites of old, are in the midst of the wilderness and want to go back. They've experienced an exodus-like redemption in Christ, but now they find the way through the wilderness of this world to be more difficult than they'd imagined.

Yet theirs isn't a peculiar struggle. Rather, the temptation to turn back is never far from any Christian convert, especially not when he or she finds himself or herself in the midst of a wilderness of difficulties. No wonder it was Paul's method to circulate around to formerly planted churches, "strengthening the souls of the disciples, encouraging them to continue in the faith, and saying that through many tribulations we must enter the kingdom of God" (Acts 14:22).

The wilderness of this world is fraught with troubles. But turning back isn't an option; it's not the way forward. There's indeed only way forward, only one way we can enter the kingdom of God: by continuing in the faith.

Brothers, I entreat you, become as I am, for I also have become as you are. You did me no wrong.

4:12

17

Imitation Is the
Solution, Part 1

GALATIANS 4:12

Note: This particular study was preached at the church where I serve as senior pastor during a major crisis in our church. Though this sermon was given in a particular context in a specific local church, the principles and insights contained in it are helpful for believers and for pastors generally and thus this sermon has been slightly adapted for this commentary, maintaining the original personal elements and appeals.

WE BEGAN THE PREVIOUS STUDY on Galatians 4:8–11 with the question, have we ever found ourselves at a place in life where the way forward looked so hard that we wanted to turn around and go back? Because of how things have unfolded in the life of our church, many of us feel like we're in the wilderness. The way forward looks hard, and the temptation is to go back. As a church we're in the midst of a significant trial. What is going on, and where do we go from here?

Crucifying the Visionary Dreamer

God has orchestrated this entire situation as a major trial for us—for us as a church but also, I believe, for me personally as your pastor. In fact, if I'm honest I'd have to say that these first three years at Calvary Memorial Church have felt like one long extended trial, with lots of little and big trials along the way, culminating with the huge mess we have on our hands right now.

Over the last three years things have not worked out exactly as I'd planned or hoped. God has done some wonderful things, and we've made some exciting strides as a church, but things haven't gone as smoothly or as straightforwardly as I would have expected. Nor have they met as much success as I would have hoped. There have been many more setbacks and a lot more pushback than I would have imagined.

When pastors find themselves in the throes of challenges like we're up against now, they often sink into a bitter and self-protective attitude toward the church. Or they simply start brushing up their resumé and preparing their resignation letter. It happens all the time.

Of course, I recognize that some of the difficulties we've experienced over the past three years of my ministry are of my own making; they're the result of a lack of judgment born of youthful impatience and sometimes a failure to love others as I would want to be loved.

I also recognize that Satan isn't on vacation. The church's archenemy is alive and well and at work. And because Calvary Memorial Church is a strategic beacon of light in a godless community, and because the enemy no doubt sees that we as a church are starting to gain some traction and make strides in gospel advance, he's gotten nervous. But more than that, he's gotten aggressive.

I received an email from an individual who has visited our church only a few times. But this person is aware of what's going on and wanted to write to express how she sees things:

> Dear Pastor Wilson,
>   I am not a member of your church. I have attended two events at your church. I think that Calvary Memorial Church is doing amazing things for God. It is great to see. . . .
>   I will pray for your church. I feel strongly that Satan is attacking Calvary b/c of the good works that the church is doing in the name of Jesus. If you were lukewarm, Satan would be content. Because so many of your flock are on fire for God I can see him viewing your church as a threat. I wish that I was wise enough to offer advice. I will pray that God will be victorious in all matters regarding your church, that He will humble everyone involved and His children will repent/submit to Him. Above all I pray that through this God will be glorified.

But do you know who I see ultimately at work in all of this, not least in my own life and struggles over the past three years? I see a sovereign God who loves me and you and this church, even at times with severe mercy and humbling grace.

Why, God?

Why does God have us where we are right now as a church? Why has God placed me as the pastor of this church in this place at this time? What is God doing in the midst of all this?

Perhaps you've been asking yourself that question, and perhaps you're coming to some conclusions. *What I see God doing in my own life is crucifying the visionary dreamer in me.* What God seems to be grinding into my soul, through difficult circumstances, disappointments, and suffering, is the painful realization for me personally that while visionary dreamers like me often make great leaders for God's people, *they don't always make the best lovers of God's people.* What God is teaching me is that the people I'm called to pastor don't want simply to be a part of my vision, they want to be a part of my heart.

A section in Dietrich Bonhoeffer's classic little book on Christian community entitled *Life Together* really nails this; in fact, it nails me—to the cross of Christ. I'd read this section many times before, and I've always been sensitive to what he says. But I think the Lord has brought this current fiery trial into my life to force me to deal with this underlying issue in my own heart, even though, I might add, I don't think it's necessarily *directly* related to our current situation. Here is what Bonhoeffer says:

On innumerable occasions a whole Christian community has been shattered because it has lived on the basis of a wishful image. Certainly serious Christians who are put in a community for the first time will often bring with them a very definite image of what Christian communal life should be, and they will be anxious to realize it. But God's grace quickly frustrates all such dreams. A great disillusionment with others, with Christians in general, and, if we are fortunate, with ourselves, is bound to overwhelm us as surely as God desires to lead us to an understanding of genuine Christian community. By sheer grace God will not permit us to live in a dream world even for a few weeks and to abandon ourselves to those blissful experiences and exalted moods that sweep over us like a wave of rapture. For God is not a God of emotionalism, but the God of truth. Only that community which enters into the experience of this great disillusionment with all its unpleasant and evil appearances begins to be what it should be in God's sight, begins to grasp in faith the promise that is given to it. The sooner this moment of disillusionment comes over the individual and the community, the better for both. However, a community that cannot bear and cannot survive such disillusionment, clinging instead to its idealized image, when that should be done away with, loses at the same time the promise of a durable Christian community. Sooner or later it is bound to collapse. Every human idealized image that is brought into the Christian community is a hindrance to genuine community and must be broken up so that genuine community can survive. Those who love their dream of a Christian community more than the Christian community itself become destroyers of that Christian community even though their personal intentions may be ever so honest, earnest, and sacrificial.

God hates this wishful dreaming because it makes the dreamer proud and pretentious. Those who dream of this idealized community demand that it be fulfilled by God, by others, and by themselves. They enter the community of Christians with their demands, set up their own law, and judge one another and even God accordingly. They stand adamant, a living reproach to all others in the circle of the community. They act as if they have to create the Christian community, as if their visionary ideal binds the people together. Whatever does not go their way, they call a failure.[1]

Bonhoeffer then applies all of this specifically to pastors and other zealous congregants.

That also applies in a special way to the complaints often heard from pastors and zealous parishioners about their congregations. Pastors should not complain about their congregation, certainly never to other people, but also not to God. Congregations have not been entrusted to them in order that they should become accusers of their congregations before God and their fellow human beings. When pastors lose faith in a Christian community in which they have been placed and begin to make accusations against it, they had better examine themselves first to see whether the underlying problem is not their own idealized image, which should be shattered by God. And if they find that to be true, let them thank God for leading them into this predicament. But if they find that it is not true, let them nevertheless guard against ever becoming an accuser of those whom God has gathered together. Instead, let them accuse themselves of their unbelief, let them ask for an understanding of their own failure and their particular sin, and pray that they may not wrong other Christians. Let such pastors, recognizing their own guilt, make intercession for those charged to their care. Let them do what they have been instructed to do and thank God.[2]

So, brothers and sisters of Calvary Memorial Church, as your pastor I say to you that I am sorry. I have not loved you in Christ Jesus the way I should. Please forgive me for often loving my own visionary dream more than you. What God is painfully teaching me is that you don't want simply to be a part of my vision but a part of my heart. God is teaching me that lesson, but it's not coming very quickly or easily because it is requiring the crucifixion of the visionary dreamer in me. So please pray for me, that he who has begun a good work in me may be faithful and just to complete this work in me, for my good and for your good and for his glory.

Crucifixion with Christ Is the Only Way Forward

Brothers and sisters, we're in the midst of the wilderness. And the way forward is going to be hard. We still have a lot of work to do in the days and weeks ahead.

But turning back isn't the way forward. Going back to Egypt isn't the way to the land of promise. Resorting to the old attachments and patterns of behavior of the past isn't the way to press on toward the future God has for us.

The way forward, indeed the only way forward, is *to embrace the cross of Christ more fully and more freely*. The way forward through the mess we find ourselves in is the same way forward that the Apostle Paul recommends to the Galatians: "Brothers, I entreat you, become as I am, for I also have become as you are" (4:12).

If we're going to move forward, out of this wilderness of affliction, we have to do what Paul is calling the Galatians to do when they find themselves in a big mess, and that is to imitate Paul, to become like him in being crucified with Christ. "I have been crucified with Christ. It is no longer I who live, but Christ who lives in me. And the life I now live in the flesh I live by faith in the Son of God, who loved me and gave himself for me" (2:20).

Imitating the crucified Paul as he imitates the crucified Christ—that is the way forward for each and every one of us, both in our current situation as a church and also in every other difficult situation in which we find ourselves. Letting our own desires and ambitions and wishes and dreams and preferences—our very life—be crucified on the cross with Christ, for the good of others, as an expression of the life and love of Christ working in and through us—that's the call of the gospel on all our lives. And that's the only way forward as a church.

Philippians 2:1–11 captures just what we need: the mind of Christ.

> So if there is any encouragement in Christ, any comfort from love, any participation in the Spirit, any affection and sympathy, complete my joy by being of the same mind, having the same love, being in full accord and of one mind. Do nothing from selfish ambition or conceit, but in humility count others more significant than yourselves. Let each of you look not only to his own interests, but also to the interests of others. Have this mind among yourselves, which is yours in Christ Jesus, who, though he was in the form of God, did not count equality with God a thing to be grasped, but emptied himself, by taking the form of a servant, being born in the likeness of men. And being found in human form, he humbled himself by becoming obedient to the point of death, even death on a cross. Therefore God has highly exalted him and bestowed on him the name that is above every name, so that at the name of Jesus every knee should bow, in heaven and on earth and under the earth, and every tongue confess that Jesus Christ is Lord, to the glory of God the Father.

Having the mind of Christ is the only way forward. The mind of Christ is what I so desperately need as a pastor. And the mind of Christ is what each and every one of you desperately needs.

May the song "May the Mind of Christ, My Savior" be our heartfelt prayer to the Lord today and in the days to come.

May the mind of Christ, my Savior,
Live in me from day to day,
By His love and power controlling
All I do and say.

May the Word of God dwell richly
In my heart from hour to hour,
So that all may see I triumph
Only through His power.

May the peace of God my Father
Rule my life in everything,
That I may be calm to comfort
Sick and sorrowing.

May the love of Jesus fill me
As the waters fill the sea;
Him exalting, self abasing,
This is victory.[3]

Crucifixion with Christ—exalting him—abasing self—this is victory!

Brothers, I entreat you, become as I am, for I also have become as you are. You did me no wrong. You know it was because of a bodily ailment that I preached the gospel to you at first, and though my condition was a trial to you, you did not scorn or despise me, but received me as an angel of God, as Christ Jesus. What then has become of your blessedness? For I testify to you that, if possible, you would have gouged out your eyes and given them to me. Have I then become your enemy by telling you the truth? They make much of you, but for no good purpose. They want to shut you out, that you may make much of them. It is always good to be made much of for a good purpose, and not only when I am present with you, my little children, for whom I am again in the anguish of childbirth until Christ is formed in you! I wish I could be present with you now and change my tone, for I am perplexed about you.

4:12–20

18

Imitation Is the Solution, Part 2

GALATIANS 4:12–20

THIS IS ONE OF THE MORE IMPORTANT and yet often overlooked passages in Galatians. Its truth can be summarized succinctly: *imitation is the solution*. Imitating Paul as he imitates the crucified Christ—this is the way forward for the Galatians. This is also the way forward for every Christian, regardless of the situation or circumstances.

To help get the Galatians back on track, Paul might have said a thousand different things. But as his first and primary appeal he says, "Brothers, I entreat you, *become as I am*, for I also have become as you are" (4:12).[1]

Understanding imitation as Paul's solution to the crisis in Galatia opens for us a critical new window on the letter. Evidently Galatians isn't only about ideas but actions. The Galatians must not only endorse Paul's gospel but must also conform to his gospel-rooted way of life. Paul's clarion call to imitate him thus invites us to look beneath the surface of theological controversy to the even more fundamental issue at stake in Galatia: *gospel-rooted living*.[2]

In fact, from Paul's perspective it's fair to say that the problem isn't ultimately theological but moral.[3] Yes, the agitators, the Judaizers, are preaching aberrant theology (1:7), which Paul confronts in the central theological portion of the letter (2:15—4 :7). Yet the root of the problem isn't the agitators' heterodoxy but the Galatians' cowardice: *they're no longer willing to imitate Paul in suffering for the cross of Christ.*

In fact, Paul thinks this is why the wheels have come off the proverbial wagon. The Galatians have abandoned the call to discipleship; or at least they've turned costly grace into cheap grace, which is no grace at all. They're acting like the face-saving agitators. But if the Galatians would only imitate Paul in his suffering for Christ, they could bring the whole crisis to a swift conclusion.

Gladly Embracing a Marked Man (4:13, 14)

This spinelessness of the Galatians stands in sharp contrast to how they began their life in Christ. Indeed, as Paul reminds them, when they initially received the gospel they were more than willing to suffer for the cross of Christ. They were even prepared to go to great lengths of self-sacrifice and service to meet Paul's own needs. "You would have gouged out your eyes and given them to me," the apostle reminds them fondly (4:15).

Modern readers of this letter need to realize that when the Apostle Paul arrived in Galatia, he gave every appearance of being a marked man—a dangerous contagion in fact. Paul reminds the Galatians that he first preached the gospel to them on account of "a bodily ailment" (4:13), and that this proved to be for the Galatians a "trial" or temptation (4:13, 14). Paul thus reminds them (albeit in an enigmatic way) of the fact that he bore on his body the visible signs of suffering, or what he will later cryptically refer to as "the marks of Jesus" (6:17).[4] But in the ancient world grave suffering indicated that you stood on the wrong side of the gods; your physical afflictions were treated as a telltale sign of divine retribution. Perhaps you were even under a curse, and the gods were set on punishing you—and anyone else associated with you.[5]

This way of construing things would have been natural for the Galatians. Consequently they would have had every reason to shun this bedraggled and disfigured Jewish preacher from Tarsus. Yet they didn't reject him but gladly received him. Neither did they "scorn or despise" him; literally they didn't try to ward off evil by spitting in his presence (4:14).[6] On the contrary, they embraced Paul as God's very own messenger—"as an angel of God," yet more than that, "as Christ Jesus" (4:14).

This was a risky decision for the Galatians, since their conversion would inevitably lead to greater challenges. For their adherence to Paul's gospel would have entailed some measure of social fallout and perhaps outright persecution, whether from their own pagan associates, local Jewish authorities, or some combination of the two. On the one hand, by embracing Paul's gospel the Galatians had to relinquish the worship of other deities (4:8, 9; cf. 1 Thessalonians 1:9), which would have made continued participation in at least some of the cultic and civic activities of their communities much more difficult, if not impossible.[7] Their sitting loose to their ancestral traditions and social responsibilities would have inevitably raised a few eyebrows.

On the other hand, Paul's gospel did not require the assimilation of his

Gentile converts into the larger Jewish communities. While the Galatians may, for example, have sought refuge through association with their local synagogue (if one was present), they were not yet circumcised and would therefore have not stopped, so to speak, being Gentiles, certainly to Jews and probably also to their own kinsmen. As a result, the Galatians would have found themselves in the awkward position of having abandoned at least some of their familial, social, and religious affiliations, yet without simultaneously embracing the new status and identity that belonged to full-fledged Jewish proselytes. They would have thus found themselves in an extremely tenuous and delicate position vis-à-vis both the Jewish community and their (former) pagan coreligionists.[8]

It would have been tremendously apropos, therefore, for Paul to say to the Galatians what is said to the saints addressed in Hebrews: "After you were enlightened, you endured a hard struggle with sufferings, sometimes being publicly exposed to reproach and affliction, and sometimes being partners with those so treated" (10:32, 33).

And yet the Galatians' embrace of Paul is more than an embrace of his gospel. It is an embrace of his cruciform way of life, as one who suffers for Christ Jesus. And thus Paul would say to the Galatians what he says to the Thessalonians: "And you became imitators of us and of the Lord, for you received the word in much affliction, with the joy of the Holy Spirit" (1 Thessalonians 1:6).

A Self-Serving Persuasion (4:15–17)

Clearly, however, something has happened to the Galatians. Paul sees a marked difference, first of all, in their response to suffering. They're no longer blessed by hardships. Hence Paul's rhetorical question: "What then has become of your blessedness?" (4:15).[9]

Paul also sees a shift in their attitude toward him. They began hot but have gone cold, even hostile. "Have I then become your enemy by telling you the truth?" (4:16). Although the Galatians were previously willing to gouge out an eye for Paul, now they won't loan him a dime.

What a sad development—for Paul, yes, but also for the Galatians! How did this happen? Was it because they discovered the Old Testament or heard about Abraham or learned about the covenant of circumcision?

No. What happened is this: certain mischievous individuals, whom Paul calls agitators, began misleading these young converts. And their influence proved to be so devastatingly effective that Paul lamentingly wonders out loud to the Galatians, "You were running well. Who hindered you from obeying the truth? This persuasion is not from him who calls you" (5:7, 8; cf. 1:6).

Why do Christians, like the Galatians, veer off course? Typically what happens is that they come under the unhelpful or even harmful influence of others. The crisis in Galatia is a case in point. The agitators got traction in Galatia only because they were able to persuade the Galatians of their point of view.

The agitators' tactic is twofold. On the one hand they flatter the Galatians with their words and gestures: "They make much of you" (4:17). On the other hand they marginalize the Galatians with their outlook and actions: "They want to shut you out" (4:17). Thus they sweet-talk the Galatians while withholding from them the very thing they desire.

Paul draws on the language of courtship and romance to describe this farcical scene.[10] The agitators are flirting with the Galatians; yet they're keeping their distance as well. And as every junior high boy understands, mixed messages from a significant other can be terribly vexing. The agitators are being teases, if you will. And their goal is as manipulative as a self-centered flirt; they simply want the Galatians in their back pocket.

One thing is clear to Paul, and he desperately wants it to be clear to the Galatians: *the Judaizers aren't self-giving but self-serving.* Yes, they say wonderful things about the Galatians, but as Paul points out, "for no good purpose" (4:17). Rather, theirs is a very self-serving and self-promoting purpose: "They want to shut you out, that you may make much of them" (4:17).[11] There it is: the aim and ambition of the agitators is *to be made much of!*

Practically what this means in Galatia is that the agitators are using the Galatians to avoid suffering for the cross of Christ. While in this passage Paul implies as much, he only states it plainly at the close of the letter: "It is those who want to make a good showing in the flesh who would force you to be circumcised, and only in order that they may not be persecuted for the cross of Christ" (6:12).

With carefully chosen Bible proof-texts and fancy-sounding theological arguments, the agitators have put up an impressive front and are now poised to take full advantage of the Galatians. They've in effect closed the door of salvation in their face, threatening them no doubt with this sort of claim: "Unless you are circumcised according to the custom of Moses, you cannot be saved" (Acts 15:1). These Gentiles must submit, therefore, to the knife and embrace circumcision; otherwise they'll be shut out of the kingdom of God.

But for Paul it's all a farce. The agitators are only playacting; they're concealing their actual designs behind the veil of their earnest appeals (cf. Romans 16:17, 18). As Paul will later make plain about the agitators, "Even those who are circumcised do not themselves keep the law, but they desire to have you circumcised that they may boast in your flesh" (6:13).

Paul's Purposeful Pain (4:18–20)

The agitators are self-centered, not Christ-centered. They want to use the Galatians, not serve them. They share in "the leaven of the Pharisees, which is hypocrisy" (Luke 12:1).

But Paul worries that they've leavened the whole lump (cf. 5:9). So he further strengthens his appeal to the Galatians by drawing a sharp contrast between himself and the agitators. Paul, we must remember, is calling the Galatians not simply away from the agitators but back to himself. Thus he presents the Galatians with two divergent portraits—one of the agitators and one of himself—and leaves the Galatians to choose which they'll have.

Paul has already displayed the aims and intentions of the agitators (4:17). Now he must paint his own portrait in the remaining verses of this passage (4:18–20). And as he does so, the contrast at once becomes clear. While the agitators pursue the Galatians for *personal gain*, the suffering apostle serves them with his *purposeful pain*.

"It is always good to be made much of for a good purpose," Paul says to the Galatians, "and not only when I am present with you" (4:18). He labors for them not only when he is with them but while he's away from them (cf. 2:5). Like a loving and longsuffering mother, Paul's spiritually wayward ones weigh heavily on his heart: "My little children, for whom I am again in the anguish of childbirth until Christ is formed in you!" (4:19).

Paul's anguish is palpable, and the Galatians' situation is serious. They're in a desperate place and need a radical solution. Indeed Paul implies that they need to be born all over again; Christ must be formed within them once more. Jesus' own self-giving life must take shape within their lives together as congregations. In a word they need to imitate the Apostle Paul as he patterns his life after the example of Christ.

Conclusion

While we know how easy it is to let the self take center stage, even in our service of others, we must strive to keep Christ at the center. For only when we're willing to endure suffering ourselves for the sake of others, so that Christ can take shape in their lives, are we truly imitating the Apostle Paul.

This is the essence of what it means to imitate Paul: to walk in the way of discipleship, to take up our cross and follow Jesus, to serve one another in love, and to be led by the Spirit. And this passage invites you and me, as it does the Galatians, to imitate this crucified apostle as he imitates his crucified Christ.

Imitation is the solution. It is the only way forward.

Tell me, you who desire to be under the law, do you not listen to the law? For it is written that Abraham had two sons, one by a slave woman and one by a free woman. But the son of the slave was born according to the flesh, while the son of the free woman was born through promise. Now this may be interpreted allegorically: these women are two covenants. One is from Mount Sinai, bearing children for slavery; she is Hagar. Now Hagar is Mount Sinai in Arabia; she corresponds to the present Jerusalem, for she is in slavery with her children. But the Jerusalem above is free, and she is our mother. For it is written, "Rejoice, O barren one who does not bear; break forth and cry aloud, you who are not in labor! For the children of the desolate one will be more than those of the one who has a husband." Now you, brothers, like Isaac, are children of promise. But just as at that time he who was born according to the flesh persecuted him who was born according to the Spirit, so also it is now. But what does the Scripture say? "Cast out the slave woman and her son, for the son of the slave woman shall not inherit with the son of the free woman." So, brothers, we are not children of the slave but of the free woman.

4:21–31

19

Children of the Free Woman

GALATIANS 4:21-31

THE ONLY WAY TO BE FREE is to be Biblical. If we fail to heed the teaching of Scripture, we're enslaved. Freedom, on the other hand, comes to those who hear God's Word and respond with obedient faith. Jesus puts it this way: "If you abide in my word, you are truly my disciples, and you will know the truth, and the truth will set you free" (John 8:31, 32).

Christians, however, easily forget this truth. We may affirm a love for the Bible, yet fail to listen to what it says; or we articulate a desire to obey Scripture, yet remain ignorant of its teaching.

As a result a very sad and potentially dangerous situation can develop. A person can think he's gaining greater and greater freedom because of his fidelity to the Bible when actually he's plunging himself deeper and deeper into the bondage of self-deception because of his ignorance of the Bible.

This was the mistake of the Pharisees. Presuming to be mighty in the Scriptures, they were pseudo-Biblical at best. Recall how Jesus chided them for their dutiful observance of the Law that was little more than a sophisticated effort to downplay, if not altogether avoid, the real heart of the Law (Matthew 23:23). To be sure, the Pharisees could strain out exegetical gnats with the best of them. The problem is, in the process they swallowed camels whole!

I've never swallowed a camel, but I suspect it's not pleasant. The thought reminds me of the old lady who swallowed not a camel but a fly. I don't know why she swallowed a fly. Perhaps she'll die. But she swallowed a spider to catch the fly. Then she swallowed a bird to catch the spider. Then she swallowed a cat to catch the bird, and she swallowed a dog to catch the cat, and she swallowed a cow to catch the dog, though I admit it's never been clear to me how cows catch dogs! In any event she eventually decided to catch the cow by swallowing, get this, a horse. Yes, there was an old lady who swallowed a horse. She's dead of course!

This old children's rhyme is humorous, but sadly death is precisely what happens to those who fail to heed the teaching of Scripture. This is the peril currently confronting the Galatians. In their supposed effort to be Biblical and thus follow the teaching of the agitators, the Judaizers, they have regressed into un-Biblical ways of thinking and living. As a result they're forfeiting the freedom they have in Christ and are being enslaved all over again (4:9).

So Paul must lead them back to the Bible, indeed to what the Scriptures actually say. For Paul doesn't think the Galatians—despite their current allegiance to the inflated yet hollow teaching of the agitators—are being half as Biblical as they should be, and not a tenth as Biblical as they presume to be! In fact, from Paul's perspective the Galatians have failed at the most basic level—namely, *they are failing to listen to the Bible*.

Paul thus launches into this new section of the letter with a stinging rebuke in the form of a loaded rhetorical question: "Tell me, you who desire to be under the law, do you not listen to the law?" (4:21). Ironic, isn't it, that the Galatians are ready to embrace circumcision in order to be more faithful to Scripture, yet they fail to grasp the very heart of the Bible's teaching.[1]

Despite the complexity of this exegetical tour de force through the Old Testament, Paul's purpose with this passage is still fairly clear. He wants to help the Galatians hear what the Law says. To that end he's chosen *three Scriptural words of exhortation* that the Galatians, if they hope to recover their freedom in Christ (cf. 5:1), will do well to heed.

The Story of Abraham's Two Sons: Rely upon Divine Initiative (4:22–24)

Paul first takes the Galatians to Genesis and the story of Abraham's two sons, Ishmael and Isaac. Offspring of one father, these boys have two different mothers, Hagar and Sarah. The former is a slave, while the latter is free.

But Paul is primarily interested in the two very different processes that led to their births. Ishmael is the result of *mere human* initiative, what Paul associates with "the flesh." Isaac, on the other hand, is the fruit of *divine* initiative, what Paul associates with "promise." "But the son of the slave was born *according to the flesh*, while the son of the free woman was born *through promise*" (4:23).

Paul thus sees in this story a picture of how *God begets spiritual children*, how a person can become a part of God's family, the people of God. Under the old covenant you could become a part of the people of God simply by taking on circumcision and the Law; thus you could be born into God's people by means of the flesh—by taking on circumcision as an expression of mere human initiative. This sort of thing is what the agitators are telling the Galatians: "Get circumcised, for only then will you truly be a part of the people of God!"

But here's the problem with trying to bring about spiritual birth by human initiative. *Human initiative will only get us human results.* Or to put it even more simply, flesh will only beget flesh. Sinful human beings will only reproduce more and more sinful human beings. This is why Paul insists that the old covenant, with circumcision and the Law, isn't the answer for the Galatians, for the old covenant, established at Mount Sinai, is only "bearing children for slavery" (v. 24).). And because Sinai's children are all of the flesh, the Sinai covenant can only enclose its adherents under the curse of the Law (cf. 3:10–12; 3:22–25; 4:1–5). Thus, "curse begets curse."[2]

True freedom only comes through divine initiative, by resting in the promises of God, what God himself has pledged to do for us. We preserve our spiritual freedom when we rely upon God's promises, not our own ingenuity, resourcefulness, or power. In fact, the extent to which we take matters into our own hands is the extent to which we forfeit our freedom in Christ. On the other hand, the extent to which we trust in God's promises—and entrust ourselves into his hands—is the extent to which we will walk in freedom.

How do we rely upon divine, rather than human, initiative? By looking to the promises of God. But how do we *know* we're relying upon God's promises? By how well we wait. Patience is our barometer of success.[3]

Consider the temptation to retaliate. Someone has wronged us, and we want to get back or get even. But the Bible expressly forbids it. Why? Because vengeance is ultimately God's job, not ours. "Beloved, never avenge yourselves, but leave it to the wrath of God, for it is written, 'Vengeance is mine, I will repay, says the Lord'" (Romans 12:19).

The prospect of God's vengeance is sobering. But it's also liberating. We don't have to bear the burden of vengeance on our backs. Instead we lay it down at the foot of the cross and entrust ourselves to our faithful Creator, who promises to right every wrong at the bar of perfect justice.

A Prophecy of Isaiah to a Barren People: Rejoice in God's Power (4:25–27)

If the Galatians want to preserve their freedom in Christ, there's another word they need to hear. It's a word from the prophet Isaiah. It's to Israel in exile, a barren people. And it's a word we too need to hear: *our freedom is preserved by rejoicing in God's power.*

Even though Israel was scattered among the nations, the prophet Isaiah promised that one day the Lord would cure her of barrenness and indeed cause her to give birth. "Rejoice, O barren one who does not bear; break forth and cry aloud, you who are not in labor! For the children of the desolate one will be more than those of the one who has a husband" (v. 27; Isaiah 54:1).[4]

As a nation, Israel was floundering. She was like a woman who could not conceive; no life came forth from her. But that wasn't the end of the story. God would turn this all around. A day was coming when Israel would flourish spiritually. And that day has indeed come with the coming of Christ and the dawning of the Church! Indeed, Paul wants to insist, Isaiah's prophecy is being fulfilled in the Galatians' midst. They are the promised children of the desolate one, offspring of Abraham, heirs of promise. "Now Hagar is Mount Sinai in Arabia; she corresponds to the present Jerusalem, for she is in slavery with her children. But the Jerusalem above is free, and she is our mother" (vv. 25, 26).

God has a remarkable way of bringing something out of nothing. My brother and sister-in-law struggled for years with infertility. Eventually, with the help of fertility technologies, my sister-in-law was able to give birth to a pair of twins. The twins are now eighteen months old. But would you believe that just a year later she conceived again, though entirely naturally. When I talked to my brother, I hardly needed to tell him that this pointed to the power of God. He was already there and understood that fully. But I did encourage him to rejoice in it. God can bring into existence that which does not exist. And what is impossible with man is possible with God.

Disappointing setbacks and difficult circumstances give us the impression that we're trapped, with no way out. Many across the country and in the congregation I pastor have felt trapped, or even imprisoned, as a result of the dramatic downturn in the economy over the last several years. People feel trapped in unemployment or underemployment, in a mortgage that outstrips the value of their home, or in a work arrangement they feel they can never leave.

Yet we ought to rejoice in the God who brings something out of nothing, the one who causes even the barren to give birth! Besides, when we fail to rejoice in God's power, we'll be tempted to trust in our own. And we'll find ourselves rushing into all sorts of dead ends. But it's precisely in these desperate moments that we should rely upon the promises of God and rejoice in his miracle-working, life-giving power.

A Request from Sarah: Root out Whatever Might Enslave You (4:28–31)

But if God's people are going to preserve their freedom in Christ, they must hear and heed a third word from Scripture. It's a surprising and perhaps even startling word, but it's one the Galatians needed to hear, as do we. *In order to preserve freedom, we must root out whatever enslaves us.*

If the Galatians are serious about being Biblical, and truly listen to what the Law says, then they would hear this word from Scripture: "Cast out the slave woman and her son, for the son of the slave woman shall not inherit with the son of the free woman" (v. 30; Genesis 21:10). Paul takes these words from the lips of Sarah, the mother of Isaac, that she spoke when she saw Ishmael, Hagar's son, "laughing" at Isaac—that is, teasing, mocking, or making sport of Isaac.

Paul here points to the long-standing sibling rivalry between the children of the flesh and the children of the promise and Spirit, which goes all the way back to the time of Abraham and his two sons. We read in Genesis 21 that the child born to the slave woman, Ishmael, laughed at the child born to the free woman, Isaac (v. 9). What is likely intended is that Ishmael scorned or mocked Isaac, held him in derision. Early Jewish interpreters of this passage understood this to indicate a hostility between Ishmael and Isaac. One text, for example, says that Ishmael "made war" on Isaac. Another describes how Ishmael, while pretending to play, covertly shot arrows at his brother Isaac.[5] This was a real sibling rivalry!

But Paul expands our understanding of this sibling rivalry, giving it enormous historical significance. In fact, Paul says that what happened between these two warring brothers way back then continues into the present day. "But just as at that time he who was born according to the flesh persecuted him who was born according to the Spirit, *so also it is now*" (v. 29).

This verse tells us what church history confirms: there's always been animosity between the children of the flesh and the children of the Spirit. For the flesh and the Spirit "are opposed to each other" (5:17), whether in our own lives or in the life of the church or in the life of our community or country. Sometimes this animosity expresses itself in social pressure; at other times it gets hostile, even violent.

If the Galatians are going to preserve the freedom they have in Christ, they must root out the children of the flesh, in this case the Judaizers. They have no other choice. If they don't, they'll be overrun by the mind-set and methods of these individuals. In fact, Paul is concerned this has already happened. And should the Galatians succumb to the flesh, with its desires and works, they too will be barred from entering the kingdom of God (5:21). They will have fallen from grace and thus find themselves severed from Christ (5:4).

The Judaizers, with their false gospel and fleshly schemes (cf. 4:17), have already stirred up much trouble in these churches. From Paul's description of things, the Galatian churches are in an uproar. Accusations are running wild, people are grasping for power, friends are choosing sides. In short, Paul sees the works of the flesh on display and thus knows the desires of the flesh are at work. It's not a pretty sight.

There's only one remedy: root out the Judaizers. Paul is calling the Galatians to do, in effect, what we today refer to as church discipline. It's often a difficult and heart-rending work, but it's essential, not only for the preservation of the truth of the gospel but for the integrity of the Body of Christ. And just as this gutsy and yet grace-promoting practice was needed in the ancient churches of Galatia, so too it's needed in our churches today.

But we should also hear in this a call for personal, spiritual self-discipline. For it's not enough to expel the Judaizers. Paul knows the Galatians must also root out what enslaves them personally. The sins that so easily entangle must be laid aside. And Paul sees all sorts of petty and fleshly behavior in play in Galatia: enmity, strife, jealousy, fits of anger, rivalries, dissensions, divisions, envy. Yet these are the very practices that lead to disinheritance, to being excluded from the kingdom of God (5:19–21).

Conclusion

Being Biblical—truly, deeply Biblical—is the only sure path to freedom. If we fail to hear and heed the teaching of the Bible, we will find ourselves enslaved, both morally and spiritually. True freedom only comes to those who listen to God's Word and respond with faith. Jesus put it this way: "If you abide in my word, you are truly my disciples, and you will know the truth, and the truth will set you free" (John 8:31, 32).

"For freedom Christ has set us free" (5:1). This is the gospel: sinners set free from sin, Satan, and themselves because of the life, death and resurrection of Jesus Christ.

And this is the key to gospel-rooted living: *listening to what the Bible says!* We must rely upon divine initiative, rejoice in divine power, and root out whatever might cause us to turn away from the life of faith, hope, and love.

For freedom Christ has set us free; stand firm therefore, and do not submit again to a yoke of slavery. Look: I, Paul, say to you that if you accept circumcision, Christ will be of no advantage to you. I testify again to every man who accepts circumcision that he is obligated to keep the whole law. You are severed from Christ, you who would be justified by the law; you have fallen away from grace. For through the Spirit, by faith, we ourselves eagerly wait for the hope of righteousness. For in Christ Jesus neither circumcision nor uncircumcision counts for anything, but only faith working through love.

5:1–6

20

What Ultimately Counts?

GALATIANS 5:1-6

FREEDOM IS THE CLARION CALL of Galatians because God wants you to be free. As Paul declares here at the outset of this passage, "For freedom Christ has set us free; stand firm therefore, and do not submit again to a yoke of slavery" (5:1).[1]

But freedom has an enemy. His name is Legalism, and he's a tyrant who would love nothing better than to have you bend your neck to his enslaving yoke.

What is legalism? A simple definition would be this: Legalism is treating that which is good as though it were essential. Whenever Christians turn something valuable into something ultimate, legalism is at work and freedom is forfeited.

On the other hand, we preserve our freedom in Christ when what is essential to God is essential to us, and everything else is kept in its place.

Many Christians come from legalistic backgrounds. They grew up in churches where it seemed like almost everything was ultimately important— except that which in fact was. They recall painful congregational meetings where individuals seemed just as incensed about a change in the music ministry or the color of the carpet in the fellowship hall as they did about the adulterous affair of the choir director or the pastor's tendency to soft-pedal substitutionary atonement. These are toxic places to be.

Yet legalism lurks in the shady corners of nearly every Christian community. This is why we can go for months, if not years, and never notice it's there. Legalism's lurking presence in our lives reminds me of a bizarre incident at one of the park district pools in the Chicago area. A nine-year-old boy went down a waterslide, plunged into the pool, and bumped into the dead body of a woman near the bottom of the pool. Much to everyone's horror and disgust, however, they discovered that the body had been in the pool for several days, even though the pool was open, lifeguards were on duty, and people were swimming. Health inspectors explained that because the pool was so murky no one could see the dead body submerged several feet under the surface.

A dead body lurking in the murky waters of a pool—that's the way legalism works in the life of a church and in the life of a Christian. This is because legalism lurks in the corners of every Christian heart. And it is often the case that the most susceptible are the most intensely religious.

Legalists lose sight of what ultimately counts. They start thinking that nonessentials are essential; they begin to insist that good things are in fact necessary. And the result is that they look with pity or suspicion on anyone who would think or do otherwise.

The Judaizers, the agitators, sought to convince the Galatians that circumcision ultimately counts. Paul doesn't tell us what they said to his Gentile converts. But with help from another Bible book we can assume their appeal sounded like this: "Unless you are circumcised according to the custom of Moses, you cannot be saved" (Acts 15:1). And evidently this tactic was persuasive enough to cause the Galatians to lose sight of what ultimately counts and want to get circumcised.

When You Lose Sight of What Ultimately Counts (5:2–4)

But what happens if you lose sight of what ultimately counts, allow legalism to set in, and slip back into slavery? Paul says quite plainly that we *lose Christ*. We lose the benefit of the blood that Christ shed for us (vv. 2, 3). Christ is no longer any advantage to us because we have sought spiritual benefit elsewhere.

The Galatians sought spiritual benefit from the act of circumcision. But Paul insists that if they embrace circumcision, they should go all the way and embrace "the whole law" (v. 3). That is, they should become Jews.[2]

But, Paul adds, if they do that, they in effect forsake the blessings of the new covenant, purchased with Christ's blood, and are left only with the provisions of the old covenant, living as if Christ had never been slain. "You are severed from Christ, you who would be justified by the law; you have fallen away from grace" (v. 4). We are then cut off from the life that Christ gives (v. 4a). We fall away from the grace that Christ offers (v. 4b).

If we try to do it all ourselves, we will be left to fend for ourselves. We won't have Christ's blood, we won't have Christ's life, and we won't have

Christ's grace. All we'll have is our sinful, silly, little, dissatisfied self, which isn't all that much comfort.

We know we've lost sight of what ultimately counts in the Christian life when we begin to lose the joy of living the Christian life. This is the telltale sign.

The Methodist movement began in the mid-eighteenth century with a small band of intensely devout students at the University of Oxford. These were towering figures like John and Charles Wesley and George Whitefield. They would meet regularly for study and devotion; they were known as the Holy Club because they practiced strict methods of increasing their spiritual zeal for God. Yet amid all the religious devotion and moral striving, these men had lost sight of what ultimately counts.

In fine, the Holy Club men knew little or nothing of grace as taught in the Scriptures. Their ironclad régime was one of human effort, that provided no assurance and left the all-important salvation of the soul a distant uncertainty. *Its practices brought little joy.* . . . These ardent men strove on and on, yet saw no point of arrival.[3]

Following his conversion, George Whitefield admitted how he'd gotten off track by losing sight of what ultimately counts: "God showed me that I must be born again, or be damned! I learned that a man may go to church, say his prayers, receive the sacrament, and yet not be a Christian."[4]

What Ultimately Counts—and What Doesn't (5:6)

We see, then, why nothing is more important than crystal clarity on what ultimately counts. We stand firm in freedom and avoid the spiritual slavery of legalism by maintaining laser focus on what ultimately matters. Whenever we lose sight of this, spiritual slavery is never far away.

Paul couldn't be more clear with the Galatians as to what ultimately counts—and what doesn't: "For in Christ Jesus neither circumcision nor uncircumcision counts for anything, but only faith working through love" (v. 6).

This is one of the most surprising arguments in this letter, if not in the whole Bible. Why? Because Paul just told the Galatians that if they get circumcised, they've fallen from grace! And yet the reason he gives for this dreadful possibility is not what one would expect: getting circumcised has such dire consequences not because circumcision is bad or sinful or stupid or old-fashioned. Rather, it's because circumcision ultimately doesn't matter!

When Paul says that neither circumcision nor uncircumcision counts for anything, he has a specific context in mind. Obviously, the Galatians might say in response, "Are you kidding? Circumcision counts a whole lot, Paul. You know that as well as we do!" But what Paul is envisioning is the effect of circumcision on *one's standing before God on the Last Day*.[5] And his powerfully provocative point is simply this: whether we're circumcised or uncircumcised, whether we're Jew or Gentile, won't make any difference on the day of judgment.

Here, then, is a revolutionary insight and a key to gospel-rooted living that we find in Galatians and the rest of Scripture: *what ultimately counts in this life is what ultimately matters on the day of judgment.*

And what will make a difference on the day of judgment? The very same thing that makes all the difference on the day we're justified—namely, *faith*.[6]

But the kind of faith that makes a difference on the day of judgment, indeed, the kind of faith that justifies, isn't what the demons possess: mere mental assent to the facts of the Christian faith (cf. James 2:19). Instead, it's the kind of faith that so trusts in Jesus that it inevitably expresses itself in love for both God and others. It's the kind of faith that is "working through love" (v. 6).

This is the *only* kind of faith that will count on the last day. This is the only thing that ultimately matters—faith in Christ expressed in love for God and others.

But why is this relevant to Bible-believing Christians? Because no earnest Christian is going to insist that what ultimately counts is stealing or lying or cheating or murder. But we might insist that water baptism ultimately counts, or our political views, or the kind of church we go to, or the view we hold on some interesting point of doctrine. Like those good Bible-believing Christians in Galatia, we are tempted to turn good things like circumcision and Biblical fidelity into ultimate things.

Neither premillennialism nor amillennialism ultimately counts, but only faith working through love. Neither Arminianism nor Calvinism ultimately counts, but only faith working through love. Neither Congregationalism nor Presbyterianism ultimately counts, but faith working through love. Neither traditional music nor contemporary music ultimately counts, but only faith working through love. Neither teetotaling nor enjoying a glass of wine ultimately counts, but faith working through love. Neither voting Republican nor voting Democrat ultimately counts, but faith working through love. Neither six-day young earth creationism nor old earth progressive creationism ultimately counts, but faith working through love. Neither pre-tribulational rapture nor post-tribulational or even mid-tribulational rapture ultimately counts, but faith working through love.

Now this is not to say you shouldn't care about these things. Nor does it mean these issues are unimportant. Not at all! Instead it means we must realize these things are important only insofar as they promote faith and produce love. If they don't, then we're missing what ultimately counts; for if we have not love, we gain nothing (1 Corinthians 13:3).

It's critical, then, for Christians to live with the end always in mind. Not only because the day of judgment will be the biggest day of our lives, but also because it has a way of putting everything else in proper perspective. In fact, I suspect the less we think about the final judgment, the more we're tempted to treat what's good as though it were ultimate.

So whenever we're tempted to turn something good into something ultimate, we should ask ourselves the question, what good will this do at the final judgment? We must apply the "faith working through love" test to everything we believe and everything we do. This will help us stand firm in freedom and avoid submitting to a yoke of spiritual slavery or legalism.

Living in Light of What Ultimately Counts (5:5)

Living in light of the final judgment may sound distressing to some. But here's the good news: doing so paves the way to greater and greater freedom, the kind of unhindered spiritual vitality Paul himself enjoys, and to which he testifies with these words: "For through the Spirit, by faith, we ourselves eagerly wait for the hope of righteousness" (v. 5).[7]

What ultimately counts is what puts us in right relationship with God. Paul has a very special word for this: *righteousness*. This is Paul's way of referring to those who are rightly related to God: they are righteous.

The Bible says righteousness is something a person receives now. But the Bible also says that righteousness is something for which we hope for the future; as Paul says here, "We ourselves eagerly wait for the hope of righteousness" (v. 5). Don't mistakenly conclude from this, however, that someone who hopes for righteousness cannot at the same time already have received righteousness.[8]

We often treat good things as though they were ultimate things. Why? Because we're hoping that it will enhance our relationship with God. Whenever we take something good and begin to think that it puts us into a right relationship with God, we are in dangerous territory. What the Bible says is that God puts us into right relationship with him when we place our faith in Jesus Christ—and him alone.

How then shall we live now in light of what ultimately counts then? Like Paul, we eagerly wait for God to work. For we realize only God can establish and secure and improve our relationship with him. And so we wait, not with resignation, but expectation.

Which is why we live *by faith*, trusting in God's promises.

And why we live *through the Spirit*, relying upon God's power.

Here's where we see such a stark contrast with the way of the legalist. For when we think of a legalist, we don't think of someone filled with hope, eagerly waiting for God to work, trusting in the promises of Jesus, and relying upon the power of the Spirit. Instead we think of someone who worries rather than waits, someone who strives rather than rests, someone who depends upon his own resources rather than resting in the sufficiency of Jesus.

What Ultimately Counts to Us?

British historian Paul Johnson says Winston Churchill did more for humanity than any other figure of the twentieth century. "No man did more to preserve freedom and democracy and the values we hold dear in the West."[9]

But what, according to Johnson, was the key to Churchill's remarkable success as a statesmen, leader, and champion of freedom? *Knowing what counts.* "Churchill had an uncanny gift for getting priorities right."[10]

Do you know what ultimately counts, not only in this life, but on the last day? What are you prioritizing in your prayers? To what are you devoting your time and energy? In what have you placed your hope? What are you striving to see accomplished in your own life and the lives of others?

When your life is rooted in the gospel, you realize that *"faith working through love"* is what ultimately counts. This is what ultimately matters to God and what ultimately makes a difference on the day of judgment.

But does this ultimately count to you? It will then. But does it now?

You were running well. Who hindered you from obeying the truth? This persuasion is not from him who calls you. A little leaven leavens the whole lump. I have confidence in the Lord that you will take no other view, and the one who is troubling you will bear the penalty, whoever he is. But if I, brothers, still preach circumcision, why am I still being persecuted? In that case the offense of the cross has been removed. I wish those who unsettle you would emasculate themselves!

5:7–12

21

Free to Run

GALATIANS 5:7-12

I PLAYED SOCCER IN HIGH SCHOOL. On the whole I loved it. But I must admit I always dreaded tryouts, especially the first day. Tryouts always began the same way: a one-mile run in under six minutes. By the end of the season that was no problem. But in mid-August, after a lazy summer of lollygagging, I always found it a grueling experience!

Entering my senior year I was in particularly lousy shape. And I knew it. So I decided my only hope of finishing at the front of the pack—and persuading the coaches that I was in good shape—was to get off to a quick start and then pray that momentum would carry me across the finish line.

So that's what I did. The whistle blew, signaling the start, and I bolted to the front of the pack on lap one. On lap two I was still in front. By lap three I was fatiguing, my heart was pounding, my legs were weakening. By lap three-and-a-half, others began to pass me. And what began as a trickle of runners turned into a deluge! By lap four I'd slowed to the point that nearly everyone was blazing by! And by the time I finished lap six and staggered across the finish line, I found myself at the back of the pack.

It was a humiliating experience. And despite being one of the stronger players on the team, this pathetic first-day effort nearly cost me a place on the team.

But it also taught me an immensely valuable lesson. You can start well, yet not finish well. You can bluff your way through a few laps, but if you're not in shape, you won't be able to sustain the pace you need to finish the race.

This even happens to professing Christians. They start well but don't finish well. Sometimes they don't even finish. Jesus was familiar with this problem, recognizing there are people who receive the Word with joy, make an enthusiastic profession of faith, yet eventually fall away. They're rootless, Jesus says, and thus won't endure (cf. Matthew 13:20, 21).

Paul is worried this is happening to the Galatians. "You were running well," he says. "Who hindered you from obeying the truth?" (5:7). They'd gotten off to a good start, but something had gone terribly wrong. They'd stopped running the race; or at least they weren't running well, running with strength, running to finish.

Perhaps that's where some of us are. When we first heard the gospel, we received it with joy and got off to a great start. But over time, as the race continued, we found ourselves running out of gas. Perhaps someone or something has gotten in our way, making it more difficult for us to run with endurance the race set before us.

The Christian Life Is a Race

The Christian life is a race. There's a beginning and an end. There's also a path on which to run, and a prize to obtain.

The beginning of the Christian race is, of course, conversion. The end or finish line is the final judgment. And the prize? Well, it's nothing less than eternal life itself, what the Bible refers to as "the crown of life," held out for those who endure all the way to the end (James 1:12).[1]

What is the path on which we run? That's the gospel. What God has done in Christ Jesus to free sinners from their bondage to sin—this is the track. The Christian life, then, is a gospel race. Or as John Bunyan says in his classic allegory *The Pilgrim's Progress*, it is the "race of saints in this our Gospel-day."[2]

Yet what does it mean to run this race? Here's where Paul's answer may come as a surprise: believers run the race by obeying the truth of the gospel (5:7). The track is gospel truth, and obedience to it is how we run.

Free to Finish (5:9, 12)

Through the gospel God sets us free to run the race. "For freedom Christ has set us free" (5:1). Yet the truth is, we have an uncanny way of allowing certain things to jeopardize our freedom and compromise our ability to run.

Imagine running the Boston Marathon with a suitcase in one hand, a duffel bag in the other, and a sixty-pound backpack draped over your shoulders. You'd never finish. Those unnecessary weights would make it impossible to run. That's what unaddressed sin in our lives is like; it undermines our ability to run the race set before us. Thus we need to lay aside such weights—the love of money, the lust of the eyes, the pride of life, covetousness, an unforgiving spirit.

Hindrances can undermine our race altogether. Some are caused by our own sin. Believers are challenged to "lay aside every weight, and sin which clings so closely" in order to "run with endurance the race that is set before us" (Hebrews 12:1).

But the Bible says that not only our own sin but *other people* can actually hinder us from running the race. This is what happened to the Galatians. Others have stepped onto the track and are troubling the Galatians, boxing them in, causing them to veer away from their original obedience to the truth.

Paul recognizes that the Galatians have been knocked off course. But he wants them to know that this isn't God's doing because he never undercuts his own runners. He may introduce a few surprising twists and turns, but he is not the one who hinders us from running the race. As Paul reminds the Galatians, "This persuasion is not from him who calls you" (5:8).

Instead a small group of people within the church is corrupting the whole. They've boxed the Galatians in and are disrupting their race, hindering them from finishing well.

At the 1938 NCAA Championships in Minneapolis, Louie Zamperini was the man to beat. Coaches from rival schools had even ordered their runners to sharpen the spikes on their shoes and to slash Louie. "Halfway through the race, just as Louie was about to move ahead for the lead, several runners shouldered around him, boxing him in. Louie tried repeatedly to break loose, but he couldn't get around the other men. Suddenly, the man beside him swerved in and stomped on his foot, impaling Louie's toe with his spike. A moment later, the man ahead began kicking backward, cutting both of Louie's shins. A third man elbowed Louie's chest so hard that he cracked Louie's rib."[3]

This is what the Judaizers, the agitators, were doing to the Galatians. They had come onto the track and surrounded the Galatians; they had boxed them in. They were stomping on their feet, slashing at their shins, even elbowing them in the chest, perhaps breaking a few ribs. And Paul recognizes that there's no way the Galatians will finish the race set before them if they don't break free of the agitators' influence. But the only way they're going to break free is by removing this hindrance from their midst.

That's why Paul quotes the proverb, "A little leaven leavens the whole lump" (v. 9). Not only does he want the Galatians to realize the source of their defection—he also wants to them to take bold action to deal with it. And bold action is what that proverb implies. Paul uses this proverb on only one other occasion, and there the point is clear. "Your boasting is not good. Do you not know that a little leaven leavens the whole lump? Cleanse out the old leaven that you may be a new lump, as you really are unleavened" (1 Corinthians

5:6, 7). So desirous, in fact, is Paul that he finally simply wishes the agitators would disqualify themselves: "I wish those who unsettle you would emasculate themselves!" (v. 12).

Some of us need to lay aside a few weights; we're carrying around some heavy bags. We're having difficulty running the Christian race because unaddressed sin in our lives is easily entangling us. If we feel a lack of energy and vitality, it may well be because we're struggling to run under the undue weight of unconfessed sin.

For others of us, a certain individual in our life is hindering our obedience to the truth. We need to remember that "a little leaven leavens the whole lump." What's true of churches is also true for individual Christians. A little bad influence can do great damage to our ability to run the race. We need to put some distance between us and that person; we need to have a blunt conversation with him or her; we may even need to part ways to avoid being weighed down any further by that person's influence.

Even When We're Free, It Still Won't Be Easy (5:11)

As we lay aside unnecessary weights and remove the hindrances in our way, we'll find ourselves running faster and faster and faster, with greater and greater strength and confidence.

But don't think this means the challenges to finishing the race will all disappear. They won't. In fact, what we often find is that the faster and faster we run, the more and more pushback we'll receive.

No one ran faster or with greater abandonment and focus than the Apostle Paul. "But I do not account my life of any value nor as precious to myself, if only I may finish my course and the ministry that I received from the Lord Jesus, to testify to the gospel of the grace of God" (Acts 20:24).

At the same time no one experienced more pushback than Paul, and he reminds the Galatians of this very thing: "But if I, brothers, still preach circumcision, why am I still being persecuted? In that case the offense of the cross has been removed" (v. 11). Paul is in essence saying to them, "Even when you're free to run, as I am, it still won't be easy. Even when the hindrances are removed from your own life or from within the church, you'll still face hostility from outsiders. Even if you're not running with unnecessary weights, and even if others aren't cutting in on you and blocking your way, you'll nevertheless have the jeering of the crowds to contend with."

The pushback, Paul says, never goes away if you're faithful to the gospel and the cross of Christ. The only way to remove all pushback is to stop obeying the gospel. Paul knows if he removes the offense of the cross of Christ, he can stop all pushback against him. But if he does that, he destroys the gospel—and will destroy his own soul, having run and labored in vain.

Running and Resting (5:10)

But the pushback shouldn't cause us to fret or worry or lose hope or quit before we've gone too far. Nor should this undermine our assurance or our confidence, either toward ourselves or toward others. Instead a Biblical perspective on the Christian life as a race would suggest this: *as you run the race, rest confidently in the Lord.* "I have confidence in the Lord that you will take no other view [than mine]" (v. 10).

God is able to sustain us all the way to the end. He is able to pour grace into our hearts in such a way that we remain "steadfast, immovable, always abounding in the work of the Lord" (1 Corinthians 15:58), even to our last breath. God is also able to deal with those who might want to keep us from finishing the race; this is also a part of Paul's confidence in the Lord about the Galatians: "The one who is troubling you will bear the penalty, whoever he is" (v. 10). Evidently Paul's not sure who all is responsible before God for the chaos that has erupted in Galatia, but he's nevertheless completely confident that God knows who's responsible and that he will most assuredly deal with that person.

Left to ourselves, we would be without hope of ever finishing the race. Apart from God, who could successfully complete the Christian life? Yet with a strong belief in the grace of God, we can rest confidently in the Lord, even as we run the race set before us with all endurance. And even when the setbacks come or we stumble along the way, we can still rest confidently in the Lord, knowing this: "He who began a good work in you will bring it to completion at the day of Jesus Christ" (Philippians 1:6). Or as Paul says to the Corinthians, "Our Lord Jesus Christ . . . will sustain you to the end, guiltless in the day of our Lord Jesus Christ. God is faithful, by whom you were called into the fellowship of his Son, Jesus Christ our Lord" (1 Corinthians 1:7–9). "He who calls you is faithful; he will surely do it" (1 Thessalonians 5:24).

We can start well, yet not finish well. Left to ourselves, this *can* happen, but it *won't.* On our own we not only *could* fail to finish but most certainly would. However, because of the grace of God, this won't happen because God himself has pledged to keep us.

Confident runners are unhurried even when they're running at a lightning-fast pace. This has been true of great Olympic sprinters; when you watch the race in slow motion, they sometimes don't even look like they're trying. The have poise; there's a coolness to the look on their face; they don't look worried, much less anxious. This is a picture of how a Christian can run the race with endurance, resting confidently in the Lord.

Running the Race, Looking to Jesus

So we must learn to rest in the grace of God as it works powerfully within us to cause us to run the race with endurance to the end. We must learn to say with the Apostle Paul, "But by the grace of God I am what I am, and his grace toward me was not in vain. On the contrary, I worked harder than any of them, though it was not I, but the grace of God that is with me" (1 Corinthians 15:10).

If we're struggling to run well, then we must lean all the more on the God "who works in you, both to will and to work for his good pleasure" (Philippians 2:13). If we have stumbled and are struggling to return to our feet, we can cry out to "the God of all grace, who has called you to his eternal glory in Christ, [and who] will himself restore, confirm, strengthen, and establish you" (1 Peter 5:10, 11). We can also cry out to other runners to come alongside us to encourage us every day, so we can keep running the race.

But what if we've stopped running altogether? Consider the prize we're forfeiting: "Blessed is the man who remains steadfast under trial, for when he has stood the test he will receive the crown of life, which God has promised to those who love him" (James 1:12; cf. Revelation 2:10). May the sheer prospect of losing the reward of eternal life with God cause us to repent, return to the Lord, and return to the track of the gospel and the Christian life and "while the promise of entering [God's] rest still stands" cause us to "fear lest any of you should seem to have failed to reach it" (Hebrews 4:1).

Finally, we run the race by looking to Jesus. "Therefore, since we are surrounded by so great a cloud of witnesses, let us also lay aside every weight, and sin which clings so closely, and let us run with endurance the race that is set before us, *looking to Jesus*, the founder and perfecter of our faith, who for the joy that was set before him endured the cross, despising the shame, and is seated at the right hand of the throne of God" (Hebrews 12:1, 2).

The Lord Jesus Christ has already crossed the finish line. And now, having finished his race, Jesus Christ is "crowned with glory and honor" (Hebrews 2:9). And he is coming again, "conquering, and to conquer" (Revelation 6:2). We who want to finish the race set before us must therefore fix our gaze upon him who has gone before us.

Looking to Jesus is the key to finishing the race set before us. Jesus is the source of our freedom to run free; he is the model of what it means to finish the race; he is the focus of our gaze as we make our way through this life; he is the source of motivation because he holds out to us the prize, the crown of life;

and he is the one who can work in us that which is pleasing in his sight—the intentionality, endurance, and exertion we need to complete the race.

Then, by the grace of God and all because of Jesus, we will be able one day to say with the Apostle Paul:

> I have fought the good fight, I have finished the race, I have kept the faith. Henceforth there is laid up for me the crown of righteousness, which the Lord, the righteous judge, will award to me on that Day, and not only to me but also to all who have loved his appearing. (2 Timothy 4:7, 8)

For you were called to freedom, brothers. Only do not use your freedom as an opportunity for the flesh, but through love serve one another. For the whole law is fulfilled in one word: "You shall love your neighbor as yourself." But if you bite and devour one another, watch out that you are not consumed by one another.

5:13–15

22

Through Love Serve One Another

GALATIANS 5:13–15

SOME MESSES ARE WORTH MAKING, but some aren't. Turning your kitchen into a disaster zone to put on dinner for close friends, that's a mess worth making. Letting your two-year-old finger-paint on the dining room table— that's probably not a mess worth making!

Church is often a messy place, but it's a mess worth making. At least God thinks so. The Church is the precious blood-bought bride of Christ (Ephesians 5:25) and now the means by which God is displaying his "manifold wisdom" in the heavenly places (Ephesians 3:10). Clearly, God is convinced the church is a mess worth making!

Unfortunately, many Christians aren't. They'd prefer church to be a mess-free zone and are easily upset when they see the mess that's so often a part of this messy business we call church.

But as Timothy S. Lane and Paul David Tripp rightly point out in their excellent book *Relationships: A Mess Worth Making*, "While we would like to avoid the mess and enjoy deep and intimate community, God says that it is in the very process of working through the mess that intimacy [and true community] is found."[1]

So if we truly desire meaningful Christian community, the question we must ask ourselves is this: how do we work our way through the mess?

The churches of Galatia had made a real mess of things. And Paul writes this letter to help them sort through the mess, both Biblically and theologically. He does this in the first four and a half chapters. But then in 5:13—6:10, the so-called "ethical section" of the letter,[2] he turns more practical and provides the Galatians with specific instructions as to how to work through the mess in which they find themselves. And as students of Galatians recognize, this concluding section of the letter is "the crux for understanding Galatians as a whole."[3]

The opening few verses of this section of Galatians identify the key to working successfully through the mess we call church: "Through love serve one another" (v. 13). But Paul surrounds this call to love with words intended to motivate the Galatians in that often difficult and sacrificial path. First, a reminder (v. 13a), second, a warning (vv. 13b, 15), and, third, an encouragement (v. 14). Each is meant to stir up the Galatians—and us—to serve one another in love, the very thing Paul believes will enable the Galatians to find their way through their current crisis.

Free from Yourself, Free for One Another

This passage reminds us that *freedom is the foundation of life together*.[4] Neither human relationships nor human communities will flourish without being grounded in the freedom that Jesus Christ alone provides.

Americans tend to think of freedom primarily in political or economic terms. We live in a "free country," people will say, or we're living "debt-free."

Biblically speaking, however, freedom is essentially relational. You're free insofar as you're rightly related to God. Otherwise you're in moral and spiritual bondage, slavery to sin, regardless of whether you live in the United States or North Korea, the United Kingdom or Afghanistan. While we may feel like we are autonomous and free, each one of us is under the lordship of powers stronger than ourselves.[5]

On the other hand, the more vibrant and intimate your relationship with God, the more freedom you enjoy.

We were called to freedom when God called us into relationship with himself through his Son Jesus Christ. When God calls us to himself, he frees us from ourselves.[6] Apart from this powerful and effectual call in our lives, we are enslaved to ourselves. We are enslaved to what the Bible calls "the flesh."[7] The flesh is the fallen self. This is the self turned in upon itself. And we experience our fallen self every single day, every single hour; sometimes it can feel like every single moment.

We experience the fallen self or the flesh in the unruly passions and illicit desires that we find coursing through our bodies. In this section of Galatians Paul talks about "the desires of the flesh" (5:16); a few verses later he refers to "the flesh with its passions and desires" (5:24).

Now the flesh wouldn't be nearly as lethal if it would only keep to itself.

But the flesh is forever busy acting up and acting out in what Paul calls "the works of the flesh": specific behaviors that run contrary to God's will and undermine human community. Paul mentions a number of them in verses 19–21, but he's clearly interested in directing the Galatians' attention to the eight vices he clusters together in the middle of this longer list: namely, "enmity, strife, jealousy, fits of anger, rivalries, dissensions, divisions, envy" (vv. 20, 21).[8]

How does God call us to freedom? He calls us to freedom by calling us to himself and by uniting us to his Son.

Abusing Freedom Is a Dead End

While the flesh has been crucified, it is not entirely gone. When God calls us to himself through the gospel and unites our lives to the life of his crucified and risen Son, our flesh is summarily executed. This liberating spiritual reality is what we celebrate in the line of that great hymn of Charles Wesley: "He breaks the power of canceled sin, he sets the prisoner free." We become free only by being executed: our sinful, fallen self is crucified with Jesus Christ.

But here's the challenge: even though the flesh is crucified, it is not altogether eliminated. We still live in sinful, fallen bodies, and we still inhabit the sinful, fallen world. Therefore, although we eagerly await "the freedom of the glory of the children of God" (Romans 8:21), we all still live in "the present evil age" (Galatians 1:4).

As a result the flesh is constantly looking for an opportunity not only to invade our lives and take back control of what's been lost, but also to wage war in us and through us into the lives of other people. The flesh is the sworn enemy of relationships and community; self-centered passions and desires are what wreak all the havoc in our relationships. And the flesh is always looking for a beachhead in our lives, which can then become a base of operations from which the flesh can work to undermine every single one of our relationships, whether with God or with our spouse or with our children or with our employer or neighbor or roommate or classmate.

The flesh is utterly ruthless and will seize every opportunity we give it. It's always with us, and the world around us is always encouraging us to let down our defenses and let it gain ground.

In what ways do we give the flesh an opportunity to establish a beachhead or a base of operations in our lives? Here are some of the most common:

- We provide opportunity for the flesh when we coddle an unforgiving spirit or harbor a grudge toward another person.
- We provide opportunity for the flesh when we fail to overlook minor offenses. As fallen, sinful human beings, we continually throw pebbles

into one another's path. That's inevitable. But Proverbs 19:11 says it is wisdom to overlook an offense. And yet because our flesh is so vain and proud, it is easily offended—often by even the slightest little thing!

- We provide opportunity for the flesh when we allow ourselves to put a negative spin on the actions of others. In that magnificent celebration of love found in 1 Corinthians 13, the Apostle Paul says that love "believes all things" (v. 7).

- We provide opportunity for the flesh when we indulge ourselves in speaking negatively about others. "Do not speak evil against one another, brothers" (James 4:11). "Let no corrupting talk come out of your mouths, but only such as is good for building up, as fits the occasion, that it may give grace to those who hear" (Ephesians 4:29). It is in view of passages like these that Dietrich Bonhoeffer came to the following bold conclusion: "Thus it must be a decisive rule of all Christian community life that each individual is prohibited from talking about another Christian in secret." Why? As he says, "Often we combat our evil thoughts [i.e., the flesh] most effectively if we absolutely refuse to allow them to be verbalized."[9] He then offers this encouragement: "Where this discipline of the tongue is practiced right from the start, individuals will make an amazing discovery. They will be able to stop constantly keeping an eye on others, judging them, condemning them, and putting them in their places and thus doing violence to them. They can now allow other Christians to live freely, just as God has brought them face to face with each other."[10]

- We provide opportunity for the flesh when we engage in conversation with those who are negative or when we continue in conversation when the conversation turns negative. Conversations can turn negative in various ways, as soon as one of those respectable little vices of the tongue shows up on the scene, things like gossip, critical speech, harsh words, insults, sarcasm, ridicule.[11] We also, frankly, need to avoid negative people. Even some believers are chronically negative; they consistently spew criticism or harsh words or sarcasm. As a result it's tough to be around them without coming away feeling oily and dirty, as if somehow we've been defiled. Pray for those folks. Seek to build them up in love. But as a rule avoid going out for coffee with them.

- We provide opportunity for the flesh when we fail to deal with our personal grievances swiftly and directly. In Ephesians 4 we find the instruction, "Be angry and do not sin; do not let the sun go down on your anger" (v. 26). But notice what Paul adds: "And give no opportunity to the devil" (v. 27). When we are slow to deal with our personal grievances, we give not only the flesh but the devil himself an opportunity to make inroads into our lives and into our communities. We must deal with personal grievances swiftly. But we also need to deal with them directly— that is, person-to-person and, whenever possible, face-to-face. Here is where we all need to be much more cautious about using technologies for communication. I have come to the conclusion that email is a high-speed landing craft for the flesh, and I'm increasingly convinced that we would all be far better off if we committed to never deliver any bad news to anyone by means of email but only face-to-face, or if that's impossible, by telephone, and if that's impossible, by a handwritten letter. It's far too easy to dehumanize the person we're addressing when all we have of that person's presence is his or her name in the address bar of the email we're ready to fire off.

These are six common ways we give the flesh an opportunity to gain influence in our lives and, through us, into the lives of those around us. These are the ways in which the Evil One destroys relationships and kills communities. If we stopped doing these six things, that would change the culture of our churches overnight. It would raise the spiritual temperature of our congregations massively.

When the flesh takes over within the life of a church, that community can quickly become a chapter out of *The Lord of the Flies*.

My family has both a dog and a cat. Big mistake. All they do is fight. Clemmie, our dog, can't see Brooklyn, our cat, without chasing her around the house, nipping at her along the way. Now I understand more fully the expression, "They fight like cats and dogs." Sadly, our churches sometimes bear a sad resemblance to our quarreling pets.

Fulfilling the Law, Foreshadowing Heaven

When we abuse our freedom, we lose our freedom. By turning freedom into an opportunity for the flesh, we become not more free but more enslaved to our own selfish passions and desires. But more than that, we let the flesh make inroads into our lives and into our relationships.

This is why it is so important to be vigilant in guarding against the flesh. We should put up rows of barbed wire, bury landmines, build gun turrets, mount missile defenses, and put in high-tech radar and alarm systems.

This passage reminds us that freedom is the foundation of community. Therefore, we should not abuse that freedom by pursuing our own self-centered passions and desires, but rather "through love serve one another."

This passage seeks to motivate us to serve one another, first, by offering a powerful incentive to loving service of one another and, second, by giving us a sober warning about what happens when we fail to serve one another that way.

The Apostle Paul says an astonishing thing to the Galatians: by serving one another through love, they in fact fulfill the whole Law. This is because, as Paul says, "The whole law is fulfilled in one word: 'You shall love your neighbor as yourself'" (5:14; cf. Leviticus 19:18).

What an astonishing thing for the apostle to say! And what an encouraging—and motivating—thing for the Galatians to hear! No doubt, the Galatians worried about their own standing vis-à-vis the Jewish law; this is why they were considering circumcision, to make sure they were doing God's will, which the Judaizers were telling them was to be found in observing the Old Testament Law, which includes circumcision.[12]

I want to conclude this study by pointing us to Heaven. Heaven is the "world of love," as Jonathan Edwards called it, that final resting place where we will at last be free from the desires and works of the flesh forever and will therefore dwell with one another in perfect loving service, joy, and delight forever and ever.

> Oh! what tranquility will there be in such a world as this! And who can express the fullness and blessedness of this peace! What a calm is this! How sweet, and holy, and joyous! What a haven of rest to enter, after having passed through the storms and tempests of this world, in which pride, and selfishness, and envy, and malice, and scorn, and contempt, and contention, and vice, are as waves of a restless ocean, always rolling, and often dashed about in violence and fury!
>
> And oh! what joy will there be, springing up in the hearts of the saints, after they have passed through their wearisome pilgrimage, to be brought to such a paradise as this!
>
> Every saint in heaven is as a flower in that garden of God, and holy love is the fragrance and sweet odour that they all send forth, and with which they fill the bowers of that paradise above. Every soul there, is as a note in some concert of delightful music, that sweetly harmonizes with every other note, and all together blend in the most rapturous strains in praising God and the Lamb forever. And so all help each other, to their utmost, to express the love of the whole society to its glorious Father and Head, and to pour back love into the great fountain of love whence they are supplied and filled with love, and blessedness, and glory. And thus they will love, and reign in love, and in that godlike joy that is its blessed fruit, such as eye hath not seen, nor ear heard, nor hath ever entered into the heart of man in this world to conceive; and thus in the full sunlight of the throng, enraptured with joys that are forever increasing, and yet forever full, they shall live and reign with God and Christ forever and ever![13]

But do you know what is the best thing to do to keep the flesh at bay? What is most effective is doing the exact opposite: rather than giving in to the desires and passions to protect and promote the self, instead we "through love serve one another" (v. 13c).

But how do we do this? There are many ways in which we can serve one another through love.

We serve one another through love when we pray for one another. This is a vital and yet often overlooked way of serving one another. "Pray for one another" (James 5:16). We should be praying for our church body in general but also praying for specific people within the body. It is nearly impossible to harbor negative feelings toward someone we pray for regularly.

We serve one another through love when we bear with one another. "I therefore, a prisoner for the Lord, urge you to walk in a manner worthy of the calling to which you have been called . . . bearing with one another in love" (Ephesians 4:1, 2). This means deciding to overlook offenses and not let them trip us up. This means letting go of the ways in which others have injured us rather than carrying them around. This means, in sum, heeding Peter's challenge: "Above all, keep loving one another earnestly, since love covers a multitude of sins" (1 Peter 4:8).

We serve one another through love when we encourage one another with edifying words. "Let no corrupting talk come out of your mouths," writes the Apostle Paul in Ephesians 4, "but only such as is good for building up, as fits the occasion, that it may give grace to those who hear" (v. 29). Let's strive to be a community that outspeaks the negative 10 to 1.

We serve one another through love when we esteem those who are over us in the Lord. "We ask you, brothers, to respect those who labor among you and are over you in the Lord and admonish you, and to esteem them very highly in love because of their work" (1 Thessalonians 5:12, 13). It might sound self-serving for a pastor to quote this verse to his congregation (as I did to mine). But note what Paul says next: "Be at peace among yourselves" (1 Thessalonians 5:13). Could it be that the peace of a church body is directly related to the esteem that body shows toward its leadership? I believe that is what the Word of God is saying to us.

We serve one another through love when we count others more significant than ourselves. "So if there is any encouragement in Christ, any comfort from love, any participation in the Spirit, any affection and sympathy, complete my joy by being of the same mind, having the same love, being in full accord and of one mind. Do nothing from selfish ambition or conceit, but in humility count others more significant than yourselves. Let each of you look not only to his own interests, but also to the interests of others" (Philippians 2:1–4). This is the mind of Christ.

Conclusion: The Mind of Christ

Martin Luther said it so well: "Each of us should become a Christ to the other. And as we are Christs to one another, the result is that Christ fills us all and we become a truly Christian community."[14]

"Through love [we] serve one another." Yet I suspect everyone realizes that love is not all that easy to come by. Love points not to ourselves but away from ourselves. It occurs only "through the Spirit, by faith" (5:5).

"We love because he first loved us" (1 John 4:19). Faith is our response to the gracious love of God displayed in the death and resurrection of our Savior, Jesus Christ. And as faith is born in our hearts, so too God causes his own love to be shed abroad in our hearts as well (Romans 5:5).

There is no one more free than the Lord Jesus Christ. Yet there is no one who is a greater servant of mankind than the God-man, Jesus Christ, "who, though he was in the form of God, did not count equality with God a thing to be grasped, but emptied himself, by taking the form of a servant" (Philippians 2:6, 7). It is this mind—the mind of Christ—that each one of us is to have.

But not only are we to imitate the example of Christ—we are also to live with one another in light of the work of Christ. We are to treat one another with grace and mercy because we have been treated that way by Christ. We are to walk by the power of the Spirit of Christ, whom God has sent into our lives and who has shed his love abroad in our hearts. Thus the love with which we are called to love one another is none other than the love of God coursing through us toward others. And we are to live in light of the faith that God has given us as a free gift, faith that looks away from the self and toward Christ, faith that seeks satisfaction not in pursuit of one's own passions and desires but in the promises of God.

Some messes are worth making; some aren't. Church is one of those messes worth making. But the key is knowing how to work through the messes when they arise, which they inevitably will.

This passage calls us to work through the messes we make, whether in church or in life, by serving one another through love. "Therefore be imitators of God, as beloved children. And walk in love, as Christ loved us and gave himself up for us, a fragrant offering and sacrifice to God" (Ephesians 5:1, 2).

But I say, walk by the Spirit, and you will not gratify the desires of the flesh. For the desires of the flesh are against the Spirit, and the desires of the Spirit are against the flesh, for these are opposed to each other, to keep you from doing the things you want to do. But if you are led by the Spirit, you are not under the law. Now the works of the flesh are evident: sexual immorality, impurity, sensuality, idolatry, sorcery, enmity, strife, jealousy, fits of anger, rivalries, dissensions, divisions, envy, drunkenness, orgies, and things like these. I warn you, as I warned you before, that those who do such things will not inherit the kingdom of God. But the fruit of the Spirit is love, joy, peace, patience, kindness, goodness, faithfulness, gentleness, self-control; against such things there is no law. And those who belong to Christ Jesus have crucified the flesh with its passions and desires. If we live by the Spirit, let us also keep in step with the Spirit. Let us not become conceited, provoking one another, envying one another.

5:16–26

23

The Sufficiency
of the Spirit

GALATIANS 5:16–26

THE CHURCH IS A MESS WORTH MAKING. The only question is, how can we work our way through the mess? The answer we find in Galatians is counterintuitive: we work through the relational messes by leaning into love; or as Paul says, "Through love serve one another" (5:13).

But that's easier said than done. What if we don't want to love people in the midst of the mess? What if we don't have any desire to love others, no motivation? It's not easy to serve others, even on a good day, much less in the midst of a mess, when harsh words have been spoken, thoughtless comments made, and sides taken. What do we do then, especially when biting and devouring others comes much more naturally and, in the moment, can feel much more satisfying?

Scripture's answer to these questions is at first blush discouraging: We don't have the ability to love others as we ought. We're constantly tempted, however, to think we can muster the necessary moral resources we need to love others well. But the fact is, greater moral resolve won't get us there. Nor will our redoubled effort at sincerity and good intentions.

On the other hand, the Bible's answer is thoroughly encouraging because the Bible teaches us that love comes from outside us. "God is love" (1 John 4:8).

Love, then, comes from God, through the Holy Spirit. And unless God, as Paul says elsewhere, pours his love into our hearts through the Holy Spirit, we will not be able to love others as we ought, at least not in any robust or truly Biblical sense.

Serving one another through love becomes, therefore, all about the Spirit: relying upon the Spirit to work in our hearts, so that we can be who God calls us to be for each other and the world. Or to put it in terms of the flow of thought in Galatians, we won't be able to do what 5:13–15 calls us to without the reality to which Paul points in 5:16–26.

Setting forth the sufficiency of the Spirit is Paul's purpose in this passage. He wants to convince the Galatians of the Spirit's inexhaustible power and thus inspire them to rely wholly upon the Spirit in the nitty-gritty of their daily lives.

This is the secret to the Galatians' success in moving forward in the midst of the mess; it's also the secret to our moving forward through whatever mess we find ourselves in. Like the Galatians, we too must "walk by the Spirit" (5:16), be "led by the Spirit" (5:18), and "sow to the Spirit" (6:8). In short, believers must be utterly convinced that we do indeed "live by the Spirit" and must therefore walk by the Spirit (5:16, 25).

Sufficient to Overcome the Flesh (5:16, 17)

Paul begins by drawing our attention to the sufficiency of the Spirit to overcome the flesh. "But I say, walk by the Spirit, and you will not gratify the desires of the flesh" (v. 16).

Now, this is an amazing promise! Victory over the flesh in the warfare of daily life! Indeed, the original Greek is even stronger than the English.[1] What Paul in effect wants to say is this: "If you walk by the Spirit, you will in no way, not a chance, absolutely not fulfill the desires of the flesh!" In our fight against the flesh, Paul's confidence in the Spirit is boundless!

Of course, the flesh is strong. We know from many a painful experience how potent is the flesh with its "passions and desires" (5:24). But we must nevertheless fully believe that the Spirit is stronger still and that the Spirit will most certainly ensure our victory over the flesh.

But, to be sure, this isn't baseless confidence. As Paul explains, the Spirit's victory over the flesh is hard fought for. "For the desires of the flesh are against the Spirit, and the desires of the Spirit are against the flesh, for these are opposed to each other, to keep you from doing the things you want to do" (v. 17).

Although the precise point of this puzzling verse continues to elude interpreters, the thrust of what Paul wants to say is clear enough: the mutual antagonism between the flesh and the Spirit doesn't end in a stalemate. The Spirit is the victor, and if we yield to the Spirit, we'll find we ourselves will triumph over the flesh.

Hence, resisting the flesh isn't about willpower, but the Spirit's empowerment. In fact, it's not even about our overcoming the desires of the flesh with the Spirit's help. Rather, the Spirit wins the victory; we simply march under his banner (cf. 5:25).

How confident are we of the sufficiency of the Spirit? Christians are often as confident in the Spirit as they are in the weather forecast, believing both to be too mysterious and unpredictable to merit much confidence.

We can ask ourselves these questions: When we find ourselves frustrated by the desires of the flesh, how do we avoid discouragement? What keeps us engaged in the fight against the flesh, striving against a short temper or bitterness, jealousy, indulgent desires, gluttony, lust, or despondency? Sad is the Christian who has signed a truce with his sin because he has so little confidence in the Spirit.

Sufficient to Avoid the Curse (5:18–21)

The Spirit is sufficient not only in our daily battle against the flesh, but also in our pursuit of entrance into the kingdom of God. For when the Spirit frees us from the flesh, he keeps us from God's judgment. Or, in Paul's own words, "If you are led by the Spirit, you are not under the law" (v. 18).

This is the fifth and final use of the phrase "under the law" in Galatians, and as we've seen elsewhere in this letter, we have good reason to suppose that Paul uses this phrase as shorthand for "under the curse of the law" (cf. 3:23; 4:4, 5, 21).[2] Hence, Paul is referring to the Spirit's ability to enable us to avoid divine judgment.

Paul's point, then, is that while those who practice the works of the flesh are under a curse and will therefore not inherit "the kingdom of God" (5:19–21), those who exhibit "the fruit of the Spirit" are not under a curse and can therefore expect to inherit "the kingdom of God" (5:22, 23; cf. 5:5, 6). Hence, in 5:19–23 Paul elaborates the thesis-like statement of 5:18 that those who are led by the Spirit are not under the curse of the Law. He begins in 5:19–21 by explicating the converse of the conditional statement of 5:18: those who practice the works of the flesh are under a curse and will therefore not inherit "the kingdom of God" (5:21b).[3]

In other words, if the Galatians do not follow the leading of the Spirit, they can expect a curse and, as a result, exclusion from the eschatological inheritance. Alternatively, in 5:22, 23 Paul further explicates the conditional statement of 5:18 itself: those who are "led by the Spirit" (5:18) and exhibit "the fruit of the Spirit" (5:22, 23a) are not under a curse (5:23b) and will thus receive an eschatological reward (cf. 6:7, 8).

Paul wants to assure the Galatians that the leading of the Spirit and love, which is the chief mark of the Spirit (cf. 5:22; 5:5, 6), are sufficient to enable them to avoid the curse of the law (5:18; 5:23b). If the Galatians follow the leading of the Spirit, they need not entertain any doubts about the Law's curse. If they succumb, however, to "the desires of the flesh" (5:16) and manifest its works (5:19–21), which is what they appear to be doing (5:15, 26), Paul can only warn them that they will be excluded from "the kingdom of God" (5:21b; cf. Matthew 25:41).

While it is important to stress Paul's emphasis upon providing the Galatians with present assurances about the Spirit's ability to enable them to avoid the Law's curse, we should not let this overshadow Paul's equally strong interest in warning the Galatians about the consequences of succumbing to the flesh and its desires. The centralized warning in 5:21b underscores this point,[4] as do a number of similar warnings elsewhere in 5:13—6:10 (cf. 5:13b, 15, 21, 26; 6:7, 8).

There is an irony in this dual aspect of warning and assurance in this passage. On the one hand, Paul assures the Galatians that the leading of the Spirit will enable them to avoid the curse of the Law (5:18, 23b). On the other hand, he warns them, at least implicitly, that the works of the flesh will only be met with the Law's curse and thus exclusion from "the kingdom of God" (5:21b).

Hence, while the Galatians were attracted to circumcision at least in part as a way to ensure that they would avoid coming under a curse, Paul warns them that unless they get back on track with following the leading of the Spirit, that which they are trying to avoid will be the very thing that comes upon them: the curse of the Law.

While the immediate aim, then, of this passage is to call the Galatians to "walk by the Spirit" (5:16), this serves both to warn and to assure the Galatians about the curse of the Law: if they follow the leading of the Spirit, they are exempt from the Law's curse (5:18; 5:22, 23), whereas if they succumb to "the desires of the flesh" (5:16), they will come under a curse and face exclusion from "the kingdom of God" (5:19–21).

Sufficient to Fulfill the Law (5:22, 23)

The Spirit is sufficient, then, not only to enable us to avoid the curse of the Law but also *to empower us to fulfill the Law*. We fulfill the Law through love; this is the sum and substance of the whole Law, as Paul has already said (5:14; cf. Romans 13:8–10). And love is *the* very thing the Spirit creates in the life of the believer and in the believing community. Love is the chief of the Spirit's fruits. We see love mentioned first in the list of the fruit of the Spirit. "But the fruit of the Spirit is love, joy, peace, patience, kindness, goodness, faithfulness, gentleness, self-control; against such things there is no law" (5:22, 23). That's not only to give love pride of place as the most important fruit but also to suggest that love is itself a summation of all the other fruit. Love contains the whole of all that God desires and requires of us.[5]

This is why Paul can say so confidently about the fruit of the Spirit, "Against such things there is no law" (5:23). He is simply reiterating what he has already said in 5:18 about the leading of the Spirit. The Law is not against the fruit of the Spirit; indeed, the fruit of the Spirit—love—is the very thing for which the Law itself calls. Thus the leading of the Spirit produces the fruit of the Spirit, which is the fulfillment of the Law and thus avoids its curse.[6]

Love, then, ought to mark our lives as Christians. Indeed, love ought to be the hallmark of the Christian. We ought to be known by how we love one another—and the world. In fact, our love for one another is an indication of whether we're walking by the Spirit.

Love ought to mark the church as well. The church ought to be filled with the fruit of the Spirit. We ought to be like a garden, the garden of God, embodying the presence of the Spirit, recapturing the love that was present originally in the garden of Eden. And this garden-church ought to be filled with fruit, new-creation fruit born of the Spirit of God within the lives of his people. Thus the church ought to be an oasis in the midst of a barren wasteland, a place of nourishment and rest and healing and life smack-dab in the middle of this present evil age.[7]

Conclusion—Let Us Walk by the Spirit! (5:24–26)

But in order for love to mark our own lives or the lives of our congregations, we must draw upon the source of life, the Lord Jesus Christ. We must, then, learn to abide in Jesus Christ. As Jesus himself says, "Apart from me you can do nothing." He is the vine; we are the branches. And unless we abide in him, we cannot bear fruit. No branch can bear fruit of itself; it must draw its resource from the vine. And if we learn the secret of abiding in Jesus, he promises we will indeed bear much fruit to his Father's glory (John 15:1–5).

Hudson Taylor, who spent five decades serving the people of China with the gospel of Jesus Christ, experienced a great turning point in his life when he understood the spiritual secret of abiding in Jesus Christ. God used a letter from a friend of Taylor's to open his eyes to the secret of the Christian life.

> To let my loving Savior work in me his will, my sanctification, is what I would live for by his grace. Abiding, not striving nor struggling; looking

oft unto him; trusting him for present power . . . resting in the love of an almighty Savior, in the joy of a complete salvation, "from all sin"—this is not new, and yet 'tis new to me. I feel as though the dawning of a glorious day had risen upon me. I hail it with trembling, yet with trust. I seem to have got to the edge only, but of a boundless sea; to have sipped only, but of that which fully satisfies. Christ literally all seems to me, now, the power, the only power for service, the only ground for unchanging joy. . . . Not a striving to have faith . . . but a looking off to the Faithful One seems all we need; a resting in the Loved One entirely, for time and for eternity.[8]

The sufficiency of the Spirit and not ourselves—this ought to be the best news in the world for all of us. It ought to be especially sweet music in the ear of a few folks. I'm thinking especially of *tired legalists* who are convinced that Christianity is all about coloring within the lines. And it ought to be good news to *grumpy moralists* who deep down are really depressed by the fact that despite their best efforts to live a good Christian life, they don't seem to be able to do it very well, perhaps not at all. And it ought to be good news to *insecure hypocrites*, those who know their life—especially their private life—doesn't match their profession; they don't walk the talk. So they are insecure, hoping no one pulls back the curtain to discover who they really are.

Through the gospel God has done what needs to be done to put us in good standing in our warfare against the flesh. When we embrace Christ Jesus by faith, we are crucified together with him (2:20), and thus our "flesh with its passions and desires" is crucified (5:24). But not only are we put to death, we're raised to newness of life by the Spirit. In fact, as Paul says, "We live by the Spirit" (5:25). This simple statement summarizes the whole. The Spirit is sufficient for life; "we live by the Spirit."

This in turn is the confident basis upon which we stand—or rather the sure path upon which we are called to walk: "Let us also keep in step with the Spirit" (5:25b). We are to walk no longer according to the ways of this world, giving expression to the desires of the flesh. "Let us not," Paul says, "become conceited, provoking one another, envying one another" (5:26). Instead let's walk in newness of life, bearing the fruit of the Spirit, fulfilling the law of love.

To walk by the Spirit means to walk by faith. God pours out his Spirit in our lives in response to our faith. Remember Paul's statement: "Through the Spirit, *by faith*" (5:5). The Spirit is the power; faith is how we open ourselves up to that power. And as we learned earlier in the letter, God supplies the Spirit to us in one way: by faith (3:5). When we hear the Word of God and respond to it with trust, God pours out his Spirit into our lives in an increased way.

We must feed upon the Word of God by faith. The Word of God is food for the soul. Faith feeds until it is full, and then the soul is happy—happy in God. And when we are happy in God, satisfied with all that he is and promises to be for us in Christ, then we are far less likely to be distracted by the attractive pull of the flesh, with its passions and desires.

What I know from my own life, I also find confirmed in my counseling with many individuals. Unless we are feeding upon the Word of God, we will not experience the empowering presence of the Spirit. God has chosen to honor his Son by joining the giving of the Holy Spirit to the receiving of the Word of Christ.

This is the God-appointed means of being "filled with the Spirit" (Ephesians 5:18). As the word of Christ dwells in us richly (Colossians 3:16), we will find that we are filled with the Spirit. And the result is the same: love, joy, peace, patience, kindness, goodness, faithfulness, gentleness, self-control. We will not be able to walk by the Spirit and enjoy the empowering presence of the Spirit in our daily life if we are not feeding upon the promises of the Word of God, Scripture, on a daily basis as well.

As we look to Scripture for daily nourishment, we find Christ there, standing forth in the pages of the Bible. And the Holy Spirit loves to see Jesus Christ treasured and trusted in, so he empowers us in our encounter with God's Word and as a result of our encounter with God's Word. This is, then, the one major practical application of this study: *we must read the Bible on a daily basis; otherwise we will not—indeed cannot—walk by the Spirit in our daily life.*

But this isn't only about personal Bible reading. There are many other ways in which believers can take in and feed upon the Word of God. That's why Christians of the past often referred to preaching and the Lord's Supper and corporate worship as *means of grace*. These are the ways in which ordinary Christians encounter the Word of God by faith and in turn can receive fresh infusions of the presence of the Spirit in their lives.

Brothers, if anyone is caught in any transgression, you who are spiritual should restore him in a spirit of gentleness. Keep watch on yourself, lest you too be tempted. Bear one another's burdens, and so fulfill the law of Christ. For if anyone thinks he is something, when he is nothing, he deceives himself. But let each one test his own work, and then his reason to boast will be in himself alone and not in his neighbor. For each will have to bear his own load.

6:1–5

24

Burden Bearing, Part 1:
Spiritual Restoration

GALATIANS 6:1–5

WHAT DOES A SPIRIT-LED COMMUNITY LOOK LIKE? When we see people who are truly led by the Spirit, what sorts of things do we see them doing?

In this passage we have a snapshot of a Spirit-led community in action. And what do we see? Paul captures the action of a Spirit-led community with a single phrase: burden bearing. "Bear one another's burdens," he says, "and so fulfill the law of Christ" (6:2). This is the main point of this passage: a call to bear one another's burdens. And this is the main thing a Spirit-led community does.

Certainly, burden bearing includes providing practical help to one another. But what Paul specifically has in mind is bearing the burden of one another's sin.[1] And the primary way we do this is through the practice of spiritual restoration, which is what Paul calls the Galatians to in the opening verse of this passage: "Brothers, if anyone is caught in any transgression, you who are spiritual should restore him in a spirit of gentleness" (v. 1).

The church is a mess worth making. But the challenge and heartache of the church's messiness is this: it almost always involves people. We're the mess and the mess makers! Dealing with the mess we call the church, then, requires knowing how to work through the messes we ourselves make.

This is just what the Galatians need to do. If they're truly going to serve one another in love (5:13) and follow the leading of the Spirit (5:18), they're going to have to come alongside erring members of their congregations and restore them to spiritual wholeness.

Surely the practice of spiritual restoration is needed not only in ancient

Galatia but in every church community. Indeed, every Christian ought to be prepared to lovingly respond to a brother or sister who falls into sin.

Regrettably, however, this is not something Christians do very often, or very well. Too often we act like a timid medical student who sees a patient with a bone fracture but is too insecure or immature to say anything about it. Or worse yet, we can be too proud or preoccupied with ourselves even to notice, much less care. In fact, we may even be annoyed that the person did something so stupid as to break his arm. So we let the person go on with the pain without addressing it with the person in need in a straightforward way that brings about that person's healing.[2]

Pride and Conceit: Roadblocks to Spiritual Restoration (5:26)

Spirit-led communities, and Spirit-led individuals, do spiritual restoration. But they only do it—or at least only do it well—when they're not tempted by their own pride and conceit. Thus Paul warns the Galatians, "Keep watch on yourself, lest you too be tempted" (v. 1).

Tempted in what way? Certainly we may be tempted to stumble in the same way the erring person has. But more to the point, we may be tempted—and almost certainly will be tempted—to gloat over others who are overtaken in sin. Not that we would ever intend to, but sin is just that subtle, and pride and conceit are just that powerful.

The proud, the conceited, are too exalted in their own hearts to bend low to carry other people's burdens. Inflated egos inhibit burden bearing.[3] Burden bearing is, after all, a slave's task; it's a menial, messy, and often thankless job. It's not a job for the proud.

An inflated ego, however, causes you not to love others but rather to envy and provoke them (5:26). The conceited heart envies others and what they have in comparison to what we have. This is why we find a certain insidious satisfaction in the faults of others being found out. And this is why our news and entertainment media have an obsession with sensational problems of other people (consider, for example, the popularity of *The Jerry Springer Show* or *Jersey Shore*).

Rather than grieve over another's sin, we sometimes revel in realizing we have a leg up on someone. We're tempted to posture ourselves toward others like that Pharisee did toward the tax collector in Jesus' parable: "God, I thank you that I am not like other men, extortioners, unjust, adulterers, or even like this tax collector" (Luke 18:11).

Yet this kind of contemptuous attitude toward others is positively fatal to burden bearing. Paul understands this and so proffers in this passage several antidotes to pride and conceit, which are ultimately designed to enable better burden bearing.

Remember the Way of the Crucified Christ (6:2)

First of all, we kill conceit, and enable burden bearing, by remembering the way of the crucified Christ. "Bear one another's burdens, and so fulfill the law of Christ," Paul says (v. 2).

Here Paul coins a fascinating phrase: "the law of Christ." And while it has long puzzled students of Galatians, it's clearly intended to point to the person and work of Christ. Hence we do well to take a good, hard look at how it is that Jesus Christ bore the burdens of others. This, in fact, is the best place to start: with the Burden bearer par excellence.

Bearing one another's burdens is the way of Christ, who "came not to be served but to serve, and to give his life as a ransom for many" (Mark 10:45). The Lord Jesus Christ "bore our sins in his body on the tree" (1 Peter 2:24). Or as the prophet Isaiah anticipated long ago:

> Surely he has borne our griefs and carried our sorrows . . . he was pierced for our transgressions; he was crushed for our iniquities . . . . All we like sheep have gone astray; we have turned—every one—to his own way; and the LORD has laid on him the iniquity of us all. (Isaiah 53:4–6)

Jesus Christ, the God-man, is the supreme Burden bearer.[4] And if we truly remember the crucified Christ—his humility, his sacrifice, his suffering, his love—we won't be able to entertain high thoughts of ourselves. We'll quickly realize that "none is righteous, no, not one" (Romans 3:10). Contemplating the full scope of our Savior's ministry thus has a remarkable way of subduing, if not eradicating, conceit in our hearts.

Beware of the Subtlety of Self-Deception (6:3)

But there's a second antidote to conceit found in this passage: *beware of the subtlety of self-deception.* "For if anyone thinks he is something, when he is nothing, he deceives himself" (6:3). How easy it is to think we're something we're not. And how prone we all are to deceiving ourselves. How easy it is, for example, to congratulate ourselves on our humility or to applaud ourselves for being so kind!

Paul was in tune with what C. S. Lewis called "The Great Sin," the sin of pride or self-conceit. Pride or self-conceit is, as Paul says, thinking you are something when in fact you're nothing (v. 3). "There is no fault which makes a man more unpopular, and no fault which we are more unconscious of in ourselves. And the more we have it ourselves, the more we dislike it in others."[5] And, I would add, the more we have it ourselves, the less likely we are *even to see it in ourselves.*

Psalm 36 describes how this happens. There David says, "Transgression speaks to the wicked deep in his heart; there is no fear of God before his eyes. For he flatters himself in his own eyes that his iniquity cannot be found out and hated" (vv. 1, 2). Sin speaks to us. Sin flatters us. Sin convinces us that we are something we're not: less vile, less vain, less self-centered, or more patient, more faithful, more gracious than we really are. No wonder that great theologian of the human heart, Jonathan Edwards, concludes: "'Tis inexpressible, and almost inconceivable, how strong a self-righteous, self-exalting disposition is naturally in man; and what he will not do and suffer, to feed and gratify it."[6]

Self-conceit is fatal for burden bearing because it turns us into *judges* rather than burden bearers. In his Sermon on the Mount Jesus warns us how self-deception leads to self-conceit and disposes us to be quick when it comes to judge others. "Why do you see the speck that is in your brother's eye, but do not notice the log that is in your own eye?" (Matthew 7:3). Jesus knows we easily deceive ourselves into thinking we're something we're not or fail to see what we truly are, especially when it comes to comparing ourselves with others, and thus judging others.

The best antidote to self-deception, then, is *confession.* The one who acknowledges his or her own sin before God is at least halfway to rooting it out, or at least to getting a better handle on it. Listen to Lewis: "If anyone would like to acquire humility, I can, I think, tell him the first step. The first step is to realize that one is proud. And a biggish step, too. At least, nothing whatever can be done before it. If you think you are not conceited, it means you are very conceited indeed."[7]

It is always good, then, to have the closing line of Psalm 139 close at hand, ready to pray in any circumstance: "Search me, O God, and know my heart! Try me and know my thoughts! And see if there be any grievous way in me, and lead me in the way everlasting!" (vv. 23, 24).

May prayers like this be a regular part of our walk with the Lord, and we'll find, not conceit, but humility blossoming in our souls. And this will turn us into better burden bearers.

Grade Our Own Work and Let Others Do the Same (6:4)

The third antidote for conceit is to grade our own work and let others do the same.[8] "But let each one test his own work," Paul urges, "and then his reason to boast will be in himself alone and not in his neighbor" (6:4).

In school nobody liked the know-it-all who was always interested in giving a grade to everyone else's work. But that's what we do when either pride or conceit has its way with us, since both are competitive and comparative by nature. We're not satisfied with how we're doing; we're preoccupied with how we're doing *in relation to those around us.* That is precisely why the apostle connects conceit or pride with "provoking one another, envying one another" (5:26).

But how do we test our own work? By what standard? The standard we use has already been mentioned: *"the law of Christ"* (v. 2). This is the Law of Moses as it has been embodied in the life and teaching of Jesus.[9] Or you can think of it as the law of love (cf. 5:13), though not as some mushy abstraction, but as it came to life in the self-giving life of Jesus.

If then we're going to grade ourselves, we should do so not on a curve we ourselves have set but rather by the law of love, the Law of Christ. And we shouldn't worry about comparing ourselves with others but instead simply look to Christ, and let our lives be measured against his.

Or we can follow the example of the Apostle Paul who understood the temptation to play the comparison game but resisted it by looking past the horizon of this life and into the next.

> This is how one should regard us, as servants of Christ and stewards of the mysteries of God. Moreover, it is required of stewards that they be found faithful. But with me it is a very small thing that I should be judged by you or by any human court. In fact, I do not even judge myself. For I am not aware of anything against myself, but I am not thereby acquitted. It is the Lord who judges me. Therefore do not pronounce judgment before the time, before the Lord comes, who will bring to light the things now hidden in darkness and will disclose the purposes of the heart. Then each one will receive his commendation from God. (1 Corinthians 4:1–5)[10]

We ought to adopt this same attitude. It will not only free us from insecurity but also from pride. We won't feel the need to prop up our fragile egos with comparisons with others; we'll wait patiently and confidently for God's evaluation of us. We must be content to let our praise come from God alone, not from man (Romans 2:29). And this in turn will free us to bear one another's burdens.

Keep Your Eye on the Judgment (6:5)

This leads to the fourth and final antidote to conceit. *If we want to kill conceit, we must keep the horizon of judgment always in view.* "For each will have to bear his own load" (v. 5).

Luther was right about this verse. These words "are forceful enough to frighten us thoroughly, so that we do not yearn for vainglory."[11] And that's precisely Paul's point, and the ultimate reason why we ought to bear burdens with both gentleness and humility.

The prospect of standing before the bar of Heaven and the majesty of the risen Lord to give an account for "every careless word" (Matthew 12:36) has a remarkable way of disabusing us of self-deception or self-conceit. It's not hard to feel spiritually spiffy when we measure ourselves against others. But when we envision our sinful, little selves before the One from whom even earth and sky will flee away (Revelation 20:11), grandiose ideas about who we are or what we've done will themselves flee away.[12]

Gazing at the final judgment ought to be a regular part of our Christian discipleship. I know that may sound counterintuitive at first, but it's entirely Biblical. It's not only taught in Scripture, it's taught plainly, abundantly, and throughout both Old and New Testaments. And this is no peripheral doctrine, but one with immense personal significance. "For we must all appear before the judgment seat of Christ, so that each one may receive what is due for what he has done in the body, whether good or evil" (2 Corinthians 5:10).

But more than that, keeping our eye on the judgment is a great antidote to conceit and thus a great help to bearing burdens rather than judging one another.

> Why do you pass judgment on your brother? Or you, why do you despise your brother? For we will all stand before the judgment seat of God; for it is written, "As I live, says the Lord, every knee shall bow to me, and every tongue shall confess to God." So then each of us will give an account of himself to God. (Romans 14:10–12)

In fact, we might summarize the entire burden of this passage as follows: *Bear one another's burdens now because you'll have to bear your own load later.* Today we ought to serve one another through love because on the last day we will be judged according to the law of love, the Law of Christ.[13]

Practical Steps toward Better Burden Bearing

We've seen how this passage provides several antidotes to kill conceit and thus enable us to better bear one another's burdens. But it's worth briefly reflecting on a few questions pertinent to bearing one another's burdens, as well as a few practical steps we might take toward better burden bearing.

First, we ought to ask, *who should bear burdens?* This text says, those who are spiritual; that is, Spirit-led people. It's tempting to treat this as a designation for a separate class of Christians, as though there were the "spiritual" and the "unspiritual." But the New Testament doesn't know of two classes— only one. Every truly born-again Christian is to be a Spirit-led Christian.[14] So this is a charge to everyone who is born again by the Spirit of God. If we are born again we are by definition spiritual and so should engage in the work of spiritual restoration.

And yet the immature need to be cautious.[15] And the spiritually mature and strong need to take full responsibility and initiative: "We who are strong have an obligation to bear with the failings of the weak, and not to please ourselves" (Romans 15:1). Luther says this difficult work of burden bearing requires that a Christian "have broad shoulders and husky bones" because the burden of another's sin isn't easy to carry.[16] It's not for the weak or halfhearted but for the spiritually strong and mature.

But, secondly, we might ask, *when should we bear one another's burdens?* Whenever anyone is overtaken "in any transgression." The word "transgression" in English connotes sins of a fairly serious nature: e.g., sexual immorality, idolatry, apostasy, drunkenness, and other works of the flesh like these (cf. 5:19–21). But we should not limit the scope to just these. In fact, Paul no doubt also has in mind other works of the flesh, which include more subtle but no less insidious vices like the following: "enmity, strife, jealousy, fits of anger, rivalries, dissensions, divisions, envy" (5:20, 21).

This, in turn, leads to a third question: *How should we do it?* The first and arguably most important thing to say is that whenever we seek to restore someone, we should, heeding Paul's explicit instruction, do so "in a spirit of gentleness" (6:1; cf. Ephesians 4:1–3).[17] Besides, if we've been personally offended, we in all likelihood could use some time to cool down. Otherwise we'll be tempted to react to an offense the way James and John did when their Lord was rejected by villagers in Samaria. "Lord," they asked, "do you want us to tell fire to come down from heaven and consume them?" (Luke 9:54). That sounds like a couple of hotheaded junior-high boys who like to play with pyrotechnics. Jesus swiftly rebuked James and John, no doubt admonishing them that they had no idea what Jesus is really all about.

We should also make it a rule to do spiritual restoration as privately and as discreetly as possible. Don't use the church bulletin to announce that someone's been overtaken in a trespass, and resist the temptation to post their misstep on Facebook. Instead, as Jesus so wisely and graciously advises, "If your brother sins against you, go and tell him his fault, between you and him alone" (Matthew 18:15).[18]

And as we anticipate doing the sensitive, spiritually requiring work of restoring an erring brother or sister, we'd do well to bathe ourselves and the whole situation in prayer. Tell a close friend or confidant as well, so this person can pray for you and lovingly hold you accountable to pure motives and right actions.

Spiritual restoration is—or at least ought to be—part of the regular business of any small group. If you're in a small group and this kind of work never happens, it may be time to ask some honest questions about the depth of spiritual maturity of the group, or the depth of intimacy and commitment within the group.

Beyond these Biblical instructions on how to do spiritual restoration, we need to conclude with a simple exhortation to get on with it! Do the hard but rewarding work of seeking to restore anyone who's been overtaken in a trespass. This is what Spirit-led Christians and Spirit-led communities do. They bear one another's burdens by doing spiritual restoration.

Conclusion

When you see the Spirit in action among believers, you see a community marked by love, though not of a saccharine or sentimental kind. It's love that's humble, gentle, and gracious, yet strong, courageous, and full of conviction.

It's love that restores. It's love that always seeks, first, the glory of God, then the good of the one being restored, and finally the purity and unity of the Body of Christ as a whole.

Martin Luther saw this passage as an all-out attack on "the poisonous vice of vainglory."[19] The Apostle Paul would doubtless have approved of the reformer's insight. So, too, we suspect, would he have approved of Luther's accompanying counsel, which we do well to heed for ourselves: "The Holy Spirit alone is able to preserve us from being infected by this poison."[20]

May God grant us grace, therefore, to walk by the Spirit, bear the fruit of the Spirit, and do the work of Spirit-restoration, for the glory and praise of God, the good of souls, and the building of the Church, both now and forevermore!

Let the one who is taught the word share all good things with the one who teaches. Do not be deceived: God is not mocked, for whatever one sows, that will he also reap. For the one who sows to his own flesh will from the flesh reap corruption, but the one who sows to the Spirit will from the Spirit reap eternal life. And let us not grow weary of doing good, for in due season we will reap, if we do not give up. So then, as we have opportunity, let us do good to everyone, and especially to those who are of the household of faith.

6:6–10

25

Burden Bearing, Part 2:
Pay Your Pastor

GALATIANS 6:6–10

I CHOSE AN ALMOST CHEEKY TITLE for this sermon: "Pay Your Pastor."
When I preached this I told my congregation, "If my sermon title makes you
feel a bit uncomfortable, you should know it makes me even more so!"

As a general rule pastors don't like talking about money. Even the fearless Reformer Martin Luther was a bit squeamish about preaching on this
particular verse: "I do not like to interpret such passages, for they seem to
commend us [i.e., pastors], as in fact they do. In addition, it gives the appearance of greed if one emphasizes these things diligently to one's hearers."[1]

Evidently the Apostle Paul wasn't all that fond of talking about money
either, at least not directly and explicitly. Whenever he does, he speaks in
highly theological and relational terms, as he does in these verses. "Let the one
who is taught the word share all good things with the one who teaches" (v. 6).[2]
And yet Paul is, in effect, simply telling the Galatians to pay their pastor.

There is an exchange that ought to take place within the life of every
healthy church. On the one hand pastors are to share with congregants the
spiritual resources of the Word of God, so that congregants can be nourished
and equipped to live for Christ. On the other hand congregants are to share
with pastors their financial resources, so that pastors are free of the burden
of having to provide financially for themselves and are thus free to devote all
their time and energy to feeding the flock.

Thus within the Spirit-led community of faith, there is to be *mutual
burden bearing* (6:2).[3] Both pastor and congregation are to share with one
another the good things they have from God for the benefit of each other.

But what we're reminded of from this passage is that this financial burden bearing is in our best interest. Let me state it even more plainly, and more precisely. *It's in believers' long-term spiritual best interest to provide financially for the teaching ministry of their local churches.*

They stand to benefit immensely—immeasurably, eternally even—by sharing their financial resources with their local churches, so their local churches can be all the more active in sharing the Word of God. In other words, believers should pay their pastor and provide financially for their local church. This is for their own good.

To some this might sound a bit sub-Christian, as though God saw fit to pander to our selfishness to get us to do what he wants. Here is where we do well to remind ourselves of something C. S. Lewis pointed out in his brilliant essay "The Weight of Glory," where he grapples with precisely this problem:

> The New Testament has lots to say about self-denial, but not about self-denial as an end in itself. We are told to deny ourselves and to take up our crosses in order that we may follow Christ; and nearly every description of what we shall ultimately find if we do so contains an appeal to desire.[4]

In this passage in Galatians there is a call to self-denial and sacrificial giving. But there's also an appeal to desire, to what we will find if we do what this text enjoins.

Some believers already live grace-filled, generous lives. But perhaps others have only given out of habit and haven't really seen the point. There may be others who don't give at all, not because they're opposed in principle, but because they've never understood why they should give or been challenged to do so.

Sowing and Reaping Is Reality (6:7, 8)

There are different reasons why people struggle to provide financial support to their local church. I suspect the main reason is not that people don't have the resources to give; even the widow with her mite gave something. I suspect the main reason we don't give generously to the church is because we don't, in our heart of hearts, believe it ultimately matters. On the other hand, we're all acutely aware of how much it will matter to our own budget if we part with another $50 or $500 a month! That'll leave a dent we can see. But will giving generously to the church really make any difference in this life or the next?

No doubt this is why Paul feels it necessary to fire a shot across the bow of the Galatians' boat: "Do not be deceived: God is not mocked, for whatever one sows, that will he also reap" (v. 7). It is very easy to slip into thinking that our actions don't matter. But this verse reminds us that just as God has created a world in which the law of gravity holds true, he's created a world in which *the law of the harvest* holds true as well: we reap what we sow.

The dynamic of sowing and reaping is reality; the law of the harvest is part of the warp and woof of this world. Just as it would be unwise to test the law of gravity by driving a car off the top of a parking garage, so too it would be unwise to test the law of the harvest by living a life centered upon ourselves. The consequences would be just as ugly. Flaunting either law will only end in destruction or even death.

So don't be deceived! Our actions have serious, long-term consequences. Indeed, God's designed it to be that way, as Paul points out in verse 8, where he reinforces the reality of sowing and reaping: "For the one who sows to his own flesh will from the flesh reap corruption, but the one who sows to the Spirit will from the Spirit reap eternal life."

If you sow to your flesh by constantly seeking to satisfy your own selfish desires, then you will get exactly what you seek: corruption. On the other hand, notice how the apostle links sowing to the Spirit with eternal life itself. He has in mind not simply eternal rewards in addition to eternal life, as many might simply assume; rather, he here explicitly and, to some, provocatively weds what we do with the gift of salvation.

We must not miss that point, which is a surprising connection for Paul to make. We've always assumed that eternal life is given in response to faith and not to works. What we need to understand is that sowing to the Spirit is simply another way to describe walking by faith; it's a life lived by faith and in reliance upon the Holy Spirit of God as both the motivation and means of giving sacrificially.

We Will Reap If We Stick with It (6:9)

Of course, sowing to the Spirit isn't easy. In fact, it's often quite hard. This is because sowing to the Spirit involves self-denial. And self-denial requires putting to death the self, which is never an easy thing to do! Besides, the flesh, with its self-serving desires (cf. 5:17), and the world, with its sin-inducing, ubiquitous presence (cf. 1:4), only compounds what's an already difficult task. As a result, believers often grow weary when attempting to sow to the Spirit.

Weariness in well-doing or sowing to the Spirit is another reason why Christians fail to give. Perhaps they have in the past, but somehow they've run out of gas. Now, for whatever reason, their strength to give is gone, and so they decide to stop and rest awhile.

This is a very common experience for believers, which is why this passage includes a word of encouragement to stick with sowing and not give up. "And let us not grow weary of doing good, for in due season we will reap, if we do not give up" (v. 9). This statement has application to all of life, whenever we grow weary in doing good. But within the context of this particular passage, we ought to take it as an encouragement to persevere in providing financial support to the ministry of the local church.

And the key, Paul says, to not growing weary is to keep your eyes fixed on the future, God's end-time harvest. We get ourselves in trouble when we allow ourselves to get too immersed in our own troubles. Instead, as Martyn Lloyd-Jones encourages:

> We need to look ahead, to anticipate, to look forward to the eternal glories gleaming afar. The Christian life is a tasting of the first-fruits of that great harvest which is to come. . . . Go on with your task whatever your feelings; keep on with your work. God will give the increase, He will send the rain of His gracious mercies as we need it. There will be an abundant harvest. Look forward to it. "Ye shall reap."[5]

Remember our Lord Jesus Christ. His entire life was devoted to sowing to the Spirit and not the flesh—indeed, every single moment of every single day. And he was sustained by constantly keeping his eyes fixed on "the joy that was set before him" (Hebrews 12:2). This is how Jesus endured the cross and a myriad of other hardships and sacrifices.

Is the joy of the harvest in view for us? Do we have our eyes fixed on what is to come? Are we seeking the things that are above, where Christ is seated at the right hand of God? And is our mind set on things above, not on the things that are on earth? Or have we forgotten that if we're Christians, we've died? Our lives are now hidden with Christ in God, so that when Christ, who is our life, appears, we also will appear with him in glory on that great day (cf. Colossians 3:1–4).

And what a glorious day that shall be! For we will discover that what we reap is completely out of proportion to what we've sown. The sacrifices we've made in this life will appear small, even to the point of insignificance, on that great and majestic day!

Prioritize Giving to the Local Church (6:10)

We have, then, every reason to live generously. For not only is sowing and reaping reality, but we can be confident that one day we will reap if we stick with it. This is all good news.

But Paul offers a third and final word to the Galatians. It's a broad and general encouragement to do good to others, and it captures the overall ethical imperative of the letter as well as of the Christian life: "So then, as we have opportunity, let us do good to everyone . . ." (v. 10a).[6]

To some this may sound trite, but still it's worth saying: Christians ought to do good. Goodness is, after all, one of the fruits of the Spirit (5:22); so our lives ought to bless and enrich the lives of others. We ought to follow in the way of our Lord Jesus, who went around "doing good" (Acts 10:38).

And yet notice that while this closing verse calls us to open-ended generosity, it does not do so without qualification. Rather, as we live generously and do good, we ought to continue to prioritize the local church. Yes, do good to everyone—believer and unbeliever alike. But as Paul is concerned to point out, Christians ought to do good "especially to those who are of the household of faith" (v. 10b).

The local church, then, must be our top priority. Why? Because it is our primary family; it is, the apostle says, "the household of faith." It is where we find identity and security, receive nurture and nourishment, get encouragement and support, benefit from teaching and training, modeling and mentoring, discipline and discipleship. The local church is our spiritual home, and those who gather week by week are, Biblically speaking, our true brothers and sisters.

The Gospels record a time when Jesus' mother and brothers came to the house where he was busy ministering to people. When Jesus heard they wanted to speak with him, he asked this provocative question of those who were gathered: "Who are my mother and my brothers?" And then, looking intently into the eyes of those gathered to hear him, he said this: "Here are my mother and my brothers! For whoever does the will of God, he is my brother and sister and mother" (Mark 3:33–35).

Those who do the will of God belong to Jesus' family and are members of what Paul calls "the household of faith." And it is they, our brothers and sisters in faith, who deserve our primary support, not of course to the neglect of our blood relations (cf. 1 Timothy 5:8), but not as a leftover or afterthought either.

Here's the bottom line. We'll only prioritize giving to the local church when we're convinced the local church is the one-of-a-kind institution it truly is. Remember, Jesus is the head of no other institution and claims no other institution as his body (cf. Colossians 1:18). No other institution serves as the dwelling place for God or the residence of the Holy Spirit (cf. Ephesians 2:21, 22). There is no other institution that has so remarkable or far-reaching a history, tracing its roots back to before the foundations of the world (cf. Ephesians 1:4). Nor is there any other institution with the church's future, extending as it does into eternity (cf. 1 Thessalonians 4:17). Nor is there any other institution as global in scope or diverse in membership (cf. Revelation 5:9, 10). We won't find any other institution that's easier to enter, yet so impossible to forsake once we've truly joined (cf. Matthew 28:18–20). And let's not forget the spiritual benefits of belonging to this unique institution: the grace of our Lord Jesus Christ, the love of God the Father, and the fellowship of the Holy Spirit (cf. 2 Corinthians 13:14).

But practically speaking what does all this mean? Simply this: as we give, we must begin with our local church. Then, as we're able, we can contribute to other Christian ministries or worthy causes. But we should not find ourselves in a place where we have nothing to give to the church because we've extended our resources everywhere else. That would be to fall short of Scripture's counsel to do good to all, especially to the household of faith.

Is there a good rule of thumb, though, to help us think concretely about what prioritizing our giving to the local church might look like? I think there is. And I'm not alone. Christians through the ages and across the denominations have identified this as a benchmark for generous giving: 10 percent or what's sometimes referred to as a tithe. Let me be very clear and direct in saying this: If we want to give generously and prioritize the local church, we should start by giving 10 percent of our income to support the church's ministries.

The church is a one-of-a-kind institution. And it ought to have first place in our affections and the pride of place among all the other concerns and commitments in our lives. After all, the church is our family. It is the household of faith.

Conclusion

Surprisingly, the body of Paul's letter to the Galatians concludes with a word on giving (6:6–10). And with it we hear the challenge, first, to provide financially for the church, second, to persevere in doing so, and, third, to prioritize the church above everything else—all because it's in our best, long-term interest to do so. Indeed, we have everything to gain, both now and for eternity.

And yet we see how profoundly God-centered this passage is. Giving is ultimately between us and God, no one else. Sharing in all good things with the one who teaches the Word of God has nothing to with whether we like the one who teaches or his teaching. It's not ultimately about the one who teaches. It's about God, to whom you and I both will ultimately answer. Honoring and pleasing him ought to be our chief concern.

This passage is also rigorously *future-oriented*. The strong warnings in this passage point us to the future, and they remind us of the eternal consequences that follow from our actions, whether good or bad. We can't read this passage and not be confronted with the value of maintaining an eternal perspective on all of life, not least when it comes to what we do with our money. This life is not the be-all and end-all of our existence. There's more to come. In fact, the best is yet to come!

In addition, we must realize that generous giving requires we live *Spirit-empowered* lives. It would be a tragic mistake to think generosity comes simply from trying harder or being more disciplined. It doesn't. We cannot sidestep the Spirit and still expect to be generous with our time, treasure, or talents. Instead we have to walk by the Spirit (5:16) and be led by the Spirit (5:18) if we want to abound in the fruit of the Spirit (5:22–23).

Finally, we need to see that the teaching of this passage is deeply Christ-focused. By sharing in all good things with the one who teaches, we bear burdens in the most practical ways, and so we fulfill the Law of Christ (cf. 6:2). Christ is the great Burden bearer who out of his own wealth shares all good things with spiritually impoverished sinners like you and me. "For you know the grace of our Lord Jesus Christ, that though he was rich, yet for your sake he became poor, so that you by his poverty might become rich" (2 Corinthians 8:9).

Do you know this grace of which the Scriptures speak? Do you know the grace of our Lord Jesus Christ, who was one with the Father and yet, for our sakes, took on human flesh to die in our place on the cross? Do you know the grace of forgiveness, healing, redemption, cleansing, pardon, freedom, restoration, hope, and new life?

You can. In fact, you will, if you will only turn from yourself and from serving your own sinful desires and turn to the Savior who loves you and gave himself for you. Cry out to him for grace, and you will find him to be the most generous Giver imaginable!

See with what large letters I am writing to you with my own hand. It is those who want to make a good showing in the flesh who would force you to be circumcised, and only in order that they may not be persecuted for the cross of Christ. For even those who are circumcised do not themselves keep the law, but they desire to have you circumcised that they may boast in your flesh. But far be it from me to boast except in the cross of our Lord Jesus Christ, by which the world has been crucified to me, and I to the world. For neither circumcision counts for anything, nor uncircumcision, but a new creation. And as for all who walk by this rule, peace and mercy be upon them, and upon the Israel of God. From now on let no one cause me trouble, for I bear on my body the marks of Jesus. The grace of our Lord Jesus Christ be with your spirit, brothers. Amen.

6:11–18

26

Boast Only in the Cross

GALATIANS 6:11–18

THIS FINAL SECTION OF GALATIANS is more than a wrap-up. It's a reitera-tion of the letter's central thrust and chief aims. In the scope of just a few verses, Paul reinforces the argument of Galatians and applies it to his hearers in as forceful a fashion as possible.[1]

With this in mind, it's worth asking about the central thrust of this portion of the letter, for therein one finds the burden of Galatians as a whole. Arguably this can be found in the first part of verse 14, where Paul says, "But far be it from me to boast except in the cross of our Lord Jesus Christ."

Evidently, then, this fiery little letter is just a call to boast in the cross of Christ alone!

Now, most who are acquainted with the Christian tradition have some idea of what the cross of Christ is. But it's worth reminding ourselves of the ignominy associated with this ancient method of execution. When we strip away the religious sentimentality that surrounds the symbol of the cross, we're confronted with what is in fact a weapon of torture and intimidation. The cross was the guillotine or firing squad or electric chair of the ancient world. Only it was far worse: less humane, more gruesome, an altogether hideous way to die.

What, then, could it possibly mean to boast in the cross of Christ? We don't typically commend boasting, and when we do, it's certainly not in weapons of torture and execution. That would be like saying, "I'm thrilled about the electric chair!" or "Guillotines are great!"

But we need to remember that boasting is how we verbalize our confi-dence. It's how we make hope audible. Boasting is hope you can hear. No one can peer into your soul to see the source of your confidence or the object of your hope. But they can hear what you talk about, the things that get you excited, and what it is you commend or celebrate.

In that sense each of us boasts all the time. We're always expressing our confidence in one thing or another. We can't help it. We're hardwired for hope and preprogrammed to verbalize this hope in our various acts of boasting.

Often we boast in objects that we think will provide us with a happy tomorrow. So we say enthusiastic things about a car and how reliable it is, or a pair of shoes and how comfortable they are, or a computer and how fast it is, or an investment and how lucrative it will be. Sometimes we boast in other people, commending them as reliable sources of hope. And sometimes we boast in ourselves, expressing confidence in our own future, whether near or distant, because of some quality we possess, whether real or imagined.

Against this backdrop, we're prepared to take a closer look at Paul's remarkable claim that he himself, and Christians by implication, ought to boast in this one thing: the cross of Christ. For the apostle, this means we're to see the cross as the source of every good in our lives or in the world. And it means we're to put zero confidence in anything else, knowing the cross alone secures a bright future for us with God.

A Good Showing in the Flesh (6:12–14)

Unfortunately, not everyone boasts in the cross of Christ. For many, whom Scripture calls unbelievers, the cross is foolishness. To those without the eyes of faith, Jesus' death is folly, not wisdom (cf. 1 Corinthians 1:18, 23).

But sadly, even some professing Christians regard the cross of Christ as a reason for embarrassment rather than a ground for boasting. They prefer to profess the cross rather than live the cross.

This was Peter's posture, once he realized Jesus was going to Jerusalem not to take up residency in a king's palace but to be strung up alongside other condemned criminals. At this point the rock upon which Jesus promised to build his church was more interested in his Lord receiving a crown than in his hanging from a tree.

Paul says the Judaizers in Galatia took a similar stance. They boasted in themselves rather than in the cross of Christ. "It is those who want to make a good showing in the flesh who would force you to be circumcised, and only in order that they may not be persecuted for the cross of Christ. For even those who are circumcised do not themselves keep the law, but they desire to have you circumcised that they may boast in your flesh" (vv. 12, 13).

The Judaizers weren't concerned with anyone's best interest except their own. They'd devised a clever plan to avoid persecution, to save face, or literally, as in the ESV, "to make a good showing in the flesh" (v. 12).[2] But it entailed the Galatians getting circumcised so that they would become look-alike Jews. This was the Judaizers' way of avoiding harassment from non-believing Jews who loathed the fact that they were fraternizing with Gentiles.[3]

But from Paul's perspective, the Judaizers were dodging the costly impli-cations of the cross of Christ. He sees them trying to save their lives rather than lose them for Jesus' sake in the service of others (cf. Mark 8:35). Like some who profess Christ today, the Judaizers didn't treat the cross of Christ as a narrow road to trod for the good of others, but as a card you play when you want to get out of jail free.

That's what happens when the cross is no longer a reality to embrace, but a symbol to display. Particularly in the West, where Christianity enjoys legal protection and a degree of social acceptance, it's easy to content ourselves with displaying the cross, even if we're not living the cross. We're glad to adorn our churches with the cross, but aren't we also quick to turn away from its imposing presence in our own lives?

Death to This Deadly World (6:14)

We see Paul, however, draw a sharp contrast between himself and the Judaizers. While their confidence is in the Galatians getting circumcised, Paul's is in the tool that took his Messiah's life.

But why? Because Paul recognizes that the cross kills this deadly world. Or as he says in appropriately personalized terms, "The world has been cruci-fied to me, and I to the world" (v. 14).

This world is a deadly place. The mortality rate is 100 percent. But the only thing more deadly than the world is the cross of Christ. There's never been a more lethal tool. And yet in the wisdom of God the world's own weapon has been turned against it, not vindictively, but in love. For through the cross God has dealt a fatal blow to this fallen world, and in due course it will breathe its last and be no more.

The cross kills the world not by inciting religious jihad but by crucify-ing the sinful nature in our souls. The Puritans had a phrase for this death-to-the-world process: the mortification of indwelling sin. Paul referred to it elsewhere as putting to death "the deeds of the body" (Romans 8:13).[4]

This is what it means to have the world crucified to you, and you to the world. And yet Paul says something definitive has already happened in the lives of those who are Christ's: "Those who belong to Christ Jesus have crucified the flesh with its passions and desires" (5:24). For believers, a crucifixion has already happened, even though we continue to put to death that which remains.

A Clearing for the New Creation (6:15)

Yet death isn't the goal of the cross. Life is. God's designs go beyond crucifixion: they move inexorably toward resurrection, new life, and new creation. By sending his Son into the world, God dealt a blow to the world, so much so that he blew open a hole large enough for the new creation. The cross thus clears the way for the new creation.

In the Christian story, crucifixion is followed by resurrection, death by life, Good Friday by Easter. Jesus Christ was crucified, died, and was buried. Yet on the third day he rose from the dead, to become "the first and the last, and the living one" (Revelation 1:17, 18), the one "who died and came to life" (Revelation 2:8).

The risen Christ is, therefore, "the beginning of God's creation" (Revelation 3:14). His own bodily presence—raised, transformed, glorified—is itself the in-breaking of the new creation. And now, as the risen and exalted Lord of history, Jesus declares this message to both the church and the world: "Behold, I am making all things new" (Revelation 21:5).

But how is Jesus bringing the reality of the new creation? And where can we see it? He is making all things new by his Spirit, who, as the Nicene Creed says, is "the Lord, the Giver of Life." And we see the dawning of this new creation in the lives of God's people as they bear the fruit of the Spirit, the first-fruits of God's new creation. Believers are the vanguard of the new creation, because this is where we see the sovereign Spirit re-creating humanity in God's image and likeness, infusing our soul with his presence, adorning our lives with his character.

The cross rescues us from "the present evil age" (1:4). The cross unleashes the powerful presence of the Spirit (cf. 3:1–5). The cross clears the way for Abraham's blessing (cf. 3:10–14). The cross ushers in the era of adoption and sonship (4:1–7). The cross gives birth to new freedom (4:21—5:1). The cross of Christ enables the presence of God.

No wonder Paul insists here again, at the close of the letter, that the only thing that counts is new creation. "For neither circumcision counts for anything, nor uncircumcision, but a new creation" (v. 15). In light of what God has done in Christ, old-creation priorities no longer matter. They still do in this fallen world, but they don't where we're headed. Nor should they among those who are headed there.

Promise of Peace and Mercy (6:16)

As the people of God, then, not only do we have the privilege of experiencing the in-breaking of the new creation in our own lives, we have the responsibility of embodying the new creation in our life together. The church is the vanguard of the new creation. We exist to point the world to that which Christ will one day fully accomplish!

But in the meantime the church bears witness to a specific promise or offer to the world: the promise of peace and mercy, the promise Paul includes here at the letter's close: "And as for all who walk by this rule, peace and mercy be upon them, and upon the Israel of God" (6:16).[5]

Peace and mercy—are these not the longings of every human heart? But where can they be found? Purchased at the cross, promised for the new creation, peace and mercy are found in Christ alone. "Therefore, since we have been justified by faith, we have peace with God through our Lord Jesus Christ" (Romans 5:1).

The Marks of Jesus (6:17)

When we're confident in the cross of Christ—even to the point of boasting—we'll start thinking radical thoughts and doing radical things. Practically speaking, we may even be willing to suffer for the good of others, confident that suffering is the proof, rather than the counterevidence, of our life in Christ.

This was Paul's attitude toward suffering. In fact, his final rebuff of his opponents and closing appeal to the Galatians points them to the fact of his suffering as the sign of his authenticity: "From now on let no one cause me trouble, for I bear on my body the marks of Jesus" (v. 17).[6]

But when Paul says he bears on his body the marks of Jesus, what does he have in mind? His male-pattern baldness, crooked nose, or rearing in Tarsus rather than Rome, each of which was evidently true of the Apostle to the Gentiles?[7]

Often we hear people refer to the "crosses" they have to bear—a cranky mother-in-law, a lousy golf swing, or an overbearing boss. But personal disappointments aren't the marks of Jesus. Personal sacrifices that involve suffering are.

The marks of Jesus to which Paul refers are those visible, tangible reminders of how he's suffered with Christ for the advance of the gospel and the good of others. He's referring to the wounds and scars he carries around with him on his body, the ones he has acquired in the service of God's gospel for Gentiles.

Do we bear the marks of Jesus in our lives, perhaps even on our own bodies? Is our identification with Jesus and service of others so vibrant that it's become costly? If we looked at our recent bank statements, would we see the marks of Jesus? If a friend perused our calendar and the way we prioritize the use of our time, would he see the marks of Jesus? Or if someone talked to our friends and neighbors, would they testify to seeing the suffering Savior in our visage?

Understand, then, that because the Christian life is sacrificial, it will be painful. If it's not, it probably isn't Christian. Or at least it's not cross-shaped, and thus patterned after Christ's own life. For our Lord's was no safe, sanitized life.

And yet he endured it all—becoming obedient to death, even death on a cross—for our sake and for our salvation.

Grace Be with You (6:18)

Galatians exists for grace. It begins with grace (1:3), and it ends with grace (6:18). But the grace of Galatians is costly, not cheap. For it propels us toward gospel-rooted living, which means boasting in the cross of Christ alone.

Is your life rooted in God's grace as found in Christ's cross? Are you looking there for every good thing in life and for eternity?

If you are, then you can bank on this: "The grace of our Lord Jesus Christ [will] be with your spirit, brothers" (v. 18).

Soli Deo gloria.

Notes

Preface

1. Todd A. Wilson, "The Supersession and Superfluity of the Law? Another Look at Galatians," in *Introduction to Messianic Judaism: Its Ecclesial Context and Biblical Foundations*, ed. Joel Willitts and David Rudolph (Grand Rapids: Zondervan, 2013, pp. 235–244); *The Curse of the Law and the Crisis in Galatia: Reassessing the Purpose of Galatians*, WUNT 2, no. 225 (Tübingen: Mohr Siebeck, 2007); "'Under Law' in Galatians: A Pauline Theological Abbreviation," *The Journal of Theological Studies* 56, no. 2 (2005): 362–392; "Wilderness Apostasy and Paul's Portrayal of the Crisis in Galatians," *New Testament Studies* 50 (2004): 550–571; "The Law of Christ as the Law of Moses: Reflections on a Recent Trend in Interpretation," *Currents in Biblical Research* 5.1 (2006): 129–150; "The Leading of the Spirit and the Curse of the Law: Reassessing Paul's Response to the Galatian Crisis," *Tyndale Bulletin* 57.1 (2006): 157–160. Naturally, I've drawn heavily on my previous work throughout this commentary.

2. Dietrich Bonhoeffer, *Discipleship*, Dietrich Bonhoeffer Works, vol. 4 (Minneapolis: Augsburg, 2003), p. 45.

3. Ibid.

4. See the recent sobering assessment offered by Ross Douthat, *Bad Religion: How We Became a Nation of Heretics* (New York: Free Press, 2012).

Chapter One: Go Back to Grace

1. See Cornelius Plantinga Jr., "Flight," chapter 10 in *Not The Way It's Supposed to Be: A Breviary of Sin* (Grand Rapids: Eerdmans, 1995), pp. 175–197.

2. On the delivery and reception of Paul's letters, see M. L. Stirewalt, *Paul: The Letter Writer* (Grand Rapids: Eerdmans, 2003), pp. 11–18; P. J. J. Botha, "The Verbal Art of the Pauline Letters: Rhetoric, Performance and Presence," in *Rhetoric and the New Testament: Essays from the 1992 Heidelberg Conference.* ed. S. E. Porter and T. H. Olbricht. JSNTSup 90 (Sheffield: JSOT, 1993): pp. 409–428.

3. I hold to what's commonly called the South Galatian theory and thus work from the assumption that the Galatian churches were founded during Paul's first missionary journey (cf. Acts 13, 14). Similar are the views of commentators like F. F. Bruce, *The Epistle of Paul to the Galatians: A Commentary on the Greek Text*, NIGTC 2 (Exeter: Paternoster, 1982), pp. 43–56; Richard N. Longenecker, *Galatians*, WBC 41 (Waco, TX: Word, 1990), pp. lxiii-lxxxvii; Thomas R. Schreiner, *Galatians*, Zondervan Exegetical Commentary on the New Testament 9 (Grand Rapids: Zondervan, 2010), pp. 22–29. It's worth noting that the so-called North-South Galatia debate appears to have shifted in favor of the South Galatian or provincial hypothesis. See J. M. Scott. *Paul and the Nations: The Old Testament and Jewish Background of Paul's Mission to the Nations with Special Reference to the Destination of Galatians*, WUNT 84 (Tübingen: Mohr Siebeck, 1995); R. Riesner, *Paul's Early Period: Chronology, Mission Strategy, Theology* (Grand Rapids: Eerdmans, 1998),

pp. 286–291; G. N. Stanton, *Jesus and Gospel* (Cambridge: Cambridge University Press, 2004), pp. 36, 37. Note also the two substantial German-language contributions by Cilliers Breytenbach, *Paulus und Barnabas in der Provinz Galatien: Studien zu Apostelgeschichte 13f.; 16,6; 18,23 und den Adressaten des Galaterbriefes.* AGJU 38 (Leiden: Brill, 1996) and Thomas Witulski, *Die Adressaten des Galaterbriefes: Untersuchungen zur Gemeinde von Antiochia ad Psidiam.* FRLANT 193 (Göttingen: Vandenhoeck & Ruprecht, 2000), as well as the forthright (if somewhat overstated) comment by the ancient historian Stephen Mitchell in his magisterial two-volume *Anatolia: Land, Men, and Gods in Asia Minor* (Oxford: Clarendon Press, 1993), 2.3: "There is virtually nothing to be said for the north Galatian theory."

4. Recognizing there are drawbacks to labeling these individuals "Judaizers," I have nonetheless opted to use this conventional designation throughout. On the challenge with labeling Paul's opponents in Galatia, see the discussion in Mark D. Nanos, *The Irony of Galatians: Paul's Letter in First-Century Context* (Minneapolis: Fortress, 2002), pp. 110–192 (especially pp. 115–131), who prefers the label "influencers."

5. The provenance, ethnicity, and tactics of the Judaizers are still hotly contested issues. Scholars continue to debate whether they hailed from Jerusalem or Antioch or were indigenous to Galatia, whether they were Christ-believers or non-Christ-believers, and whether they were Jews, Gentiles, or a mixed group. The same can be said about the much-debated issue of whether the Judaizers advocated complete law observance or adopted a more lenient approach that focused primarily on circumcision, calendar observance, and perhaps a few ethical commands. I tend to think they were largely, if not entirely, Jewish Christ-believers (or at least, professing to be such) who were indigenous to Galatia and maintained close ties with local synagogues and the native non-Christ-believing Jewish population in those areas. In addition, I don't think they cared whether the Galatians embraced the whole Law (hence Paul's reminder in 5:3), as long as they received circumcision and thus became look-alike Jews, because this would alleviate the pressure *the Judaizers themselves* felt from other non-Christ-believing Jews who strongly disapproved of their fraternizing with uncircumcised Gentiles, even to the point of persecuting them (cf. 6:12, 13).

6. John M. G. Barclay, *Obeying the Truth: A Study of Paul's Ethics in Galatians* (Edinburgh: T & T Clark, 1988), p. 68.

7. In addition, the Galatians may have had their own reasons to be attracted to Judaism and the Law. It's worth remembering that during this period some Gentiles were attracted to Judaism. See Shaye J. D. Cohen, "Crossing the Boundary and Becoming a Jew," *Harvard Theological Review* 82 (1989): 13–33. It's also worth bearing in mind that the Galatians inhabited a world filled with tokens of divine vengeance and the workings of curses and as a result would have surely feared coming under the curse of a god. Hence, they would have been deeply unsettled by the threat of a curse and would have been quite keen to avert this possibility, even if it meant getting circumcised. The Galatians would thus likely have viewed the observance of circumcision as a means of bringing their lives into alignment with the demands of the Law and thereby averting its curse. In addition, they may have been influenced by viewing the rite of circumcision, insofar as it involved the shedding of blood, as an apotropaic ritual or sacrifice, which could avert God's anger (cf. Exodus 4:24–26). For this and other suggestions about the attraction of circumcision, see S. M. Elliott, *Cutting Too Close for Comfort: Paul's Letter to the Galatians in its Anatolian Cultic*

Context, JSNTSup 248 (London: T & T Clark, 2003): pp. 249–253. See also Todd A. Wilson, *The Curse of the Law and the Crisis in Galatia: Reassessing the Purpose of Galatians*, WUNT 2, no. 225 (Tübingen: Mohr Siebeck, 2007), pp. 69–94, where I argue that the Galatians' encounter with suffering, both Paul's and their own (cf. 3:4; 4:12, 13), may have exacerbated their fears about the curse of the Law, since in a world dominated by the overseeing presence of the gods suffering could easily be interpreted as an expression of divine vengeance and the workings of a curse. I also suggest that the Judaizers may have further provoked the Galatians' anxieties about the threat of a curse by interpreting the Galatians' suffering and Paul's own suffering as evidence of the fact that a curse *had already overtaken* them both.

8. See the evidence in Robert G. Hall, "Arguing Like an Apocalypse: Galatians and Ancient *Topos* outside the Greco-Roman Rhetorical Tradition," NTS 42 (1996): 434–453 (esp. 440, 441). Note that Paul says the Judaizers "force" circumcision (6:12; cf. 2:3, 14). This is a striking accusation since the only other contemporaneous examples of compelling circumcision that use this same terminology involve cases of forced Jewish proselytism (Josephus, *Jewish Antiquities* 13.318; 13.257–58; *Life* 112, 113). It's highly unlikely that the Judaizers were using physical coercion or legal pressure to compel the Galatians to get circumcised. Paul must then be describing an intense *moral pressure*, which, as far as he was concerned, amounted to a kind of militant proselytism. In fact, Paul describes their influence as deeply unsettling, even frightening, to the Galatians (cf. 1:7; 5:10). Whatever the Judaizers were saying and doing, it evidently provided the Galatians with no other viable options; they were left with a singular choice: circumcision. For more on the Judaizers and their identity and tactics, with special attention to their use of the threat of a curse to advocate for circumcision, see Wilson, *Curse of the Law*, pp. 47–68.

9. M. L. Stirewalt, *Paul: The Letter Writer* (Grand Rapids: Eerdmans, 2003), pp. 94–106 argues on the basis of a comparison of Galatians with official letters in antiquity that the reference to "all the brothers who are with me" in the salutation (1:2) probably refers to a delegation from Galatia sent to Paul, indeed one that may even have included some of the Judaizers themselves (cf. p. 106).

10. Charles Wesley, "O for a Thousand Tongues to Sing," 1740.

11. Cf. J. Louis Martyn, *Galatians: A New Translation with Introduction and Commentary*, AB 33A (New York: Doubleday, 1997), p. 91.

Chapter Two: Apostolic Astonishment!

1. See Tullian Tchividjian, *Jesus + Nothing = Everything* (Wheaton, IL: Crossway, 2011).

2. See further Todd A. Wilson, "Wilderness Apostasy and Paul's Portrayal of the Crisis in Galatia," NTS 50 (2005): 550–571, where I argue that part of Paul's rhetorical strategy to redress the developing crisis within the Galatian churches is to portray the Galatians, like Israel of old, as on the verge of apostatizing in the wilderness. After having been miraculously delivered from servitude through an exodus-like redemption in Christ (1:1–4; 4:3–7; 4:21—5:1a; 5:13a), the Galatians are now contemplating a return to Egyptian-like bondage (1:6, 7; 4:8, 9; 5:1b). As a result, Paul tries to exercise whatever moral leverage he can over the situation, coloring his rebukes and warnings with language that evokes the Israelites' own tragic wilderness defection and ultimate disinheritance. He thus "scripts" the Galatians into the role

of wilderness wanderers, presumably because he thinks this will clarify for them the seriousness of their present situation and elicit from them the desired response: a return to the Pauline gospel (1:6, 7; 5:7).

3. For another fictional and yet realistic and sober account of a young man who abandons his Christian faith in the midst of wrestling with the intellectual challenges of the twentieth century and his own personal experiences, see Martin Gardner, *The Flight of Peter Fromm* (Amherst, NY: Prometheus Books, 1994).

4. John Calvin, *Sermons on Galatians* (Edinburgh: Banner of Truth, 1997), p. 5.

5. We shouldn't underestimate the significance of the fact that Paul opens the letter with a double anathema upon anyone who preaches another gospel (1:8, 9). To begin with, this abrupt opening salvo marks a sharp contrast in tone to Paul's typical prayers of blessing or thanksgiving (cf. Romans 1:8–15; 1 Corinthians 1:4–9; 2 Corinthians 1:3–11; Ephesians 1:3–14; Philippians 1:3–11). Although some of the Galatians may not have been familiar enough with conventional letter-writing habits to register this change in style, they would all have been struck by Paul's stinging rebuke and charge of apostasy (1:6, 7), followed by the pronouncement of an anathema upon anyone preaching contrary to what the Galatians themselves had already received (1:8, 9).

6. Charles Spurgeon, *C. H. Spurgeon Autobiography, Volume 2: The Full Harvest 1860–1892* (Edinburgh: Banner of Truth, 1973), p. 114.

7. Martin Luther, "Lectures on Galatians," *1535, Luther's Works*, vol. 26, trans. and ed. Jaroslav Pelikan, (St. Louis: Concordia, 1963), p. 58.

8. Both the form and content of these verses, as well as the immediate context (1:6, 7), suggest that Paul may have been thinking in terms of the legislation of Deuteronomy 13, the classic Old Testament passage on false prophecy. See especially K. O. Sandnes, *Paul—One of the Prophets?: A Contribution to the Apostle's Self-Understanding*, WUNT 2, no. 43 (Tübingen: Mohr Siebeck, 1991), p. 71; Todd A. Wilson, *The Curse of the Law and the Crisis in Galatia: Reassessing the Purpose of Galatians.* WUNT 2, no. 225 (Tübingen: Mohr Siebeck, 2007), pp. 25, 26. It would be natural for Paul to perceive the apostasy within his Galatian congregations as akin to the situation envisaged in Deuteronomy 13, where one is led astray to worship "other gods" and thus leads others astray. Little wonder that Paul should have viewed the situation in comparable terms. The double anathema is Paul's effort to put the Judaizers under a curse and thus serves as a means of protecting the Galatians from their corrupting influence. This point becomes more explicit later in the letter: "Cast out the slave woman and her son" (4:30; cf. 5:7–12; 1 Corinthians 5:1–5).

9. For an excellent treatment of the Biblical warnings of Scripture, see Thomas R. Schreiner and Ardel B. Caneday, *The Race Set Before Us: A Biblical Theology of Perseverance and Assurance* (Downers Grove, IL: InterVarsity, 2001).

Chapter Three: People-Pleaser or Servant of Christ?

1. Josephus, *Jewish War*, 8.203, eds. H. St. J. Thackeray, R. Marcus, A. Wikgren, and L. H. Feldman, *Josephus: Works.* Loeb Classical Library. 10 vols. (Cambridge, MA: Harvard University Press, 1926–1965).

2. Cicero, *The Verrine Orations*, 2.5.66, in L. H. G. Greenwood, *Cicero. The Verrine Orations*, Loeb Classical Library. 2 vols. (Cambridge, MA: Harvard University Press, 1953).

3. Brian J. Dodd, "Christ's Slave, People Pleasers and Galatians 1.10," NTS 42 (1996): 90–104 (cf. 94, 95) rightly relates the theme of being a slave of Christ in 1:10 to the theme of suffering-persecution in Galatians.

4. Quoted in Richard Baxter, *The Practical Works of Richard Baxter, Volume 1: A Christian Directory* (Orlando: Soli Deo Gloria, 2003), p. 188. Baxter's treatment of hypocrisy in this whole section is excellent.

Chapter Four: You Are Your Best Argument

1. While the trend recently has been to downplay the apologetic function of Galatians 1, 2, the defensive tone of these chapters cannot be wholly eliminated. Paul's sharp antithetical contrasts (1:1, 10, 11), together with his carefully crafted travelogue vis-à-vis Jerusalem (1:17—2:10), is very difficult to explain apart from the supposition that his gospel and apostleship were somehow in question. Especially telling is the fact that Paul felt the need to guarantee the veracity of what he was saying with an oath: "In what I am writing to you, before God, I do not lie!" (1:20; cf. Romans 1:9; 9:1; 2 Corinthians 1:23; 11:31; 12:19; Philippians 1:8; 1 Thessalonians 2:5, 10), which would otherwise appear "dreadfully melodramatic" were he not faced with some kind of accusations (Moisés Silva, *Interpreting Galatians: Explorations in Exegetical Method,* 2nd ed. [Grand Rapids: Baker, 2001], p. 105). Thus John M. G. Barclay, *Obeying the Truth: A Study of Paul's Ethics in Galatians* (Edinburgh: T & T Clark, 1988), p. 88, among others, thinks it is "virtually certain" that Paul's gospel and apostleship were being called into question. However, the precise nature of the charges Paul suffered is more difficult to discern. Several observations suggest that Paul may have been charged with false prophecy. Debate over true and false prophets was important at the time of the writing of the New Testament and, more importantly, often arose within contexts where competing interpretations of Scripture were at issue, as would have probably been the case in the Galatian churches. Furthermore, an accusation of false prophecy would have been an effective means of *distancing* the Galatians from Paul, which evidently is precisely what has happened (cf. 4:17). Such accusations would have cast a shadow of doubt over Paul's character and thereby discredited the validity of his message. Reading Galatians 1, 2 against the backdrop of accusations of false prophecy also has the advantage of being able to correlate Paul's defense of his divine commission (1:1, 11–17), on the one hand, with the demonstration of his unswerving commitment to "the truth of the gospel" (2:5; cf. 1:10; 2:14), on the other, without needing to choose one instead of the other, as is sometimes done. This dual emphasis may reflect, then, Paul's conviction that the prophet's ethos is inseparable from his message. Several more specific observations suggest that Paul may have faced accusations of false prophecy. First, Paul's stress upon the divine, as opposed to merely human, origin of his apostleship (1:1) and gospel (1:11, 12) is characteristic of contexts where prophetic legitimacy is at stake. Luke's record of Gamaliel's advice to the council in Jerusalem deliberating over what is to be done to Peter and the other apostles, who they suspect are spreading a false teaching about Jesus of Nazareth, is indicative of this basic outlook: "If this plan or this undertaking is of man, it will fail; but if it is of God, you will not be able to overthrow them" (Acts 5:38, 39). The validity of the prophet's message depends upon the prophet having been sent by God (cf. Mark 11:31, 32). False prophets, on the other hand, can trace their calling only to a human source. Secondly, Paul sub-

stantiates his claim to having received his gospel not "from any man" but "through a revelation of Jesus Christ" (1:12) by recounting his calling in terms reminiscent of other Old Testament prophetic callings (1:15–17). Whether this reflects Paul's own self-understanding is not my concern here. It is sufficient simply to note that Paul clearly wants to bolster his claim to legitimacy by underscoring the divine origin of his calling and gospel. Paul's description of his own dramatic reversal from persecutor to preacher (cf. 1:13–24) is arguably intended to underscore this precise point. Thirdly, Paul's contrast between "pleasing man" and pleasing God (1:10) is a stereotypical distinction to make when prophetic legitimacy is at stake. False prophets speak "smooth things" and "prophesy illusions" (Isaiah 30:10). In various strands of early Jewish and Christian literature false prophets are portrayed as being religious charlatans with impure motives. They proclaim, in Paul's words, "man's gospel" (1:11). Because they derive their message and authority ultimately from humans, they aim to please them. One of the hallmarks of genuine prophets, however, is their uncompromising moral integrity (cf. 1 Thessalonians 2:3–6). See further Todd A. Wilson, *The Curse of the Law and the Crisis in Galatia: Reassessing the Purpose of Galatians,* WUNT 2, no. 225 (Tübingen: Mohr Siebeck, 2007), pp. 64–67.

2. Cited in William H. Willimon, *Conversation with Barth on Preaching* (Nashville: Abingdon, 2006), p. 97.

3. Josiah Bull, *Letters of John Newton, with Biographical Sketches and Notes by Josiah Bull* (Edinburgh: Banner of Truth, 2007 [orig. 1869]), p. 412.

4. Josiah Bull, *The Life of John Newton* (Edinburgh: Banner of Truth, 2007 [orig. 1868]), pp. 310, 311.

Chapter Five: Seeing Grace

1. Here I work from a South Galatian view and thus see Paul founding the churches of Galatia during his first missionary journey (cf. Acts 13, 14). On the correlation of Acts with Galatians, where Galatians 2:1–10 is identified with the famine visit in Acts 11:27–30, see Richard N. Longenecker, *Galatians,* WBC 41 (Waco, TX: Word, 1990), pp. lxxx–lxxxiii.

Chapter Six: Remember the Poor

1. Richard N. Longenecker, *Galatians,* WBC 41 (Waco, TX: Word, 1990), p. 59.

2. For a characteristically Biblical, nuanced, and pastorally helpful discussion of the issues surrounding the poor and poverty, see John Stott, *Issues Facing Christians Today,* 4th edition (Grand Rapids: Zondervan, 2006), pp. 161–188 ("Living with Global Poverty") and pp. 295–321 ("Simplicity, Generosity and Contentment").

3. See the very helpful discussion in Steve Corbett and Brian Fikkert, *When Helping Hurts: How to Alleviate Poverty without Hurting the Poor—and Yourself* (Chicago: Moody, 2009).

4. Mark R. Gorink, *To Live in Peace: Biblical Faith and the Changing Inner City* (Grand Rapids: Eerdmans, 2002), p. 206.

5. Clayborne Carson, *The Autobiography of Martin Luther King, Jr.* (New York: Intellectual Properties Management in association with Warner Books, 1998), p. 295.

6. Quoted in Tim Chester and Steve Timmis, *Total Church: A Radical Reshaping around Gospel and Community* (Wheaton, IL: Crossway, 2008), p. 79. Their chapter on "Social Involvement" is an excellent place to go for further reflection

on how the church can remember the poor (pp. 69–84). See also the wealth of immensely helpful material in Timothy J. Keller, *Ministries of Mercy: The Call of the Jericho Road*, 2nd edition (Philipsburg, NJ: P&R, 1997).

Chapter Seven: Staying in Step with the Truth of the Gospel

1. Richard N. Longenecker, *Galatians*, WBC 41 (Waco, TX: Word, 1990), p. 76.

2. Note the insightful comment in *ibid.*, 76: "The pathos that reverberates in the expression καὶ βαρναβᾶς ("even Barnabas") is gripping, for Barnabas had been Paul's advocate at Jerusalem (cf. Acts 9:26–28), mentor at Antioch (cf. Acts 11:25–30), and esteemed colleague in the evangelization of Cyprus and Southern Galatia (cf. Acts 13:2—14:26)."

3. Martin Luther, "Lectures on Galatians," *1535, Luther's Works*, vol. 26, trans. and ed. Jaroslav Pelikan (St. Louis: Concordia, 1963), p. 109.

4. Ibid., p. 109.

Chapter Eight: The Truth of the Gospel

1. Thomas A. Harris, *I'm OK—You're OK* (New York: HarperCollins, 1967).

2. In this particular instance I think the subjective genitive reading is to be preferred. Cf. Ardel Caneday, "The Faithfulness of Jesus Christ as a Theme in Paul's Theology in Galatians," in Michael F. Bird and Preston M. Sprinkle, *The Faith of Jesus Christ: Exegetical, Biblical, and Theological Studies* (Peabody, MA: Hendrickson, 2010), pp. 221–246. For the objective genitive reading of this clause, together with a fair handling of the issues, see Thomas R. Schreiner, *Galatians*, Zondervan Exegetical Commentary on the New Testament 9 (Grand Rapids: Zondervan, 2010), pp. 162–166. On this whole question, one should consult the collection of essays in Bird and Sprinkle, *The Faith of Jesus Christ*.

3. On the impact of the Damascus Road encounter with the risen Christ on Paul's theology, see G. W. Hansen, "Paul's Conversion and His Ethic of Freedom in Galatians," in *The Road from Damascus: The Impact of Paul's Conversion on His Life, Thought, and* Ministry, ed. Richard N. Longenecker (Grand Rapids: Eerdmans, 1997), pp. 213–237; Seyoon Kim, *The Origin of Paul's Gospel*, American ed. (Grand Rapids: Eerdmans, 1982).

4. Note the telling title of the recent book on Christian ethics by N. T. Wright, *After You Believe: Why Christian Character Matters*, 1st ed. (New York: HarperOne, 2010).

5. Dietrich Bonhoeffer, *Life Together; Prayerbook of the Bible*, Dietrich Bonhoeffer, Works, vol. 5 (Minneapolis: Fortress Press, 1996), p. 109.

Chapter Nine: Cruciformity: The Shape of Gospel-Rooted Living

1. For further reflections on this motif in Paul, see Michael J. Gorman, *Cruciformity: Paul's Narrative Spirituality of the Cross* (Grand Rapids: Eerdmans, 2001), pp. 178–213. Although Paul's call to cruciform, suffering love runs like a thread through his letters, he does not always invoke the motif of cruciformity in the same way. The particular shape of the cruciformity to which Paul calls his churches depends upon the exigencies of their particular situation. In Corinth, cruciformity is to manifest itself in the renouncing of individual rights and the proper exercise of spiritual gifts for the edification of the whole body. In Rome, cruciformity requires non-

retaliation toward enemies and nonjudgmental attitudes toward believers. In Galatia, however, cruciformity means bearing one another's burdens by following Christ in accepting suffering for the sake of others in submission to God.

2. Paul was thus an "anomalous Diaspora Jew" in the ancient Mediterranean world; so John M. G. Barclay, "Paul: An Anomalous Diaspora Jew," chap. 13 in *Jews in the Mediterranean Diaspora: From Alexander to Trajan (323 BCE–117 CE)* (Edinburgh: T&T Clark, 1996), pp. 381–396, though I don't follow Barclay on all of his conclusions regarding Paul and the Law.

3. Cf. A. E. Harvey, "Forty Strokes Save One: Social Aspects of Judaizing and Apostasy," in *Alternative Approaches to New Testament Study*, ed. A. E. Harvey (London: SPCK, 1985), pp. 79–96.

4. See Collin G. Kruse, "The Price Paid for a Ministry among Gentiles: Paul's Persecution at the Hands of the Jews," in *Worship, Theology and Ministry in the Early Church*, eds. M. J. Wilkins and T. Paige, JSNTSup 87 (Sheffield: JSOT, 1992): pp. 260–272.

5. Paul's suffering-persecution plays an important part in his self-presentation in Galatians. On several occasions he draws an inextricable link between his own fidelity to the gospel and his willingness to endure suffering-persecution for the sake of the cross (5:11; 6:14–17; cf. 2:1–15; 4:12–20). This is a crucial aspect of Paul's moral polemic in the letter, especially insofar as he on several occasions explicitly juxtaposes his *modus vivendi* with that of the Judaizers (5:10–12; 6:12–17; cf. 2:1–14). He clearly wants to portray himself, in contrast to them, as "an unfailing and divinely ordained follower and imitator of the suffering and persecuted Christ" (Dieter Mitternacht, "Foolish Galatians?—A Recipient-Oriented Assessment of Paul's Letter," in *The Galatians Debate: Contemporary Issues in Rhetorical and Historical Interpretation*, ed. M. D. Nanos [Peabody, MA: Hendrickson, 2002], pp. 408–433 [esp. p. 412]). Cf. Brian J. Dodd, "Christ's Slave, People Pleasers and Galatians 1.10," NTS 42 (1996): 90–104 (esp. pp. 94, 95); George Lyons. *Pauline Autobiography: Toward a New Understanding*, SBLDS 73 (Atlanta: Scholars, 1985), pp. 149, 150. He is, in a word, a "servant [slave] of Christ" (1:10) whose own crucified existence is patterned after the paradigmatic self-giving of his Master (cf. 1:4; 3:13; 4:4, 5). As Paul boldly states in the passage that may constitute the hermeneutical center of the letter: "I have been crucified with Christ. It is no longer I who live, but Christ who lives in me" (2:20).

6. Cited in Arnold Dallimore, *George Whitefield: The Life and Times of the Great Evangelist of the Eighteenth-Century Revival*, vol. 2 (Edinburgh: Banner of Truth, 1980), p. 160.

Chapter Ten: There's Only One Way to Finish

1. Gordon D. Fee, *God's Empowering Presence: The Holy Spirit in the Letters of Paul* (Peabody, MA: Hendrickson, 1994), p. 384 rightly says of 3:3: "This is the question to which the entire argument of the letter is devoted as a response."

2. See John Calvin, *Sermons on Galatians* (Edinburgh: Banner of Truth, 1997), p. 79: "Paul does not charge them with having, from the outset, rejected the gospel, but with *not having persevered in obedience*" (emphasis added).

3. Some may be uncomfortable with how starkly I've stated this warning and future contingency, wondering whether it undermines a theology of perseverance

and assurance. For a nuanced treatment of this issue that maintains the Biblical tension between warning and assurance, see Thomas R. Schreiner and Ardel B. Caneday, *The Race Set before Us: A Biblical Theology of Perseverance and Assurance* (Downers Grove, IL: InterVarsity, 2001).

4. There is in 3:1 an unmistakable stress upon the *visible* nature of this portrayal (οἷς κατ' ὀφθαλμοὺς), which speaks against this language being taken simply metaphorically as a way to describe the rhetorical vividness of Paul's proclamation; so Basil S. Davis, "The Meaning of Προεγράφη in the Context of Galatians 3.1," NTS 2 (1999): 194–212; Basil S. Davis, *Christ as Devotio: The Argument of Galatians 3:1–14* (Lanham, MD: University Press of America, 2002), pp. 207–210. Paul is, therefore, doing more than "celebrating his rhetorical skills" (Robert A. Bryant, *The Risen and Crucified Christ in Galatians*, SBLDS 185 [Atlanta: Society of Biblical Literature, 2000], p. 171). Instead he wants to remind the Galatians that during his initial visit they actually saw something; they had a concrete encounter with the crucified Christ. Paul's reference to the crucifixion of Christ here should be viewed in light of the immediately preceding reference to his own cocrucifixion with Christ (2:19, 20). Hence, the implication seems to be that the Galatians saw the living Christ in the dying apostle; that is, the life of Christ was manifest in Paul's suffering. This is probably what Paul envisages when he claims that God reveals his Son "in me" (ἐν ἐμοί, 1:16, ESV margin; cf. 2 Corinthians 4:7–12). His own suffering has become "paradoxically the locus of God's gift of life, being the present form of Jesus' own death-life pattern" (cf. Colossians 1:24). See J. Louis Martyn, *Galatians: A New Translation with Introduction and Commentary*, AB 33A (New York: Doubleday, 1997), p. 569; Todd A. Wilson, *The Curse of the Law and the Crisis in Galatia: Reassessing the Purpose of Galatians*, WUNT 2, no. 225 (Tübingen: Mohr Siebeck, 2007), pp. 87, 88. Cf. Scott J. Hafemann, "'Because of Weakness' (Galatians 4:13): The Role of Suffering in the Mission of Paul," in *The Gospel to the Nations: Perspectives on Paul's Mission*, ed. Peter Bolt and Michael Thompson (Downers Grove, IL: InterVarsity, 2000), pp. 131–146 (esp. pp. 136–141), who draws upon the Corinthian correspondence for corroboration of this point (1 Corinthians 4:9; 2 Corinthians 1:9, 10; 4:10, 11; 6:3–10; 12:9, 10; cf. 2 Corinthians 2:14).

5. On the theme of communion with the Triune God, one does well to consult the classic study by Puritan divine John Owen, which is now conveniently made available in Kelly M. Kapic and Justin Taylor, *Communion with the Triune God* (Wheaton, IL: Crossway, 2007).

6. A number of scholars and translators (cf. RSV) prefer to take this verse as a reference to how much the Galatians have experienced of the Spirit; cf. W. Bauer, F. W. Danker, W. F. Arndt, and F. W. Gingrich, *A Greek-English Lexicon of the New Testament and Other Early Christian Literature*, rev. and ed. F. W. Danker, 3rd ed. (Chicago: University of Chicago Press, 2000), 'πάσχω'; W. Michaelis, 'πάσχω,' *Theological Dictionary of the New Testament*, vol. 5 (Grand Rapids: Eerdmans, 1967), p. 912. It must be said, however, that if lexicography alone determined exegesis, there would be no debate about this verse. Every other use of πάσχω in the New Testament (including Paul) and the Septuagint has a negative nuance. Taking 3:4 as a reference to the Galatians' suffering (and persecution) was evidently the consensus view among Patristic commentators: e.g., Chrysostom, Augustine, Victorinus, Ambrosiaster, Pelagius, Jerome, Theodore of Mopsuestia, Theodoret, John

of Damascus, as noted by Basil S. Davis, *Christ as Devotio: The Argument of Galatians 3:1–14* (Lanham, MD: University Press of America, 2002), p. 211. Among modern scholars and commentators, see Herman N. Ridderbos, *The Epistle of Paul to the Churches of Galatia*, NICNT (Grand Rapids: Eerdmans, 1953), p. 115; F. F. Bruce, *The Epistle of Paul to the Galatians: A Commentary on the Greek Text*, NIGTC 2 (Exeter: Paternoster, 1982), p. 150; Ernst Baasland, "Persecution: A Neglected Feature in the Letter to the Galatians," *ST* 38 (1984): 135–150 (esp. 139, 140); Charles H. Cosgrove, *The Cross and the Spirit: A Study in the Argument and Theology of Galatians* (Macon, GA: Mercer, 1988), pp. 185, 186; A. J. Goddard and S. A. Cummins, "Ill or Ill-Treated? Conflict and Persecution as the Context of Paul's Original Ministry in Galatia (Galatians 4.12–20)," JSNT 52 (1993): 93–126 (esp. 119); Sylvia C. Keesmaat, *Paul and His Story: (Re)Interpreting the Exodus Tradition*, JSNTSup 181 (Sheffield: Sheffield Academic, 1999): p. 202; Mark D. Nanos, *The Irony of Galatians: Paul's Letter in First-Century Context* (Minneapolis: Fortress, 2002), p. 189.

Chapter Eleven: Abraham's Blessing

1. See Miguel Helft, "From Young Mogul, a Gift on the Scale of Philanthropy's Elders," *The New York Times*, September 25, 2010, p. B4.

2. Given that circumcision is the point at issue in the Galatian crisis and given the prominence of Scripture as part of Paul's response in Galatians (cf. 3:6—4:31), there is very good *prima facie* support for thinking that the Judaizers were using the Jewish Scriptures to convince the Galatians of the need for circumcision. In fact, it is difficult to envisage a scenario in which Gentile Christ-believers would be urged to embrace circumcision without at least some appeal to the Scriptural sanction and rationale for the practice. This initial impression finds further support from even a cautious "mirror-reading" of Galatians (see John M. G. Barclay, "Mirror-Reading," a Polemical Letter: Galatians as a Test Case," *Journal for the Study of the New Testament* 31 [1988]). First, the sheer *density* and *subtlety* of Paul's Scriptural argumentation is most easily explained as his attempt to counter competing interpretations proffered by the Judaizers, especially if the Galatians were largely illiterate pagans with minimal familiarity with the Scriptures and little or no independent access to them. Secondly, the *tone* of at least some of Paul's appeals to Scripture suggests he is on the defensive; indeed, on several occasions he appears to be matching the Judaizers' Scriptural exegesis with his own (3:10–14; 4:21–31). Thirdly, a few of Paul's citations appear to be in *tension* with the ostensible thrust of his own arguments, which suggests he may have been struggling to find a way to respond to a competing interpretation of these same texts. Fourthly, closely related to this last point, several of Paul's citations presumably would have been *well suited* to the Judaizers' own position (e.g., Deuteronomy 27:26 in 3:10 or Leviticus 18:5 in 3:12). Finally, a comparison of Paul's use of several Scriptural passages in Galatians with his use of these same passages in his other writings (e.g., Romans) reveals certain *peculiarities* and points of emphasis, which reinforce the impression that he is engaging in Scriptural repartee with the Judaizers. It may well have been that the Galatians themselves were well acquainted with the Jewish Scriptures through their involvement in the synagogue; so, for example, Roy E. Ciampa, *The Presence and Function of Scripture in Galatians 1 and 2*, WUNT 2, no. 102 (Tübingen: Mohr Siebeck, 1998),

pp. 260–270. On the literacy levels of Paul's churches and the church in Galatian in particular, see Christopher D. Stanley, *Arguing with Scripture: The Rhetoric of Quotations in the Letters of Paul* (London: T & T Clark, 2004), pp. 38–61 and pp. 114–118 respectively.

3. Christopher J. H. Wright, *The Mission of God: Unlocking the Bible's Grand Narrative* (Downers Grove, IL: InterVarsity, 2006), p. 65.

4. The Judaizers may well have been refracting the Abrahamic promise that "in you all the families of the earth shall be blessed" (Genesis 12:3b; Galatians 3:8) through the covenant theology of Deuteronomy, arguably the way in which the Biblical tradition and some strands of early Judaism did (cf. *Jubilees* 12.23; 25.22; 26.24; 31.17, 20; Tobit 13.9–18). Blessing and life come via incorporation into Abraham, the father of a multitude of nations (cf. 4:21–31). It is hardly accidental that in Galatians Paul makes no explicit reference to Genesis 17. An advocate of circumcision would be hard pressed to find a more unambiguous text in the whole of Scripture. It is indeed telling that Justin Martyr, an early Christian apologist, is pressed hard by his Jewish interlocutor Trypho over the fact that Christians dispense with circumcision and the Law, yet still expect divine favor (cf. *Dialogue with Trypho* 10.3).

5. Abraham's blessing shouldn't be equated with justification. It certainly includes God's counting us righteous because of Christ. But it goes beyond that. In fact, God's justifying us in Christ Jesus opens the door for every other blessing God intends for humanity and indeed for the whole creation.

Chapter Twelve: Clearing the Way for God's Blessing

1. Interestingly, however, the standard narrative enshrined in Christian theology has assumed as much. See R. Kendall Soulen, *The God of Israel and Christian Theology* (Minneapolis: Fortress, 1996). Elsewhere I have argued against the view that Galatians supports the superfluity or supersession of the Law; see Todd A. Wilson, "The Supersession and Superfluity of the Law? Another Look at Galatians," in *Introduction to Messianic Judaism: Its Ecclesial Context and Biblical Foundations*, ed. Joel Willitts and David Rudolph (Grand Rapids: Zondervan, 2013), pp. 235–244.

2. As is widely recognized, this verse seems singularly ill-suited to Paul's line of thought; in fact, it seems to say precisely the opposite of what Paul wants to argue: that the curse falls upon those who *do* the "works of the law'"—not upon those who *fail* to do so, which is the ostensible thrust of Deuteronomy 27:26. Some explain the awkwardness by supposing Paul's on the defensive, offering his own counter-interpretation to the Judaizers' handling of this verse, which they presumably were already using to warn the Galatians of the consequences of failing to comply with the demands of the Law. See C. K. Barrett, "The Allegory of Abraham, Sarah, and Hagar in the Argument of Galatians," in *Essays on Paul* (London: SPCK, 1982), pp. 118–131 (esp. p. 158). J. Louis Martyn, *Galatians: A New Translation with Introduction and Commentary*, AB 33A (New York: Doubleday, 1997), p. 309, James M. Scott, "'For as Many as Are of Works of the Law are Under a Curse' (Galatians 3:10)," in *Paul and the Scriptures of Israel*, ed. C. A. Evans and J. A. Sanders, JSNTSup 83 (Sheffield: Sheffield Academic, 1993): pp. 187–221, and N. T. Wright, *The Climax of the Covenant: Christ and the Law in Pauline Theology* (Edinburgh: T & T Clark, 1991), pp. 137–156 have put forward a more promising line of interpretation that situates Paul's citation of Deuteronomy 27:26 within Israel's own experience of ex-

ile and restoration. For a refinement of this line of interpretation one should consult Rodrigo J. Morales, *The Spirit and the Restoration of Israel*, WUNT 28 (Tübingen: Mohr Siebeck, 2010).

3. On the inner-Biblical exegesis of Leviticus 18:5, as well as the use of it in Second Temple Judaism and by Paul, see Preston M. Sprinkle, *Law and Life: The Interpretation of Leviticus 18:5 in Early Judaism and in Paul*, WUNT 2, no. 241 (Tübingen: Mohr Siebeck, 2008), though I differ with some of his conclusions about Paul's view of the Law in Galatians.

4. Christopher D. Stanley, "'Under a Curse': A Fresh Reading of Galatians 3.10–14," NTS 36 (1990): 481–511 is right to see this as a warning to the Galatians.

5. See the powerful scene from John Bunyan, *The Pilgrim's Progress* (New York: Penguin, 2008), p. 39, where the main character Christian observes in the Interpreter's House a man choking on the dust he's stirred up by trying to sweep his house clean. Says the Interpreter to Christian, "This parlor is the heart of a man that was never sanctified by the sweet Grace of the Gospel: the dust is his Original Sin and inward Corruptions, that have defiled the whole man. He that began to sweep at first, is the Law."

6. Charles H. Spurgeon, *C. H. Spurgeon Autobiography, Volume 2: The Full Harvest 1860–1892* (Edinburgh: Banner of Truth, 1973), pp. 61, 62.

7. The careful reader will note a nod here to particular redemption. For a potent exposition of this theological truth, see the masterful treatment by J. I. Packer, "'Saved by His Precious Blood': An Introduction to John Owen's *The Death of Death in the Death of Christ*," in *A Quest for Godliness: The Puritan Vision of the Christian Life* (Wheaton, IL: Crossway, 1994), pp. 125–148.

8. Karl Barth, *Church Dogmatics, Volume IV.1: The Doctrine of Reconciliation* (Edinburgh: T & T Clark, 1956), p. 165.

9. On the roots of Christian mission in the Abrahamic blessing, see Christopher J. H. Wright, *The Mission of God: Unlocking the Bible's Grand Narrative* (Downers Grove, IL: InterVarsity, 2006); Richard Bauckham, *Bible and Mission: Christian Witness in a Postmodern World* (Grand Rapids: Baker, 2003); P. T. O'Brien, *Gospel and Mission in the Writings of Paul: An Exegetical and Theological Analysis* (Grand Rapids, Carlisle, Cumbria, UK: Baker; Paternoster, 1995).

10. These comments reflect my own eschatological leanings toward historic or classical premillennialism.

11. Adapted from the hymn "May the Mind of Christ My Savior," lyrics by Kate Barclay Wilkinson.

Chapter Thirteen: Why Then the Law?

1. The literature on Paul and the Law is vast and unending. It's only a little more manageable for Galatians. For general discussions of the Law in Galatians, see Michael Winger, *By What Law? The Meaning of Nomos in the Letters of Paul*, SBLDS 128 (Atlanta: Scholars, 1992), pp. 73–78; I-G. Hong, *The Law in Galatians*, JSNTSup 81 (Sheffield: JSOT, 1993): pp. 122–124; Kari Kuula, *The Law, the Covenant and God's Plan: Volume 1—Paul's Polemical Treatment of the Law in Galatians*, Publications of the Finnish Exegetical Society 72 (Helsinki and Göttingen: Finish Exegetical Society and Vandenhoeck & Ruprecht, 1999), pp. 46–57; Philip F. Esler, *Galatians*, New Testament Readings (London: Routledge, 1998), pp.

178–204; Vincent M. Smiles, *The Gospel and the Law in Galatia: Paul's Response to Jewish Christian Separatism and the Threat of Galatian Apostasy* (Collegeville, MN: Liturgical, 1998), pp. 219–230.

2. See the masterful treatment of this complex issue by Paul F. M. Zahl, *Grace in Practice: A Theology of Everyday Life* (Grand Rapids: Eerdmans, 2007), though I don't agree with him on all points.

3. Charles H. Spurgeon, *The Complete John Ploughman: Combined Editions of John Ploughman's Talk and John Ploughman's Pictures* (Hagerstown, MD: Christian Heritage, 2007), pp. 190, 191.

4. Paul's brief digression in 3:21–25 serves, then, not unlike Romans 7:7–25, to ward off a possible charge against the Law. Given what Paul has said thus far in chapter 3, one might conceivably conclude that the Law somehow opposes the promises (3:21), for Paul has denied that the Law in any way mediates the *blessing* of Abraham (3:6–14), but instead has only brought about the *curse* (3:10–14). This grim reading of the Law's function is further exacerbated by Paul's intervening claim that the Law was secondary to the promises (3:15–18) and added only "because of transgressions" (3:19), and that by an "intermediary" (3:20). Regardless of the implications one draws from these seemingly disparaging remarks, the question of 3:21 is surely to the point: is the Law against the promises? Paul's answer to this query, though, is surprisingly straightforward. The Law is not ultimately culpable for the curse—sin is. Sin blocks the reception of the promises by interposing, not the Law, but the *curse* of the Law. This again explains why Paul compares being under law (i.e., under the curse of the Law) to being "under a guardian" or pedagogue (3:24, 25). In the Greco-Roman milieu, not only was a pedagogue's role over the life of a child temporary, the very presence of a pedagogue was indicative of the child's *inability to access his inheritance*. Not insignificantly, this second nuance is precisely the one Paul develops in both 3:23–29 (cf. 3:29) and 4:1–7 (cf. 4:7). One of the underlying themes of 3:10—4:7 is that while Israel was "under the law" (3:23), Israel was unable to gain access to the promise of the inheritance. As such, Israel was, at least with respect to the inheritance, hardly any different than the nations, despite being rightfully entitled to that inheritance (4:1, 2). Speaking metaphorically, Israel was "under a guardian" during her protracted childhood (3:24, 25; 4:1, 2). Alternatively, one could say that for Israel the Law, because of its curse, became for a time a pedagogue, which precluded Israel gaining access to the inheritance. In short, until Christ came to redeem Israel from the curse of the Law (3:13; 4:4, 5), Israel was kept "under the law"—under the Law's curse.

5. Hence, when Paul says that we were kept "under the law" (3:23) by being enclosed "under sin" (3:22), he is probably referring to Israel's inability to escape from the *curse* of the Law because of her inability to come out from "under sin" (cf. 3:10–12; 4:21–27). In other words, sin foiled Israel's best attempts to find liberation from the curse of the Law *by means of* the Law (cf. Romans 8:3).

6. See David J. Lull, "'The Law Was Our Pedagogue': A Study in Galatians 3:19–25," JBL 105 (1986): 481–498; Norman H. Young, "*Paidagogos*: The Social Setting of a Pauline Metaphor," NovT 29, no. 2 (1987): 150–176; T. David Gordon, "A Note on Παιδαγωγός in Galatians 3.24–25," NTS 35 (1989): 150–154; Linda L. Belleville, "'Under Law': Structural Analysis and the Pauline Concept of Law in Galatians 3.21–4.11," JSNT 26 (1986): 53–78; but note the incisive comment by Stephen

Westerholm, *Israel's Law and the Church's Faith: Paul and His Recent Interpreters* (Grand Rapids: Eerdmans, 1988), p. 195: "It is probably pointless to ask which part of the 'pedagogue's' task Paul has in mind in applying the figure to the Law."

7. In saying this, one should be careful to note that Paul does not describe the *Law itself* as a "pedagogue," but only the particular historical *function* of the Law before the "coming [of] faith" (3:23), when it was itself enclosed "under sin" (3:22). As Paul says: ὥστε ὁ νόμος παιδαγωγὸς ἡμῶν γέγονεν εἰς Χριστόν (3:24). Thus Paul's comparison of the Law's function to that of a pedagogue tells us little about whether he thought the Law itself was of limited duration or not. His only point here is that this particular function of the Law (i.e., to enclose Israel under a curse) is of a limited duration (i.e., εἰς Χριστόν). Despite the widespread assumption to the contrary, the issue of the perpetuity of the Law *after* the coming of faith is not at issue here. In fact, one of the implications of our exegesis of 3:23–25 and 4:1–7, where the chronological nature of Paul's argument is often assumed to imply the idea of superfluity, actually revolves around the cessation of the Law's *curse* for those who participate in redemption in Christ (3:25; 4:4, 5; cf. 3:13, 14). Although Paul strongly opposes the circumcision of his Gentile converts (5:1–4), which may imply some element of superfluity in his understanding of the Law (cf. 5:6; 6:15), it has become clear nonetheless that the *basic thrust* of his polemic in Galatians centers upon the Law's inability to mediate righteousness (2:15–21; 3:21; 5:5, 6), its contrast with faith (3:11, 12), and its power to curse (1:8, 9; 3:10, 13) rather than upon its irrelevance within a *post-Christum* situation. See further Todd A. Wilson, "The Supersession and Superfluity of the Law? Another Look at Galatians," in *Introduction to Messianic Judaism: Its Ecclesial Context and Biblical Foundations*, ed. Joel Willitts and David Rudolph (Grand Rapids: Zondervan, 2013), 235–244.

8. See Todd A. Wilson, *The Curse of the Law and the Crisis in Galatia: Reassessing the Purpose of Galatians,* WUNT 2, no. 225 (Tübingen: Mohr Siebeck, 2007) for a substantiation of this thesis.

9. The perennial question of the role of the Law in the life of Paul's (largely) Gentile congregations is still an unresolved issue in Pauline scholarship, as it is in Christian theology and ethics. As Stephen Westerholm observes: "Exegetes cannot agree whether or not Paul thought Christians are subject to the law" (*Israel's Law and the Church's Faith: Paul and His Recent Interpreters* [Grand Rapids: Eerdmans, 1988], p. 198). The position taken in this commentary is that the Law continues to serve for Paul as an abiding standard of behavior for believers. This basic line of interpretation, however, has at least three different expressions within Pauline scholarship. It has been prominent among Patristic and Reformed exegetes to affirm what in Reformation nomenclature came to be referred to as the "third use" of the Law (see Gerhard Ebeling, "On the Doctrine of the *Triplex Usus Legis* in the Theology of the Reformation," in *Word and Faith* [London: SCM, 1963], pp. 62–78). Augustine, for example, was little troubled by Paul's continued references to the Law in 5:13—6:10, since the Law contained both "sacramental works" and "works having to do with good morals," the latter of which, when properly understood, continued to be obligatory for believers (Eric Plumer, *Augustine's Commentary on Galatians: Introduction, Translation (with Facing Latin Text), and Notes,* Oxford Early Christian Studies [Oxford: Oxford University Press, 2003], sections 43, 44 [on 5:13, 14]). Calvin makes similar sorts of distinctions in order to uphold the moral obligation of the Law for the life of

the Christian. John Calvin, *Commentaries on the Epistles of Paul to the Galatians and Ephesians*, trans. W. Pringle, reprinted edition, Calvin's Commentaries, 22 Vols. (Grand Rapids: Eerdmans, 1993), p. 164 (on 5:18). While the believer's conscience is not bound by the Law for salvation, this does not, Calvin insists, render the Law superfluous for Christian living (see especially John Calvin, *Institutes of the Christian Religion*, trans. F. L. Battles, The Library of Christian Classics, 2 vols. [London: SCM Press, 1960], 3.19.2). Cf. I. J. Hesselink, "John Calvin on the Law and Christian Freedom," ExAud 11 [1995]: 77–89. This was evidently the consensus among Puritan divines; see E. F. Kevan, *The Grace of Law: A Study in Puritan Theology* (London: The Carey Kingsgate Press Limited, 1964), pp. 167–223. A variation of this basic approach can be found among some scholars known as supporters of the New Perspective on Paul. James D. G. Dunn, for example, insists that Paul's criticisms of the Law are carefully targeted, not wholesale, and should not be taken to imply a complete disavowal of the Law for the Christian (cf. James D. G. Dunn, *The Theology of Paul the Apostle* [Grand Rapids: Eerdmans, 1998], p. 632). What has changed is the Law's function within the new era of salvation-history. "With the transition to a new epoch, the law's role as guardian of Israel's distinctiveness was at an end. The obligation to walk in a way appropriate to the relationship given by God remained" (James D. G. Dunn, *The Theology of Paul's Letter to the Galatians,* New Testament Theology [Cambridge: Cambridge University Press, 1993], p. 116). A third variation of this same approach is to argue that Paul, in keeping with many of the other earliest Jewish followers of Jesus, believed that the Law was obligatory for Jews and Gentiles in different ways: that is, for Jews *as Jews* and for Gentiles *as Gentiles* (Michael Wyschogrod, "A Jewish Postscript," in *Encountering Jesus: A Debate on Christology*, ed. S. T. Davis [Atlanta: Westminster/John Knox, 1988], pp. 185–187; idem., "Christianity and Mosaic Law," ProEccl 2, no. 4 (1993): 451–459; idem., *Abraham's Promise: Judaism and Jewish-Christian Relations*, ed. R. K. Soulen [Grand Rapids: Eerdmans, 2004], pp. 160–164, 188–201; Peter J. Tomson, *Paul and the Jewish Law: Halakha in the Letters of the Apostle to the Gentiles,* CRINT, Vol. 1, Sec. 3, Jewish Traditions in Early Christian Literature. [Assen/Maastricht and Minneapolis: Van Gorcum and Fortress, 1990]; idem., "Paul's Jewish Background in View of His Law Teaching in 1 Cor 7," in *Paul and the Mosaic Law*, ed. J. D. G. Dunn [Tübingen: Mohr Siebeck, 1996], pp. 251–270 [esp. p. 268]; idem., *"'If This be From Heaven . . . ': Jesus and the New Testament Authors in Their Relationship to Judaism*, Biblical Seminar 76 [Sheffield: Sheffield Academic, 2001], esp. pp. 179–190; Markus N. A. Bockmuehl, *Jewish Law in Gentile Churches: Halakhah and the Beginning of Christian Public Ethics* [Edinburgh: T & T Clark, 2000], pp. 145–173; Richard Bauckham, *James: Wisdom of James, Disciple of Jesus the Sage*, New Testament Readings [London and New York: Routledge, 1999], pp. 148–151; Alan F. Segal, *Paul the Convert: The Apostolate and Apostasy of Saul the Pharisee* [New Haven, CT: Yale University Press, 1990], pp. 187–223; idem., "Universalism in Judaism and Christianity," in *Paul in His Hellenistic Context*, ed. T. Engberg-Pedersen [Edinburgh: T & T Clark, 1994], pp. 1–29). According to the Jewish theologian Michael Wyschogrod, the Noachide commandments constitute for Paul, and for much of the early church (cf. Acts 15), the law for Gentiles (*Abraham's Promise*, p. 162). While Jews are under obligation to observe, in Paul's terms, "the whole Law"(5:3), i.e., to live as Jews, Gentiles are to conform to the basic moral standards of the Law, which includes avoiding things such as incest, murder, and robbery. Thus, when Paul refers to Gentiles fulfilling the Law, he has in mind the Law *as it applies to Gentiles* (cf. 1 Corinthians 7:19). And when he warns the Galatians that "the works of the flesh" exclude one from "the kingdom of God" (5:19–21), he identifies behavior that overlaps considerably with those cardinal sins proscribed by the Law, which Jews, generally speaking, believed even Gentiles were to observe. On the particular question of Paul's rationale for continuing to refer to the Law in the so-called ethical section of Galatians (5:13—6:10), these approaches come out looking somewhat similar. While scholars within the Reformed tradition tend to utilize the distinction between various aspects of the Law, some of which are now obsolete, those who identify with the New Perspective on Paul tend to mark different priorities within the Law, some of which now take precedence over others. The third approach mentioned above takes a slightly different tack by distinguishing between different aspects of the Law along the Jew-Gentile axis. In the end, however, each of these readings depends upon a similar line of argument: Paul's positive affirmations of the Law in 5:14 and 6:2 (and perhaps 5:23) refer to the Law as, in some sense, an abiding standard of behavior, while Paul's negative comments elsewhere in the letter should be taken to refer to a particular feature or function of the Law.

10. For an excellent treatment of this issue, see John Piper, *The Purifying Power of Living by Faith in Future Grace* (Sisters, OR: Multnomah, 1995).

Chapter Fourteen: Heirs According to Promise

1. In Galatians, Paul consistently personifies Scripture (γραφή) so that it "preached" (3:8), "imprisoned" or encloses (3:22), and speaks (4:30). This suggests he uses the term as a way to refer to what *God* has done, as witnessed to in Israel's Scriptures. The formal parallels between 3:22 and 3:8, as well as the parallels between 3:22 and Romans 11:32 (cf. Romans 9:17), corroborate this point.

2. Several commentators take "under sin" (3:22) to refer to the Law's *condemnation* of sin, thus equating "under sin" with "under a curse" (3:10). While I certainly find this a tempting proposal, a close reading of these verses argues against this line of interpretation. First, Paul says that it was Scripture (γραφή) and not the Law (νόμος, cf. 3:21; 3:23–25) that enclosed all things "under sin." Secondly, he says that Scripture enclosed not just all persons (τοὺς πάντας cf. Romans 11:32), but all things (τὰ πάντα) "under sin." This suggests that Paul may have wanted to include the *Law itself* within the scope of that which Scripture enclosed "under sin." That Paul conceives of the Law itself as "under sin" is supported by the fact that 3:22 serves as a logical contrast to the condition of 3:21 (cf. ἀλλά, 3:22). Paul denies the possibility that a law was given that could "give life" (3:21) by asserting that in reality Scripture has enclosed all things—even the Law itself—"under sin" (3:22; cf. 1:4). As a prisoner to sin, then, the Law was incapable of producing life and therefore unable to provide "righteousness" (3:21; cf. 2:15–21; 3:11, 12). It is best, then, to take "under sin" as a reference, not to the Law's condemnation of sin, but to the *power* or *authority* of sin over all things, including those who possess the Law, those of the Sinai covenant. The expression "under sin" thus refers to a more general (i.e., universal) condition than that referred to by "under the law" (3:23). The latter is a particular expression of the former; "under law" is a subset of "under sin." While everyone is "under sin," only those of the Sinai covenant are "under law"—that is, under the penalty prescribed in the Law for failure to observe its precepts, which is

itself the direct consequence of being "under sin" (cf. 3:10; 2:15, 16). This reading makes good sense of the following verse: "Now before faith came, we were held captive under the law, imprisoned [συγκλειόμενοι] until the coming faith would be revealed" (3:23). Here Paul repeats the verb συγκλείω from 3:22, though he elides the phrase "under sin," probably to avoid an unnecessary redundancy. But the point is clear: "We were held captive under the law" (3:23). Though controversial, this statement likely summarizes Paul's reflections on Israel's own experience with the Law under the Sinai covenant (cf. 3:17–21). Hence, when Paul says that we were kept "under the law" by being enclosed "under sin" (3:22–23), he is probably refer-ring to Israel's inability to escape from the *curse* of the Law because of her inability to come out from "under sin" (cf. 3:10–12; 4:21–27). In other words, sin foiled Is-rael's best attempts to find liberation from the curse of the Law *by means of* the Law (cf. Romans 8:3: τὸ ἀδύνατον τοῦ νόμου).

3. Again, see Todd A. Wilson, *The Curse of the Law and the Crisis in Galatia: Reassessing the Purpose of Galatians*, WUNT 2, no. 225 (Tübingen: Mohr Siebeck, 2007) and idem., "'Under Law' in Galatians: A Pauline Theological Abbreviation," *JTS* 56, no. 2 (2006): 362–392 for a defense of this reading.

4. Cited in Edward Gilbreath, *Reconciliation Blues: A Black Evangelical's in-side View of White Christianity* (Downers Grove, IL: InterVarsity Press, 2006).

5. See the helpful essay by Robert H. Stein, "Baptism and Becoming a Chris-tian in the New Testament," *SBJT* 2, no. 1 (Spring 1998): 6–17.

6. See Troy W. Martin, "The Covenant of Circumcision (Genesis 17:9–14) and the Situational Antithesis in Galatians 3:28," *JBL* 122, no. 1 (2003): 111–125.

7. See especially Michael O. Emerson and Christian Smith, *Divided by Faith: Evangelical Religion and the Problem of Race in America* (Oxford and New York: Oxford University Press, 2000).

Chapter Fifteen: Adoption as Sons

1. "Babies 'cry in mother's tongue,'" *BBC News*, November 6, 2009; accessed online: http://news.bbc.co.uk/2/hi/8346058.stm.

2. See especially Timothy J. Keller, *Counterfeit Gods: The Empty Promises of Money, Sex, and Power, and the Only Hope That Matters* (New York: Dutton, 2009); and the older Richard J. Foster, *Money, Sex & Power: The Challenge of the Disci-plined Life* (San Francisco: Harper & Row, 1985).

3. The progression from being "born of woman" (4:4c) and "born under the law" (4:4d) would thus be a movement from the Son's birth to his death and there-fore contain a reference to the Son's coming under the curse of the Law upon the cross, an echo of 3:13. See further Todd A. Wilson, "'Under Law' in Galatians: A Pauline Theological Abbreviation," JTS 56, no. 2 (2006): 362–392 for sustained de-fense of this reading of "under the law" as rhetorical shorthand for "under the curse of the Law."

4. Given the significance of what Paul says here in 4:3–5, J. Louis Martyn, *Ga-latians: A New Translation with Introduction and Commentary*, AB 33A (New York: Doubleday, 1997), p. 388 may be right when he claims that these verses constitute "nothing less than the theological center of the entire letter."

5. Sylvia C. Keesmaat, *Paul and His Story: (Re)Interpreting the Exodus Tradi-tion*, JSNTSup 181 (Sheffield: Sheffield Academic, 1999): pp. 202–203 (cf. pp. 74–

77) rightly suggests that the Spirit sent into the heart of the believer crying "Abba, Father" is intended as a cry of desperation in the midst of trials or suffering. Cf. Robert A. Bryant, *The Risen and Crucified Christ in Galatians*, SBLDS 185 (Atlanta: Society of Biblical Literature, 2000), p. 181n54.

Chapter Sixteen: Turning Back Isn't the Way Forward

1. There continues to be significant debate about whether this statement implies the Galatians are turning to Jewish calendar observance (still the view of the majority of commentators) or returning to some kind of pagan practices (so, e.g., Troy W. Martin, "Apostasy to Paganism: The Rhetorical Stasis of the Galatian Controversy," JBL 114, no. 3 [1995]: 437–461). A more promising line of inquiry of late has been to situate this fascinating comment within the context of imperial cult and imperial ideology of the Julio-Claudian period in Asia Minor and Galatia in particular; see especially Justin K. Hardin, *Galatians and the Imperial Cult: A Critical Analysis of the First-Century Social Context of Paul's Letter*, WUNT 2, no. 237 (Tübingen: Mohr Siebeck, 2008), pp. 116–147 (on 4:10).

2. For more on Paul's use of the exodus and wilderness traditions in Galatians, see Todd A. Wilson, "Wilderness Apostasy and Paul's Portrayal of the Crisis in Galatia," NTS 50 (2005): 550–571.

3. Augustine, *Confessions*, The Penguin Classics, L114 (Baltimore: Penguin, 1961), pp. 175, 176.

4. J. I. Packer, *Knowing God*, 20th anniversary ed. (Downers Grove, IL: InterVarsity, 1993), pp. 41, 42.

5. This statement thus constitutes more than Paul's desire for the Galatians to grow in Christian maturity; his assessment of their situation is much more radical. So Y-G. Kwon, *Eschatology in Galatians: Rethinking Paul's Response to the Crisis in Galatia*. WUNT 2, no. 183 (Tübingen: Mohr Siebeck, 2004), pp. 34, 35. See also Beverly R. Gaventa, "The Maternity of Paul: An Exegetical Study of Galatians 4:19," in *The Conversation Continues: Studies in Paul and John in Honor of J. Louis Martyn,* ed. R. T. Fortna and B. R. Gaventa (Nashville: Abingdon, 1990), pp. 189–201. Apparently the Galatians need nothing less than *rebirth* by the Spirit!

Chapter Seventeen: Imitation Is the Solution, Part 1

1. Dietrich Bonhoeffer, *Life Together; Prayerbook of the Bible*, Dietrich Bonhoeffer, Works, vol. 5 (Minneapolis: Fortress, 1996), pp. 35, 36.

2. Ibid., pp. 37, 38.

3. Kate B. Wilkinson, "May the Mind of Christ, My Savior," 1925.

Chapter Eighteen: Imitation Is the Solution, Part 2

1. On 4:12 as an (implicit) call for imitation, see Willis Peter de Boer, *The Imitation of Paul* (Kampen: J. H. Kok, 1962), pp. 188–196; Beverly R. Gaventa, "Galatians 1 and 2: Autobiography as Paradigm," NovT 28, no. 4 (1986): 309–326 (esp. 319–322); Richard B. Hays, "Christology and Ethics in Galatians: The Law of Christ," CBQ 49 (1987): 268–290 (esp. 281, 282); Andrew J. Goddard and Stephen A. Cummins, "Ill or Ill-Treated? Conflict and Persecution as the Context of Paul's Original Ministry in Galatia (Galatians 4.12–20)," JSNT 52 (1993): 93–126 (esp. 94–100); Basil S. Davis, *Christ as Devotio: The Argument of Galatians 3:1–14* (Lan-

ham, MD: University Press of America, 2002), pp. 216, 217; and the more recent contribution by Susan G. Eastman, *Recovering Paul's Mother Tongue: Language and Theology in Galatians* (Grand Rapids: Eerdmans, 2007), pp. 25–61.

2. Paul's portrayal of the crucified Christ (cf. 1:4; 3:13) and his own self-presentation as Christ's crucified apostle (cf. 2:19, 20; 5:11; 6:17) provide warrant for and give shape to his call here in 4:12 for imitation. Although imitation is less explicit in Galatians than in some of Paul's other writings, it is not difficult to discern a mimetic undercurrent in much of what he says. Regardless of whether one detects an apologetic note in Galatians 1, 2, Paul clearly presents himself as a courageous defender of "the truth of the gospel" (2:5), one whose own ethos not only inspires admiration but elicits imitation. At least, then, one of the purposes of Paul's autobiographical remarks becomes clear with the letter's first explicit imperative: Γίνεσθε ὡς ἐγώ (4:12). As Richard B. Hays rightly observes, this summons presupposes Paul's earlier narrative portrayal of himself: "The basis for this exhortation would lie in Paul's belief that his own life manifested a conformity to the normative pattern of Christ's obedient self-sacrifice" ("Law of Christ," 281). The only refinement I would want to add is that within the context of the Galatian crisis, Paul conceives of conformity to Christ as an unwavering commitment to the truth of the gospel in the face of *opposition* (2:1–14) and even *suffering-persecution* (5:11; 6:17). The Galatians are thus called to imitate Paul's own crucified commitment to Christ (2:19, 20; 6:14).

3. On the moral nature of the Galatian crisis, see Yon-Gyong Kwon, *Eschatology in Galatians: Rethinking Paul's Response to the Crisis in Galatia,* WUNT 2, no. 183 (Tübingen: Mohr Siebeck, 2004), esp. pp. 184–212.

4. While most modern commentators treat Paul's "bodily ailment" as an illness of some kind, with numerous possibilities suggested, I here endorse an interpretation popular among Patristic and Reformation commentators that the phrase should be taken as a reference to the debilitating or even disfiguring effects of Paul's persecution (cf. 6:17; 2:19, 20; 3:1; 5:11). Among modern commentators who advocate this view, see especially Goddard and Cummins, "Conflict and Persecution," pp. 93–126. Prior to founding the churches in Galatia, Paul may have already received some form of synagogue discipline, perhaps even the thirty-nine lashes (cf. 2 Corinthians 11:24). Cf. A. E. Harvey, "Forty Strokes Save One: Social Aspects of Judaizing and Apostasy," in *Alternative Approaches to New Testament Study*, ed. A. E. Harvey (London: SPCK, 1985), pp. 79–96 (esp. pp. 83–88). In fact, if we work from the assumption that the churches of Galatia are those founded during Paul's first missionary journey, then the very planting of these churches may well have entailed for Paul significant suffering-persecution (cf. Acts 14:1–20) and thus became part of his early catechesis and encouragement of the Galatians (cf. Acts 14:21, 22).

5. From what Paul says about his initial encounter with the Galatians, they evidently could have had some trouble embracing him in his own affliction. Paul refers to the fact that his "bodily ailment" proved to be a "trial" or temptation to the Galatians (4:13, 14). In fact, as he says, they had every reason to "scorn or despise" him in his suffering, even though, to their credit, they embraced him "as an angel of God, as Christ Jesus" (4:14). What this suggests is that Paul recognizes that the Galatians' own preconversion cultural and religious outlook could have inclined them to regard Paul in his suffering as a dangerous contagion, whose presence was to be avoided, for he had the appearance of one suffering under the righteous rage of a god.

6. It may be that Paul simply intended the term ἐκπτύω as a way of expressing a strong sense of disdain or rejection (see Goddard and Cummins, "Conflict and Persecution," pp. 105, 106). But his use of this rare word at least suggests that the Galatians were inclined to perform an apotropaic gesture to ward off possible demonic influence associated with Paul's physical suffering or weakness. Cf. A. Oepke, *Der Brief des Paulus an die Galater*, 5th ed., THKNT 9 (Berlin: Evangelische Verlagsanstalt, 1984), pp. 142, 143; H. Schlier, *Der Brief an die Galater*, KEK 7 (Göttingen: Vandenhoeck & Ruprecht, 1962), pp. 210, 211; Ulrich Heckel, "Der Dorn im Fleisch: Die Krankheit des Paulus in 2Kor 12,17 und Gal 4,13f.," ZNW 84 (1993), pp. 65–92 (esp. 84–86).

7. A growing number of scholars point to the pressure that may have been exerted on the Galatians to participate in imperial cult worship. See the recent discussion in Graham N. Stanton, *Jesus and Gospel* (Cambridge: Cambridge University Press, 2004), pp. 35–49 (esp. pp. 42–45); and now especially Justin K. Hardin, *Galatians and the Imperial Cult: A Critical Analysis of the First-Century Social Context of Paul's Letter*, WUNT 2, no. 237 (Tübingen: Mohr Siebeck, 2008).

8. Furthermore, we know that allegiance to this newfangled religion centered around a Jewish peasant executed as a criminal by the Romans was often a costly business, not least in Asia Minor, where it was apparently not uncommon for believers to suffer social dislocation and harassment (cf. 1 Peter 2:12–20; 3:13–16; 4:3–5, 12–16). We have little reason to doubt that the Galatians would have encountered similar sorts of reactions. This may even have gone beyond verbal abuse, libel, or slander to include actual physical mistreatment. Either way it is very likely that the Galatians would have experienced some (perhaps a significant) measure of suffering as a result of their adherence to Paul's gospel.

9. Obviously Paul intends this comment to contrast the Galatians' *former* willingness to embrace him in his suffering (4:13, 14), even to the extent of being willing to gouge out their own eyes to remedy what afflicts him (4:15), with their *present* defection from him (4:16). Paul provocatively highlights this change of posture by implying that they have forfeited their original "blessedness" (4:15). This seems like a slightly odd thing to say, but it may reflect the fact that Paul is here tapping into the well-attested early Jewish and Christian conviction that blessedness attends the righteous in their suffering (cf. Matthew 5:11, 12; 10:22; Luke 6:22; 1 Peter 3:14; 4:14; Daniel 12:12 LXX). In James 1:12, for example, we see these two terms closely juxtaposed: "Blessed is the one who remains steadfast under trial" (cf. James 5:11). First Peter is perhaps more germane to Paul's comment here: "Beloved, do not be surprised at the fiery *trial* when it comes upon you to test you, as though something strange were happening to you. But rejoice insofar as you share Christ's sufferings, that you may rejoice and be glad when his glory is revealed. If you are insulted for the name of Christ, you are *blessed*, because the Spirit of glory and of God rests upon you" (4:12–15). Paul may, then, intend this comment to serve as a subtle allusion to the Galatians' forfeiture of the Spirit, the source of eschatological joy in the midst of suffering (cf. 4:6).

10. Cf. J. Louis Martyn, *Galatians: A New Translation with Introduction and Commentary*, AB 33A (New York: Doubleday, 1997), pp. 422, 423.

11. This remark continues to puzzle commentators. Part of the difficulty is that Paul does not state from whom or what the Galatians were to be excluded: from

Christ (5:4), from God (1:6; 5:8), from the gospel (1:6; 2:5; 5:7), from the church (4:30), or from Paul himself (4:16)? Another possibility would be to view this comment within the larger context of Galatians 3, 4, where the issue of who are the rightful heirs of the inheritance is paramount. Paul would then have in mind exclusion from the *inheritance* (3:29; 4:7, 30). This may have involved interposing the threat of a curse between the Galatians and their entering into "the kingdom of God" (5:21). By insisting on the necessity of circumcision, the Judaizers were in effect excluding the Galatians from the eschatological inheritance (cf. 4:21–31; Acts 15:1).

Chapter Nineteen: Children of the Free Woman

1. That Paul is speaking polemically and, in fact, ironically in 4:21 is suggested by his use of the verb θέλω to depict what the Galatians "desire" to do. Paul uses this verb on a number of occasions to portray the motives of both the Judaizers and the Galatians. His strategy with θέλω appears to be twofold. On the one hand, Paul wants to distance the Galatians from the Judaizers by exposing the Judaizers' fraudulent motives (cf. 1:7; 4:17; 6:12, 13). On the other hand, he wants to warn the Galatians about their present apostasy by projecting their own motives in terms of the negative consequences of their actions (4:9, 21). While the Judaizers no doubt promulgated their teaching under a fair guise, and may well have done so with good intentions, as far as Paul was concerned they simply "wanted" to pervert the gospel of Christ (1:7), exclude the Galatians (4:17), "make a good showing in the flesh" (6:12), avoid persecution (6:12), and boast in the Galatians' circumcision (6:13). Paul's tactic with the Galatians, however, is more subtle. By portraying what the Galatians *want* to do in terms of what they are trying to *avoid* in both 4:9 and 4:21, Paul issues a pair of very forceful (albeit highly ironic) warnings. After having been miraculously delivered from servitude to beings "that by nature are not gods" (4:8), Paul is incredulous over the fact that the Galatians are now observing "days and months and seasons and years" (4:10). He chides them: "How can you turn back again to the weak and worthless elementary principles of the world, *whose slaves you want to be once more?*" (4:9). The Galatians, needless to say, had absolutely no intention of returning to slavery of any kind, much less bondage to the "principles" (4:9). But discerning intentions is not Paul's point here. Rather he confronts the Galatians with their own foolishness by outrageously asserting that they themselves are eager to be enslaved.

2. Susan Eastman, "The Evil Eye and the Curse of the Law: Galatians 3.1 Revisited," JSNT 83 (2001): 69–87 (esp. 75).

3. For a series of wonderful devotional reflections on this theme, see Andrew Murray, *Waiting on God: A Classical Devotional Edited for Today's Reader*, edited and updated (Minneapolis: Bethany, 2001).

4. On the use of Isaiah in this context, see Karen H. Jobes, "Jerusalem, Our Mother: Metalepsis and Intertextuality in Galatians 4:21–31," WTJ 55 (1993): 299–320; Joel Willitts, "Isa 54,1 and Gal 4,25b-27: Reading Genesis in Light of Isaiah," ZNW 96 (2005): 188–201; and Matthew S. Harmon, *She Must and Shall Go Free: Paul's Isaianic Gospel in Galatians,* Beihefte zur Zeitschrift für die neutestamentliche Wissenschaft und die Kunde der älteren Kirche (Berlin and New York: De Gruyter, 2010).

5. Cf. J. Louis Martyn, *Galatians: A New Translation with Introduction and Commentary*, AB 33A (New York: Doubleday, 1997), p. 444.

Chapter Twenty: What Ultimately Counts?

1. For a powerful and theologically robust exposition of Galatians from the perspective of the theme of freedom, see Gerhard Ebeling, *The Truth of the Gospel: An Exposition of Galatians*, trans. D. Green (Philadelphia: Fortress, 1985).

2. Thus I don't view Paul's statement about keeping "the whole law" as presupposing the impossibility of perfect law keeping. To be sure, Paul is still threatening the Galatians, though not with the impossibility of perfect law keeping, but with the necessity of taking on the whole Law and thus becoming Jewish. The problem for the Galatians resides not in the impossibility of perfect law keeping but in the adherence to the old covenant, which will render the reality of the new covenant, namely, the person and work of Jesus Christ, utterly useless, as Paul warns the Galatians: "Look: I, Paul, say to you that if you accept circumcision, *Christ* will be of no advantage to you" (5:2), and "You are severed from *Christ*, you who would be justified by the law; you have fallen away from grace" (5:4). Hence, one should hear Paul's warning in 5:3 in light of what he's already said in 3:10 about the dead-end of "works of the law" and the old covenant as a whole. On the other hand, as Paul goes on to demonstrate in 5:13—6:10, if one embraces the gifts of the new covenant—the death of Jesus Christ (3:13) and the sending of the promised Holy Spirit (3:14)—then one will in fact *fulfill "the whole law"* (5:14; cf. 6:2). Paul no doubt intends the affirmation of 5:14 about the whole Law being fulfilled in love as one walks by the Spirit (5:16; cf. 5:5, 6) to be the answer to both 5:3 and 3:10. See Todd A. Wilson, *The Curse of the Law and the Crisis in Galatia: Reassessing the Purpose of Galatians*, WUNT 2, no. 225 (Tübingen: Mohr Siebeck, 2007), pp. 97–138 (esp. 104–112 on the interplay between 3:10, 5:3, and 5:14).

3. Arnold Dallimore, *George Whitefield: The Life and Times of the Great Evangelist of the Eighteenth-Century Revival*, vol. 1 (Edinburgh: Banner of Truth, 1980), p. 72 (emphasis added).

4. Ibid., p. 73.

5. See Douglas J. Moo, "Justification in Galatians," in *Understanding the Times: New Testament Studies in the 21st Century, Essays in Honor of D. A. Carson on the Occasion of His 65th Birthday*, ed. Andreas Köstenberger and Robert Yarbrough (Wheaton, IL: Crossway, 2011), pp. 160–195, who rightly notes that the issue Paul is addressing in Galatians is "how the Galatians are to *maintain* their status of righteousness and, especially, how they can expect to be found to be in the 'right' in the judgment" (p. 189, emphasis original).

6. See ibid., pp. 178–186 for an exegetically careful restatement of the Reformation principle of *sola fide* as the teaching of Paul in Galatians.

7. See Moo in ibid., p. 170, who rightly says of 5:5: "Paul is not just stating a truth; he is inviting the Galatians to join with him in taking ownership of that truth."

8. On the timing of justification in Galatians, see especially Moo in ibid., pp. 186–190, who rightly concludes his survey as follows: "Overall, justification language in Galatians has a timeless and, if anything, future-oriented focus" (p. 189). Thus, as he goes on to note, justification functions at both ends of the eschatological spectrum: "already" and "not yet" (cf. p. 190).

9. Paul Johnson, *Churchill* (New York: Viking, 2009), p. 3.

10. Ibid., p. 123.

Chapter Twenty-one: Free to Run

1. See Thomas R. Schreiner and Ardel B. Caneday, "The Prize to Be Won: Our present and Future Salvation," chap. 2 in *The Race Set Before Us: A Biblical Theology of Perseverance and Assurance* (Downers Grove, IL: InterVarsity, 2001), esp. pp. 46–86.

2. John Bunyan, *The Pilgrim's Progress* (New York: Penguin, 2008), xxv.

3. Laura Hillenbrand, *Unbroken: A World War II Story of Survival, Resilience, and Redemption* (New York: Random House, 2011), p. 41.

Chapter Twenty-two: Through Love Serve One Another

1. Timothy S. Lane and Paul David Tripp, *Relationships: A Mess Worth Making* (Greensboro, NC: New Growth, 2008), p. 12.

2. On 5:13—6:10 as a discrete unit within Galatians, see John M. G. Barclay, *Obeying the Truth: A Study of Paul's Ethics in Galatians* (Edinburgh: T & T Clark, 1988), p. 24. For discussion of the difficulties with this particular designation see, for example, the discussion in J. Louis Martyn, *Galatians: A New Translation with Introduction and Commentary*, AB 33A (New York: Doubleday, 1997), pp. 482–484, esp. 482n41.

3. Gordon D. Fee, *God's Empowering Presence: The Holy Spirit in the Letters of Paul* (Peabody, MA: Hendrickson, 1994), p. 420. In the last twenty years, particularly within English-speaking scholarship, a widespread consensus has emerged on the question of the relevance of 5:13—6:10 to Galatians and to the situation in Galatia. In short, most scholars now agree that 5:13—6:10 is both *integral* to the letter and, at least to some extent, *relevant* to the situation. It is now commonplace for interpreters to affirm without further ado that this section of the letter is not only vital to the argument of Galatians but also pertinent to the situation in Galatia; indeed, for some these closing chapters constitute the high point of the letter. See Frank J. Matera, "The Culmination of Paul's Argument to the Galatians: 5:1—6:17," JSNT 32 (1988): 79–91; Barclay, *Obeying the Truth*, pp. 216–220.

4. This is a prominent, if not driving, theme of Dietrich Bonhoeffer's classic study of Christian community, *Life Together; Prayerbook of the Bible*, Dietrich Bonhoeffer, Works, vol. 5 (Minneapolis: Fortress, 1996).

5. Human susceptibility to "lordless powers" is a prominent theme in J. Louis Martyn, *Galatians*, as well as in a number of more recent readings of Galatians (e.g., Bruce W. Longenecker, *The Triumph of Abraham's God: The Transformation of Identity in Galatians* [Edinburgh: T & T Clark, 1998]). Cf. Karl Barth, *Church Dogmatics, Volume IV.3: The Christian Life* for a powerful exposition of this concept.

6. Thus Paul's statement in 5:13, 14 is intentionally paradoxical: we are called to freedom, but this freedom is for the purpose of being slaves to one another in love. In a recent article I have argued that this paradox reflects an exodus matrix of thought: having been redeemed from Egyptian-like bondage, the Galatians are called to enslave themselves to God (cf. 4:8, 9) and therefore to one another; cf. Todd A. Wilson, "Wilderness Apostasy and Paul's Portrayal of the Crisis in Galatia," NTS 50 (2005): 550–571 [esp. 565–567]). Paul's call to be enslaved to one another in love thus constitutes more than a "necessary nuance" to his notion of Christian freedom (so Stephen Westerholm, "On Fulfilling the Whole Law (Gal 5.14)," SEÅ 51–52 [1986–1987]: 229–237 [esp. 231]). Instead it provides freedom with its very *raison d'être*.

7. Often scholars will argue that this shift in the use of "flesh" (σάρξ) here coincides with a transition in the argument of the letter from the threat of nomism in 2:15—5:12 to libertinism in 5:13—6:10. For those unconvinced of a threat of libertinism, Paul's warning is related to the "fleshly" attitudes and communal infighting evidently already at work in the Galatian churches (cf. 5:15, 19–21, 26). While there is doubtless something to this, Paul's charge not to allow freedom to become "an opportunity for the flesh" should not be entirely divorced from the issue of circumcision (cf. 5:1, 2). For one thing, Paul uses "flesh" (σάρξ) at several key points in Galatians to refer to circumcision (3:3; 4:23, 29; 6:12, 13). Furthermore, 5:13—6:10 is bracketed by two sections that speak explicitly about taking on circumcision (5:1–12; 6:11–18). Cf. Frank J. Matera, "The Culmination of Paul's Argument to the Galatians: 5:1–6:17," JSNT 32 (1988): 79–91.

8. A close inspection of "the works of the flesh" enumerated in 5:19–21 suggests that communal infighting was a live issue for the Galatians. Paul's list focuses both structurally and numerically upon those vices naturally associated with situations of social discord. Eight of the fifteen vices mentioned (i.e., "enmity, strife, jealousy, fits of anger, rivalries, dissension, divisions, envy") are social in orientation, and their centralized location gives them emphasis. That communal infighting was a problem is also suggested by the parallel warning Paul issues in 5:26: "Let us not become conceited, provoking one another, envying one another." The Galatians, then, perhaps as a result of the influence of those heralding "another gospel" (1:6, 7; cf. 5:7), were beset by attitudes and actions that were destroying social cohesion and loving service (cf. 5:13c, 14; 6:1–10).

9. Bonhoeffer, *Life Together*, p. 94.

10. Ibid., p. 95.

11. See the excellent study by Jerry Bridges, *Respectable Sins: Confronting the Sins We Tolerate* (Colorado Springs: NavPress, 2007), especially Chapter 19, which deals with "Sins of the Tongue" (pp. 159–163).

12. If, as I have argued in my work *The Curse of the Law and the Crisis in Galatia: Reassessing the Purpose of Galatians*, WUNT 2, no. 225 (Tübingen: Mohr Siebeck, 2007), the threat of a curse was looming large in the background of the Galatian crisis, then Paul's affirmation of the total realization of God's will here in 5:14 would have been precisely what the Galatians needed to hear. While the Galatians may have had doubts about coming under a curse for failing to abide by all that the Law enjoins (3:10), they can nevertheless be confident of the fact that serving one another in love actually fulfils the whole Law (5:14). As we shall see, Paul continues to reinforce this precise point with his other three references to the Law in 5:13—6:10 (cf. 5:18, 23; 6:2).

13. Jonathan Edwards, *Charity and Its Fruits* (Edinburgh: Banner of Truth, 1969), pp. 351–353.

14. Martin Luther, *The Freedom of a Christian* (Minneapolis: Fortress, 2008), p. 84.

Chapter Twenty-three: The Sufficiency of the Spirit

1. Cf. Frederick Blass, Albert Debrunner, Robert W. Funk, *Greek Grammar of the New Testament and Other Early Christian Literature,* revised edition (Chicago: University of Chicago Press, 1961), section 365, who note that οὐ μὴ with the aor-

ist subjunctive expresses "the most definitive form of negation regarding a future event"; cited in John M. G. Barclay, *Obeying the Truth: A Study of Paul's Ethics in Galatians* (Edinburgh: T & T Clark, 1988), p. 68, who similarly notes the "resounding confidence" Paul expresses with this statement.

2. Cf. Todd A. Wilson, "'Under Law' in Galatians: A Pauline Theological Abbreviation," JTS 56, no. 2 (2006): 362–392.

3. Interpreters often note that the language of 5:21b is unusual for Paul, particularly since elsewhere in Galatians inheritance terminology is used as "reception of" rather than "entrance into" (cf. 3:18, 29; 4:1, 7, 30). But this peculiarity may be best explained by granting the influence of the wilderness narratives at this point, for they attest to the failure of the Israelites to *enter the land* precisely because they practiced the very vices Paul *now* sees at work in the Galatian churches (cf. 1 Corinthians 10:1–13). Paul fears, then, that the Galatians are threatening to repeat the folly of the Israelites who turned their exodus freedom into "an opportunity for the flesh" (5:13) by giving way to the dreaded "works of the flesh" (5:19–21; cf. 5:15, 26), which in the end brought not the inheritance of what was promised but divine judgement (cf. 5:21b; 6:7, 8). He, too, fears that if the Galatians fail to follow the leading of the Spirit, they will, like the Israelites, come under the curse of the Law and be disinherited. Cf. Todd A. Wilson, *The Curse of the Law and the Crisis in Galatia: Reassessing the Purpose of Galatians.* WUNT 2, no. 225 (Tübingen: Mohr Siebeck, 2007), pp. 127–131.

4. I. H. Thomson, *Chiasmus in the Pauline Letters*, JSNTSup 111 (Sheffield: Sheffield Academic, 1995): pp. 142–144 supports this claim by contending that the warning of 5:21b is the central element of a well-developed chiasmus from 5:13—6:2 (see pp. 116–151).

5. It is worth noting that Paul links the fulfillment of the Law with love and "the promised Spirit" (3:14), whose presence marks the realization of prophetic expectations for a future restoration of the people of God (Isaiah 32:15; 44:3; Ezekiel 11:19; 36:26; 37:14; 39:29; Joel 2:28–32; Acts 2:33, 39; Ephesians 1:13). In fact, when speaking of the fulfillment of the Law, Paul may well have in mind the new covenant prophecy of Jeremiah about the Law being written "on their hearts" (Jeremiah 31:33 [LXX 38:33]; cf. Ezekiel 36:26, 27).

6. Paul is therefore affirming the fact that the curse of the Law does not fall upon the kind of behavior that is enabled by the Spirit and embodied in love (5:22; cf. 5:5, 6, 14). This reading, of course, tallies nicely with the interpretation of 5:18 offered above. In fact, it reiterates basically the same point made in 5:18: those who are led by the Spirit (5:18) and whose lives are characterized by "the fruit of the Spirit" (5:22, 23) are not under the curse of the Law. This reading also presupposes that those who are led by the Spirit actually satisfy the Law's demands. As we saw in the previous chapter, this is one of the key points of Paul's two references to the fulfillment of the Law in 5:14 and 6:2. While a number of scholars note that walking by the Spirit (5:16) leads to the fulfillment of the Law (5:14), which in turn implies that the Galatians are not "under the law" (5:18), they often interpret this as a statement about the superfluity of the Law rather than as an affirmation of the fact that the leading of the Spirit enables one to avoid the curse of the Law. Those who are led by the Spirit fulfill the Law (5:14; 6:2) and thereby avoid its curse (5:18, 23), for when the empowering agency of the Spirit excludes "the desires of the flesh" (5:16), believers are enabled to serve one another through love and thus fulfill the Law (5:13, 14; 6:1, 2; cf. 5:5, 6).

7. Several scholars have drawn attention to the Old Testament background to Paul's use of fruit and Spirit language and imagery in 5:22, 23. See Barclay, *Obeying* (1988), pp. 120, 121; G. K. Beale, "The Old Testament Background of Paul's Reference to 'the Fruit of the Spirit' in Galatians 5:22," BBR 15.1 (2005): 1–38. In the Old Testament Israel is often depicted as a fruit-bearing tree, or at least this is the ideal; the people are often upbraided for failing to produce the requisite fruit (i.e., moral qualities). But this failure is actually taken up and transformed and becomes part of the eschatological aspirations of the prophets. For one day the Lord will revivify Israel so she becomes what she was always intended to be: an Eden-like plant whose fruitfulness stands in sharp contrast to the nation's present plight of barrenness and fruitlessness (cf. Isaiah 27:2–6; 37:30–32; Jeremiah 31:27, 28; 32:41; Ezekiel 17:22–24; Hosea 14:5–8; Joel 2:18–32; Amos 9:13–15). Several of these texts, moreover, ascribe this process of revivification to the agency of the Spirit (e.g., Isaiah 32:15, 16; Joel 2:18–32). Barclay is thus right to observe: "Paul's reference to the 'fruit of the Spirit' may therefore be intended to evoke the prophetic statements on Israel and the promise for her future: such fruit is what God has always demanded of his people and what was promised for the 'age to come'" (*Obeying the Truth*, p. 121).

8. Howard and Geraldine Taylor, *Hudson Taylor's Spiritual Secret* (Peabody, MA: Hendrickson, 2008), p. 131.

Chapter Twenty-four: Burden Bearing, Part 1: Spiritual Restoration

1. See especially Dietrich Bonhoeffer, *Life Together; Prayerbook of the Bible*, Dietrich Bonhoeffer, Works, vol. 5 (Minneapolis: Fortress, 1996), p. 100.

2. I owe this analogy to Philip Graham Ryken, *Galatians*, Reformed Expository Commentary (Phillipsburg, NJ: P&R, 2005), p. 245.

3. Cf. Todd A. Wilson, *The Curse of the Law and the Crisis in Galatia: Reassessing the Purpose of Galatians*, WUNT 2, no. 225 (Tübingen: Mohr Siebeck, 2007), p. 112.

4. Richard B. Hays, "Christology and Ethics in Galatians: The Law of Christ," CBQ 49 (1987): 268–290 thus rightly speaks of Christ's action in Galatians as "a pattern of submission to God and of accepting suffering for the sake of others" (p. 278).

5. C. S. Lewis, *Mere Christianity: A Revised and Amplified Edition, with a New Introduction, of the Three Books, Broadcast Talks, Christian Behaviour, and Beyond Personality*, 1st HarperCollins edition (San Francisco: HarperSanFrancisco, 2001), p. 94.

6. Jonathan Edwards, *Religious Affections*, Works, vol. 2 (New Haven, CT: Yale University Press, 1959), p. 315.

7. Lewis, *Mere Christianity*, p. 99.

8. Rightly captured by Ronald Y. K. Fung, *The Epistle to the Galatians*, NICNT (Grand Rapids: Eerdmans, 1988), p. 290: "It is on his own conduct and performance that each person should concentrate, not the conduct and performance of others; he is to engage in self-assessment, not in critical evaluation of another."

9. Within the history of interpretation, the Law of Christ has seldom been taken as a direct reference to the Law of Moses. While it may not be entirely unprecedented, prior to the late twentieth century it would be difficult to find anyone stating explicitly and unambiguously that Paul connects the Law of Moses with the Law of Christ. The nearly universal view has been that with this expression Paul refers to

that which *replaces* the Law of Moses. Particularly outside the Lutheran tradition, this has meant taking the Law of Christ as a reference to some kind of *nova lex* for Christians. It was not at all uncommon, for example, for Patristic commentators to interpret the Law of Christ in terms of Jesus' "new commandment" (cf. John 13:34, 35). The Law of Moses has thus been replaced by the love command as it was taught by Jesus himself. Recently, however, an increasing number of scholars are exploring the possibility that the Law of Christ in fact refers to the Law of Moses. This conclusion is based on several observations. First, the close parallels between 6:2 and 5:13, 14, where a reference to the Law of Moses is, as we have already seen, very well established, strongly suggests that Paul is also referring to the Law of Moses in 6:2. Secondly, the close proximity of 5:13, 14 to 6:2, together with the fact that 5:13, 14 precedes and thus prepares for 6:2, makes it rather unlikely that Paul intended the Law of Christ to refer to something other than what he has just referred to with the whole Law in 5:14. Thirdly, with the (possible) exception of 3:21b, every other use of νόμος in Galatians refers to the Law of Moses. As J. Louis Martyn has recently argued with some vigor: "There is every reason, then, for taking Gal 6:2 to be the thirty-first juncture in this letter at which Paul refers to *the* Law" (J. Louis Martyn, *Galatians: A New Translation with Introduction and Commentary*, AB 33A [New York: Doubleday, 1997], pp. 555, 556n41). See further Todd A. Wilson, "The Law of Christ and the Law of Moses: Reflections on a Recent Trend in Interpretation," CurBR 5.1 (2006): 129–150, where I also set this recent trend in interpretation within the exegetical and theological milieu in which it has arisen and draw out several of its implications for Pauline theology and exegesis.

10. See similarly, Martin Luther, *Lectures on Galatians, 1535*, Luther's Works, vol. 26, trans. and ed. Jaroslav Pelikan (St. Louis: Concordia, 1963), p. 121: "At the Last Judgment each man will have to bear his own load; therefore the praise of others will not do him any good there."

11. Ibid., p. 120.

12. Thus verse 5 is closely related to verse 3, as is rightly noted by John Calvin, *Sermons on Galatians* (Edinburgh: Banner of Truth, 1997), p. 176.

13. See A. Andrew Das, *Paul and the Jews*, Library of Pauline Studies (Peabody, MA: Hendrickson, 2003), p. 181: "All people, even Christians, will be judged according to the standard of the Mosaic Law according to Paul" (cf. this entire section entitled "God's Standard for Judgment," pp. 181–183).

14. So Thomas R. Schreiner, *Galatians*, Zondervan Exegetical Commentary on the New Testament 9 (Grand Rapids: Zondervan, 2010), p. 358.

15. Rightly noted by John R. W. Stott, *The Message of Galatians: Only One Way*, The Bible Speaks Today (Leicester, UK; Downers Grove, IL: InterVarsity, 1986), p. 161, even if, exegetically speaking, Paul does not intend to limit this exhortation to the mature.

16. Luther, *Galatians, 1535*, p. 113.

17. This is best seen as an explicit reference to the *Holy Spirit* rather than to the human spirit, for Paul has just reminded the Galatians that one of the fruits of the Spirit is the very quality he here commends: gentleness. See, e.g., James D. G. Dunn, *The Epistle to the Galatians*, BNTC (Peabody, MA: Hendrickson, 1993), p. 321, who suggests that the ambiguity (spirit or Spirit?) was deliberate.

18. Rightly, Schreiner, *Galatians*, p. 357.

19. Luther, *Galatians, 1535*, p. 121.
20. Ibid.

Chapter Twenty-five: Burden Bearing, Part 2: Pay Your Pastor

1. Martin Luther, *Lectures on Galatians, 1535*, Luther's Works, vol. 26, trans. and ed. Jaroslav Pelikan (St. Louis: Concordia, 1963), p. 126.

2. You can find this same pattern of speaking in highly relational and theological terms throughout Paul's letters: see Romans 1:13, "reap some harvest among you," 2 Corinthians 8:6, "this act of grace," Philippians 1:5, "your partnership in the gospel," with 4:14–20.

3. While J. G. Strelan, "Burden-Bearing and the Law of Christ: A Re-Examination of Galatians 6:2," JBL 94 (1975): 266–276 mistakenly tried to restrict the language of burden bearing to meeting one another's financial needs, he did underscore the fact that language comparable to that used in 6:2 often occurs in Paul's letters within contexts that do so.

4. C. S. Lewis, "The Weight of Glory," in *The Weight of Glory and Other Essays* (San Francisco: HarperOne, 2001), pp. 25, 26.

5. D. Martyn Lloyd-Jones, *Spiritual Depression: Its Causes and Cure* (Grand Rapids: Eerdmans, 1965), p. 201.

6. Note that 6:10 is introduced with the inferential ἄρα οὖν cf. Richard N. Longenecker, *Galatians*, WBC 41 (Waco, TX: Word, 1990), p. 282, who notes that 6:10 serves to summarize not only 6:1–10 but also 5:13—6:10.

Chapter Twenty-six: Boast Only in the Cross

1. These verses provide "the interpretive clues to the understanding of Paul's major concerns in the letter as a whole and should be employed as the hermeneutical key to the intentions of the Apostle" (Hans Dieter Betz, *Galatians: A Commentary on Paul's Letter to the Churches in Galatia*, Hermenia [Philadelphia: Fortress, 1979], p. 313). See also George Lyons, *Pauline Autobiography: Toward a New Understanding*, SBLDS 73 (Atlanta: Scholars, 1985), p. 168; Jeffrey A. D. Weima, "Gal. 6.11–18: A Hermeneutical Key to the Galatian Letter," *CTJ* 28 (1993): 90–107.

2. Bruce W. Winter, "The Imperial Cult and Early Christians in Roman Galatia (Acts Xiii 13–50 and Galatians Vi 11–18)," in *Actes Du Ier Congrès International Sur Antioche De Pisidie*, ed. T. Drew-Bear, M. Tashalan, and C. M. Thomas (Paris: Université Lumière-Lyon 2 and Diffusion de Boccard, 2002), pp. 67–75 has argued that the verb εὐπροσωπέω ("to make a good showing") refers to the Judaizers' desire to obtain a good legal or political status in the eyes of the local civic authorities. For further interaction with and refinement of Winter's thesis, see Justin K. Hardin, *Galatians and the Imperial Cult: A Critical Analysis of the First-Century Social Context of Paul's Letter*, WUNT 2, no. 237 (Tübingen: Mohr Siebeck, 2008), pp. 85–115 (on 6:12, 13).

3. There continues to be a lively debate about the reason why the Judaizers would have been exposed to persecution because of their association with the Galatian believers; for various proposals see Robert Jewett, "The Agitators and the Galatian Congregations," NTS 17 (1971): 198–212; J. Muddiman, "An Anatomy of Galatians," in *Crossing the Boundaries: Essays in Biblical Interpretation in Honour of Michael Goulder*, ed. S. E. Porter, P. Joyce, and D. E. Orton, BibIntSer 8 (Leiden: Brill, 1994), pp. 257–270; Hardin, *Galatians and the Imperial Cult*, pp. 85–115.

4. See the Puritan divine John Owen's classic study on this theme, now made conveniently accessible in Kelly M. Kapic and Justin Taylor, *Overcoming Sin & Temptation* (Wheaton, IL: Crossway, 2006).

5. Galatians thus begins with a conditional curse (1:8, 9) and ends with a conditional blessing (6:16). This blessing-curse framework for Galatians in turn offers an important clue as to how Paul intended the letter to function within the situation of crisis in Galatia. Paul addresses the Galatians with a blessing and a curse in response to perceived apostasy (1:6) on the one hand and the influence of (what he perceives to be) false teachers on the other (1:7). Invoking the motif of blessing and curse within this particular context bears some similarity to the way this same motif functions as part of the covenant renewal ceremony depicted in other early Jewish texts, like Qumran (cf. 1QS 1.16–2.19; 4Q286–87; 4Q280; 1QM 13.4–6) and *Jubilees* 1. It is also not unlike what Paul does at the end of 1 Corinthians, where he draws upon covenantal categories to separate out the faithful from the apostates: "If anyone does not love the Lord, let him be accursed. Lord, come. The grace of our Lord Jesus be with you" (16:22, 23). This may suggest that Paul intended the letter to the Galatians, its delivery and reception, perhaps within a liturgical setting of worship (1:5), to function as a kind of "covenant renewal" ceremony, wherein the entire Galatian community is presented with a stark choice: blessing or curse? "I call heaven and earth to witness against you today, that I have set before you life and death, blessing and curse" (Deuteronomy 30:19). Which it will be depends upon how the Galatians respond to Paul's *reproclamation* of his gospel, which occurs through the delivery of his personal communiqué in lieu of his actual presence (6:11; 4:20; cf. 1 Corinthians 5:1–5). But Paul does not intend his letter to effect merely a theological change of mind, devoid of social consequences. On the contrary, the conditional nature of both the blessing (6:16) and the curse (1:8, 9) signify Paul's intention to *identify* those within the mixed community who are in the right—those who walk according to Paul's apostolic "rule" (6:16)—and those who are not but who instead come under his anathema (1:8, 9). Upon hearing his letter, the community should divide between the apostates and the faithful, and the subsequent procedure should be clear: the latter group should exclude the former from the life of the community as a dangerous and defiling contagion (4:30; 5:7–12).

6. Although scholars continue to debate the exact significance of Paul's "marks" (στίγματα), there is widespread agreement that the phrase itself refers to the physical effects of Paul's own suffering-persecution. See J. B. Lightfoot, *Saint Paul's Epistle to the Galatians: A Revised Text with Introduction, Notes, and Dissertations* (London: Macmillan, 1896), p. 225; Ernst de W. Burton, *A Critical and Exegetical Commentary on the Epistle to the Galatians,* International Critical Commentary (Edinburgh: T & T Clark, 1921), p. 360; Herman N. Ridderbos, *The Epistle of Paul to the Churches of Galatia,* NICNT (Grand Rapids: Eerdmans, 1953), p. 228; J. S. Pobee, *Persecution and Martyrdom in the Theology of Paul,* JSNTSup 6 (Sheffield: JSOT, 1985): pp. 94–98; F. J. Matera, *Galatians,* SP 9 (Collegeville, MN: Glazier, 1992), p. 232; Richard N. Longenecker, *Galatians,* WBC 41 (Waco, TX: Word, 1990), p. 300; James D. G. Dunn, *The Epistle to the Galatians,* BNTC (Peabody, MA: Hendrickson, 1993), p. 347; J. Louis Martyn, *Galatians: A New Translation with Introduction and Commentary,* AB 33A (New York: Doubleday, 1997), pp. 568, 569; Richard B. Hays, "The Letter to the Galatians: Introduction, Commentary, and

Reflections," in *The New Interpreter's Bible: A Commentary in Twelve Volumes,* ed. L. E. Keck, vol. 11 (Nashville: Abingdon, 2000), pp. 181–348 (esp. p. 346). This final reference is thus as significant as it is intriguing. As Lightfoot pointed out well over a century ago: "It is his final appeal, before which all opposition and controversy must give way" (*Galatians*, p. 51).

7. One of our earliest descriptions of Paul (albeit of limited historical value) is that Paul was "a man of small stature, with a bald head and crooked legs, in a good state of body, with eyebrows meeting and a nose somewhat hooked, full of friendliness" (*Acts of Paul,* 3.1; see 2 Corinthians 10:10).

Scripture Index

General Index

Index of Sermon Illustrations

Author's infertile sister-in-law had twins thanks to fertility technology and a year later conceived naturally, 166

Pride

C. S. Lewis called pride or self-conceit "The Great Sin," 207

Lewis on pride: "There is no fault which makes a man more unpopular, and no fault which we are more unconscious of in ourselves," 207–208

Luther: "the poisonous vice of vainglory," 212

Priorities

Paul Johnson: "Churchill had an uncanny gift for getting priorities right," 176

Repentance

Author as a youth had to confess to his spiritual mentor, who is now his father-in-law, that he had thrown a wild party in his house while his parents were away, and his mentor's gentle rebuke brought tears of repentance, 145

Self-Denial

Lewis: "We are told to deny ourselves and to take up our crosses in order that we may follow Christ," 216

Self-Righteousness

Edwards: "how strong a self-righteous, self-exalting disposition is naturally in man," 208

Serving Christ

In ancient times dying on a cross was "the most wretched of deaths" (Josephus) and "so horrible a deed" (Cicero), but Jesus bore it for us, and now we can suffer the shame of the cross for him, 38–39

Bishop Thomas Wolsey: "If I had served God as faithfully as man, I had been better rewarded, and not forsaken in my distress," 41

Newton said he was "appointed to preach the faith I had long labored to destroy," 49

Just as we need friends beside us when we learn to walk on the balance beam, helping us stay in step with the beam, we need each other in our walk with Christ, 71

Luther: "No man has ever fallen so grievously that he could not have stood up again. On the other hand, no one has such a sure footing that he cannot fall," 72

Christian song: "May the mind of Christ, my Savior, live in me from day to day," 154

A letter from a friend helps Hudson Taylor grasp the secret of victorious Christian living: "abiding, not striving nor struggling; looking oft unto him; trusting him for present power," 201–202

Lewis: "We are told to deny ourselves and to take up our crosses in order that we may follow Christ," 216

Serving Others

Author's church takes up offering for the victims of an earthquake in Haiti—$14,000, 55

Christians who don't bear others' burdens are like a timid medical student who sees a patient with a bone fracture but is too insecure to say anything about it, 206

Luther: burden-bearers must "have broad shoulders and husky bones," 211

Sin

Book title *I'm OK—You're Okay* illustrates human tendency to deny our sinfulness, 76

Author watches father-in-law do heart surgery and learns that even with a strong heart, if one artery is blocked, the patient's life is in danger, and Christ came to remove our spiritual blockage—sin, 107

A society's laws, parents' rules, posted classroom guidelines, and company policies all exist because of sin, 118

Men make even good things bad; Spurgeon: "A handsaw is a good thing, but not to shave with," 119

Author as a youth had to confess to his spiritual mentor, who is now his father-in-law, that he had thrown a wild party in his house while his parents were away, and his mentor's gentle rebuke brought tears of repentance, 145

Edwards: "how strong a self-righteous, self-exalting disposition is naturally in man," 208

Sowing and Reaping

Driving a car off the top of a parking garage to test the law of gravity would be as foolish as testing the law of the harvest by living for ourselves, 217

Lloyd-Jones: "The Christian life is a tasting of the first-fruits of that great harvest which is to come," 218

Spiritual Inheritance

One day she was Kate Middleton, the next day the Duchess of Cambridge, and once we came to Christ we too became heirs to the throne, 125

Spiritual Transformation

Classic hymn: "He breaks the power of canceled sin, He sets the prisoner free," 23

John Newton, former slave trader, wrote the timeless hymn "Amazing Grace," 48

Newton said he was "appointed to preach the faith I had long labored to destroy," 49

Suffering for Christ

In ancient times dying on a cross was "the most wretched of deaths" (Josephus) and "so horrible a deed" (Cicero), but Jesus bore it for us, and now we can suffer the shame of the cross for him, 38–39

Author, soon to receive PhD from Cambridge, mentioning that he will pastor a church in the Midwest U.S. is told by an acquaintance, condescendingly, that would be a huge step down from Cambridge, 39–40

Historian's comments on early Methodist preachers: "If Methodism had not come into contact with the mob it would never have reached the section of the English people which most needed salvation," 86

Warnings

Author's children have never thanked him for yelling to his children to get out of the street, but none have been hit by a car either, 32

The Preaching the Word series is written
by pastors for pastors and their churches.

crossway.org/preachingtheword